Cabo Verdean Women Writing Remembrance, Resistance, and Revolution

Critical African Studies in Gender and Sexuality

Series Editors: Besi Brillian Muhonja, James Madison University, and Babacar M'Baye, Kent State University

Series Advisory Board

Nkiru Nzegwu, Achola Pala, Melinda Adams, Binyavanga Wainaina, Ashley Currier, Betty Wambui, Jane Rarieya, Olufemi Taiwo, Cheikh Thiam

Critical African Studies in Gender and Sexuality publishes innovative, interdisciplinary research on intersections of gender, sexuality, and other political, social, economic, cultural, and geographic identity markers. The series has particular interest in groundbreaking scholarship on herstories/histories, elements and politics of gender and sexuality that center critical African thought and philosophies within global contemporary theoretical debates across the disciplines. Thus, manuscripts exploring gender relationships, queer identities, sexualities, masculinities, and femininities within both Africa and its Diaspora in interdisciplinary contexts are highly encouraged.

Recent Titles in the Series

Cabo Verdean Women Writing Remembrance, Resistance, and Revolution

Kriolas Poderozas

Edited by Terza A. Silva Lima-Neves and
Aminah N. Fernandes Pilgrim

LEXINGTON BOOKS
Lanham • Boulder • New York • London

Published by Lexington Books
An imprint of The Rowman & Littlefield Publishing Group, Inc.
4501 Forbes Boulevard, Suite 200, Lanham, Maryland 20706
www.rowman.com

6 Tinworth Street, London SE11 5AL, United Kingdom

British Library Cataloguing in Publication Information Available

Library of Congress Cataloging-in-Publication Data Available

ISBN 9781793634894 (hardcover) | ISBN 9781793634900 (electronic)
ISBN 9781793634917 (paperback)

Contents

Acknowledgments

I Acknowledge/Um Ta Reconhese,

All Kriolas across the globe who paved the way for me to be where I am. Every Kriola who's ever attended and/or volunteered at the Poderoza Conference. My grandmothers Alice and Arsena (Dinhanha), my ancestors who always protect my path. Every woman in the armed struggle for the liberation of Cabo Verde and those who continue to fight the patriarchy.

My sister-friend Aminah, who embarked on this journey with me to render visible our experiences, our stories, and our lives. We did that! I love you.

My teachers, professors, and mentors for helping me unapologetically center my love for and commitment to Cabo Verde in my academic work and introducing me to the Historically Black College and University (HBCU) tradition where I felt at home and learned to own my identity as a Black African Feminist Kriola. Thank you, Marcelina Flor Lopes, Patricia Anderson, Roy Alves, Tony Affigne, Abi Awomolo, Fragano S. Ledgister, Mack H. Jones, Hashim Gibril, and Marvin Haire.

My colleagues at Johnson C. Smith University who supported this work in many ways. Every single one of my students past, present, and future for the many lessons and the privilege to be a part of their journey. My friend Shokanti for bringing Aminah and I together and for being an active supportive Poderoza partner.

My friends in the academy—Joseph Jones, Jennifer Guglielmo, Kim Gallon, Julia Jordan-Zachery, Tonya Williams, and Drena Lopez-Duran. Academia can be a difficult place for Black women and you've helped me navigate it.

My homies—Ndaya, Guelas, Sweeta, Josie, Dana, Kimesha, Tanisha, Terrell, Iolanda, Eliana, Jael, Lili, Viviana, Marilene, Paulinha—for growing with me through the many versions of "Terza."

Tibe (Elizabete), Tisan (Sandra), Tia Lola (Crisolita), Guta (Maria Augusta), Tia Zau, Tia Lina, Tia Marta, dinha Fernanda, Aleida, Cousin Zai, Cousin Vera, Cousin Lizy—*bsot eh nha fonte de inspirasau e exemplo de Kriolas Poderozas. Nhas primas, primos, sobrinhas, sobrinhos e nha familia inteira pa bsot apoio e amor.*

Mama e Papa, Ivone e Cesar - Obrigada pa bsot apoio desde berso e um vida de sacrificios. Sem bsot mim ka eh nada. My sisters, Lauraberth and Frandine—our sisterhood is so sweet. You are the best gifts our parents could have ever given me, *sempre junte.*

My babies, the "ELNs"—Emilio, Ema, and Eri—because of you I know the full depth of unconditional love. Thanks for reminding me when I need to chill and that "it" ain't that serious. My main goal in this lifetime is to help create a society where you can continue to be free Black children and kind humans.

Luis, my best friend, the love of my life—a partner who's always inspired me to be a better woman, human, wife, mom, and professional since the day we met in 2005. This life we have intentionally created together is what I was looking for and more. I am a lucky girl. *Vali Pena.*

I dedicate this book to the three Poderozas who inspire me to do this work: my grandmother, Maria/Mãe, my mama, Ivone, and my daughter, Ema Ivone. This collection is about telling the stories of women like Mãe and mama, recording it in texts so little girls like Ema will always feel centered, seen, inspired, and proud to write their own stories.

Um Ta Sinti Orgulhosa De Ter Nascid Cabo Verdeana
(I feel proud to have been born a Cabo Verdean woman)
Terza A. Silva Lima-Neves

First, I acknowledge and thank God for ALL that I have and ALL that I am. I would not be here—having overcome so many challenges—if it were not for the grace of God. I thank my son Akein (Akin) Pilgrim-Cardoso for sharing his mom with the world, and for being my greatest teacher. I thank my entire family, especially Ruben Pierre, for believing in me more than I have believed in myself very often. Mama (the late Inez Santos Fernandes), Mom (Minniet Fernandes Pilgrim), Dad (Hugh Gordon Pilgrim), Sister (Ayana Pilgrim-Brown), Brother (Hasani M. E. Pilgrim), and all of my nieces (Aleena, Myka, Presley), and spiritual sisters, brothers, children, nieces and nephews, you all have been the wind in my wings and my inspiration to continue working hard. Thank you my Brockton Mom, Julieta, and for my cumadre Any Veiga, for all the times you keep Akein so I can work and have peace of mind (same for all of my Brockton family—Nair, Chris, Annette—who have helped me so often).

I thank my beloved Aunt Auriel Pilgrim for her faith in me, patience with me, and for being at every Poderoza except 2020 (only due to Covid19) I thank my beloved cousin Nadine Fernandes for her presence at every Poderoza as well. Thank you to my entire SABURA family who have not only attended Poderoza but have volunteered and helped make it a success—Leny, Ivette, Bethy, Margie, Maria Eugenia (an honoree), Solange, and all others whose names are too many to mention. Thank you to my students—past, present, and future—who have taught me and inspired me and pushed me to do better. Some of you volunteered, spoke, or served at Poderoza and we appreciate you (Manny, Edna, Ailine, Sarah, Carlene, Tiffany, Sania Santos, and others). Thank you Shokanti, for connecting me with Terza and for your support of Poderoza! Thank you Val Lopes/Afryk for your early support of Poderoza and our website. Thank you to the Kriola scholars who paved the way for us to be here—Belmira Nunes, Vanessa Brito, Dawna Thomas, Claire Andrade-Watkins, Gunga Tavares, and Inês Brito—you've mentored me formally or informally and I am indebted to you. I thank my former advisor, Kim D. Butler, for mentoring me and believing in my work on Cabo Verde and Cabo Verdeans. Thank you to UMass Boston colleagues such as Shirley Tang, Lorna Rivera, Marisol Negron, Ping-Ann Addo, and those at WGSS & CECS who embraced me and supported my work. Finally, thank you to my sister-scholar Terza for rolling with me on this journey—for the laughter, tears, challenges, and triumphs. Thank you Poderozas, all over the globe for holding up Cabo Verde, its diasporas and the whole world.

Aminah Fernandes Pilgrim

Poderosa

Gunga Tavares

A Criola can be
        oh so gentle
             and oh so powerful
                  and oh so beautiful,
                      and God help so mean!

She rose up from something that is more like nothing
                    or more like everything

        Everything that would want to hate,

           but yet, she love it…

A family without a father,
        a table without food,
             a room with no windows
                  A cheated education

        And yes, a stolen innocence
               by the neighbor who played with her dreams

     but not her destiny

        Because she rises up!

And yes God, her smile filled up the room

and she raised her children as mother and father
to be human

And she allowed the light to enter their rooms
And yes!
She replaced her lost innocence with wisdom
And taught herself to love

And grabbed the control of her dreams
And yes!
her destiny became
Criola – Poderosa

Introduction

Nos Vez, Nos Voz *("Our Time, Our Voices")*

Aminah Fernandes Pilgrim and
Terza A. Silva Lima-Neves

Nos vez. Our time. Here we go. Here we tell our stories in our own voices, the stories of Cabo Verde, and her daughters and sons living in communities in most corners of the world. As a collection of writings, this book *Kriolas Poderozas* (pronounced Kree-Oh-Luhz Poh-deh-roh-Zuhs) grew out of the conference by the same name, co-founded by the co-editors. Poderoza International Conference was born out of solidarity, sisterhood, and seeking. We were two Cabo Verdean scholars of the African Diaspora, from different academic fields and different islands, yet we had similar social identities and similar political positions in regards to the portrayal and positionalities of Kriolas worldwide (including the virtual/ online world) (Pilgrim 2015; Pires-Hester 1994).[1]

In our first few conversations, we spoke with ease about our shared work—personal and professional—and we discussed all of the topics we felt strongly about. We quickly found that a mutual commitment existed and that there was a sense of urgency about the need to make a change. First, we wanted to address the persistent and predominant image of Cabo Verdean women in popular culture as over-sexualized beings and video vixens. Second, although there is a history of oral tradition, we wanted to address the limited and almost non-existing presence of Cabo Verdean women writers in African literary and scholarly traditions. We recognized what African American poet June Jordan (1978) declared, that "we are the ones we have been waiting for" (para. 5). We recognized we stood on the shoulders of queens and that although it wasn't only our idea (it was one that many pioneering Kriolas had thought of before), it *was* our moment. We agreed to partner and to declare to the world that this is our time, to reclaim our history and legacy, to amplify our voices, art, activism, and work, and to reintroduce Kriolas to the world as Poderozas or empowered women.

1

In 2016, we hosted the first installment of the Poderoza International Conference on Cabo Verdean Women. We designed the event to bridge community, popular culture, and academia. Through Poderoza, we began to institutionalize a diaspora conversation, and this conversation has become a movement—an extension of the centuries-old tradition of resistance that began within us before Kriolas were even Kriolas.[2] After more than five years on this journey and three installments of the event, this collection, then, complements the conference, the movement, and all of its offshoots. We recognize that this collection is not complete, but our intention is to lay a solid foundation upon which the nascent field of Cabo Verdean Women's and Gender Studies can be built and expanded. In this introduction, we intend to accomplish the following: (1) provide historical background on the Republic of Cabo Verde and its people, (2) discuss the significance of the idea of Cabo Verdean Women's Studies and how this book contributes to that field, (3) situate this collection in a scholarly context, (4) provide the rationale for the selections included in the anthology, and (5) to celebrate the accomplishment that this project represents. The intention of this collection is twofold—telling our stories in our own voices (as the first few sentences declared), *and* offering this documentation of the scholarship researched and written by Kriolas in diverse fields (such as academia, politics, clinical psychology, K-12 education, law enforcement, business, and the arts), as well as the creative, professional, community/grassroots, reflective and emotional labor that Kriolas perform daily in service of the culture and the transnational diaspora. We hope that while reading these beautiful selections, readers are challenged, inspired, and healed.

CABO VERDE AND ITS DIASPORA

Cabo Verde is a small archipelago of ten islands (nine are inhabited) with a strong history of migration due to colonialism and long periods of drought and famine. As a former colonial subject, this West African island nation fought and won its independence from Portugal on July 5, 1975 (Carreira 1978; Andrade 1974; Lobban 1995). Since its independence, it has experienced considerable economic and political development, often called an African success story (Resendes-Santos 2015; Amado 2015). Still, emigration has been the natural and forced choice for most Cabo Verdeans when faced with poverty and unemployment. The population of Cabo Verdeans and their descendants abroad (over 1 million) exceeds the domestic population (nearly 600,000). This figure is unconfirmed due to the way Cabo Verdeans perceive themselves in terms of racial and ethnic identity as well as legal and illegal immigration status. Cabo Verde is a Creole nation, with a mixed population of African, European, and South Asian ancestry. Because of this ethnic mix, Cabo Verdeans are phenotypically diverse; the population is of all shades and hues. This is an identity that is not necessarily unique or different from populations of Caribbean countries such as the Dominican Republic, Martinique, or Guadeloupe, for example, but is singular in the context of an African island nation. This has attracted the attention of many scholars from ethnic and racial studies (Amado 2015; Pilgrim 2008).

There are Cabo Verdean communities in the United States, Portugal, France, Italy, Spain, Angola, Senegal, Sao Tome and Principe, Holland, Brazil, and Argentina. In the United States, the New England region is home to the largest Cabo Verdean community outside of Cabo Verde, followed by Portugal (Almeida 1978; Lima-Neves 2009; Batalha and Carling 2008). Within the archipelago homeland, true to any transnational diaspora, some desire to go abroad, work hard, and return home to family. Historically, the push factors that shaped the first waves of out-migration from the ten-island nation included colonial neglect by the Portuguese, environmental changes (severe cyclical droughts), extreme poverty, and overwhelming famine. Currently, it's notable that Cabo Verdeans cite unemployment, having relatives abroad, and recurring remittances as factors in their desire to emigrate. However, easy access to social media makes Cabo Verdeans at home less enamored with the dream of going abroad as they see their fellow compatriots abroad often suffering in deplorable socioeconomic conditions. In terms of gender, there has been a balance in emigration flows. The shift changed from individual labor and education-related moves to family-related migration (where family members migrate together or family re-unification is a motivating factor). In contrast to previous times where men migrated leaving the women behind to care for the home and raise the children, present-day Cabo Verdean women are more independent and also exercise their desires to migrate and find opportunities for economic freedom and educational advancement.

Migration has allowed women the agency and freedom to seek betterment, such as baccalaureate and advanced degrees, professional training, and financial freedom, as well as general opportunities to define their own futures. Highlighting that not all development is positive, Cabo Verdean women's rights advocate Zezinha Chantre asserts that with the departure of the women, Cabo Verde suffers a loss of the educator who is responsible for the preservation of the cultural fabric of the Cabo Verdean state. Women teach their children and other community members the significance of Cabo Verde's history and culture (Nos Genti 2013).

Consider one chapter in the history of migration. The Cabo Verdean men who settled in northwestern Europe during the 1960s and 1970s brought their wives and children in the 1980s. During this period, single women also migrated. While men migrated to the Netherlands and Portugal during this particular era, women often tended to choose Italy, although not exclusively (others still migrated to Portugal). These places were major destinations for Cabo Verdean domestic workers, both documented and undocumented. The number of women migrants to Italy tripled that of men. Women in Italy were employed as hourly domestic workers instead of live-in domestic workers (Grassi 2007; Silva 2015). The migration of women to Italy also forged a new level of transnational networking. Cabo Verdean males in Holland often vacationed and visited the women in Italy. This relationship between Cabo Verdeans in Holland, Portugal, and Italy formed the Cabo Verdean European community (Pojmann 2014). They came together during social events and exchanged economic and cultural goods. The regional integration of the European community, the European Union (EU), has made it much easier for the formation of a stronger diaspora of Cabo Verdeans in Europe. It has facilitated migratory circulation in Europe. There are several actors responsible for building the transnational nature of this relationship. Women have been important actors in this process. They facilitate unifying the different diaspora communities and also connect them with the homeland. Female entrepreneurs in the informal market carry traditional Cabo Verdean products to be sold to the diaspora and in turn, bring back to the islands consumer goods, such as clothes, shoes, domestic appliances, foods, as well as other products otherwise inaccessible to the poor.

One cannot discuss female entrepreneurs without implicating social activism since they often intersect. Cabo Verdean women's commitment to community activism has taken different forms, often impacted by the socioeconomic realities of their particular host countries. For example, in the United States, the Cape Cod region—Harwich, Massachusetts, in particular—became the final home of the beloved "Cape Verdean Rosa Parks" (as she was called). Eugenia Fortes, who left Brava and migrated to the United States at the tender age of nine, began a long career of both entrepreneurship (initially selling food out of her own home) and social justice activism on behalf of Cabo Verdeans and the general Black population. Dating back to the 1940s, she led grassroots efforts to raise money for youth scholarships, protested school segregation on the Cape, and eventually became a founding President of the Cape Cod chapter of the National Association for the Advancement of Colored People (NAACP). She is said to have housed the likes of Dr. Martin Luther King Jr. at her modest Harwich home where she became legendary (Pilgrim 2005). Indeed, the U.S. Civil Rights Movement, Feminist and Black Power eras of the 1960s–1970s coincided with the Cabo Verde independence movement. In the Cabo Verdean case, local manifestations of these global trends resulted in social movements and the launching of women's organizations both led by Zezinha Chantre, Lilica Boal, Crispina

Gomes, Paula Fortes, Isaura Gomes, and others. In the diaspora, women were also actively supporting the recognition of Cabo Verde as an independent state. Romana Ramos, for example, led initiatives to create spaces in the wider New England region of the United States where the Cabo Verdean immigrant community could express cultural pride and maintain connections with the homeland. Her efforts resulted in a radio program that discussed politics at home and the Cabo Verde independence celebration which takes place in the Fox Point neighborhood in Providence, where a predominantly Cabo Verdean community resides. This event is the longest running Independence Day celebration across all diaspora locations. It demonstrates the critical role these women played in raising awareness and funds—as historical actors—in support of the independence movement in Cabo Verde (Pires-Hester 1994; Gibau 2008; Pilgrim 2015).

Claire Andrade-Watkins' well-known film *Some Kind of Funny Porto Rican* showed us Cape Verdean American women (who probably didn't consider themselves activists at the time) were among those on the frontlines of defending the very same Fox Point, Rhode Island Cape Verdean community referenced above, when it was threatened and ultimately divided by highway 195. This film is among the work of Kriolas that has often never gotten its due. Another example of a scholar who worked tirelessly, facing tremendous barriers to publication early on, is Dawna Thomas—whose work we are proud to feature in this collection. Nevertheless, past scholarship has documented the strategic ways Cabo Verdeans, both men and women built community, navigating questions of identity and ethnicity within the context of a systemically racist U.S. sociopolitical system. As historical actors, these women also acted within and navigated around African American identity politics and socioeconomic, linguistic, and citizenship barriers that often circumscribed their own existences as well as that of their family members. For instance, more work should be done within Cabo Verdean studies to document the lives of Kriolas in urban centers such as New Bedford, Boston (Dorchester and Roxbury where there are Cabo Verdean enclaves), and Brockton; Cabo Verdeans have been disproportionately affected by gun violence and gang activity in these spaces. Here we are referring to mothers, such as peace activist Isaura Mendes (who lost sons and multiple nephews to gun violence) or the late Jassy Correia (a young woman/mother whose life was cut short due to gender-based violence in the Boston area) whose case mobilized a generation to pay closer attention to the vulnerability of young Kriolas. Similarly, there are Kriolas who are on the frontlines of the fight for Black maternal health—most notably Massachusetts State Representative for the 5th Suffolk District, Elizabeth "Liz" Miranda, and community organizer Soraya Dos Santos. There are several Cabo Verdean women in local New England communities—many of whom have attended, spoken at, or been honored at a Poderoza conference and whose stories are waiting to be told.

These stories are a kind of cultural "remittance" or legacy that must be preserved and passed on. Remittances sent by women have been, in nature, more dynamic than men and often include individuals and groups beyond their immediate families (Pessar 2003). Women are more likely to help causes that are social in nature such as education, health, and anti-domestic violence initiatives. They are also less likely to engage directly and formally with government officials for diverse reasons such as high import fees and lack of confidence in elected officials (Lima-Neves 2009). As discussed previously, in her study on gender and Cabo Verdean women in Portugal, Marzia Grassi highlights the predominance of women in the informal transnational economy known as "rabidantes" as a means of helping their families back home as well as personal survival (Grassi 2007). Cabo Verdean women in Portugal face numerous challenges in settling and acculturating in their new country. Existing research points to harsh working conditions and discrimination in the job place as major challenges to their livelihood (Fykes 2000; Grassi and Évora 2007). Most women work in the private domestic and cleaning sectors, which are the lowest paid jobs requiring little to no specified qualifications. Women with children find it difficult to navigate the long working hours, securing care for their children, and actively participating in their children's academic progress. Another obstacle to the settlement process is securing legal immigration status, which can take a very long time depending on the employer's willingness to provide paperwork for the process. Additional research about the status of women in diaspora locations such as Holland, the United States, and Italy would shed light on the various ways women empower themselves and the community and raise consciousness via digital platforms.

WHAT THE COLLECTION REPRESENTS

The global call for women's empowerment has become louder and more pronounced. This was a call that was first articulated by enslaved women of African descent all over the globe who were leading maroon societies and revolts for freedom. In the United States, the enslaved women such as Sojourner Truth were the first to raise their voices for the cause of feminism—before it was even a word. Their cries about the sexual exploitation they experienced laid the groundwork for contemporary scholar-activism around gender-based violence and intersectional feminisms. Stories from across all continents emerge each moment, documenting the ongoing need for the fight for women's and LGBTQIA+ rights as human rights and demonstrating the individual and collective contributions to the struggle (Blain 2018; Busby 2019; Clark et al. 2018).

Within academia, "traditional" community activism, and digital activism, there has been a call for Black women's stories to be told in ways that recognize our full identities and affirm our humanity. The work is being done in meaningful ways in multiple disciplines. This volume adds to this interdisciplinary work. For instance, African scholars Marnia Lazreg, Chimamanda Adichie, and Minna Salami implore us to push for the decolonization of feminism in order to add a fuller story inclusive of African women's narratives, making space for an in-depth understanding of our intersectional identities and how race, gender, ethnicity, sexuality, class, religion, and so on overlap and collide to inform our lived experiences in the context of global feminism without dismissing elements of culture and history (Lazreg 2005). Adichie makes the case that African women's experiences have successfully been told through narratives, storytelling, performance, and other types of art, without the need for academic or structured feminist theory, which she reminds us is a Western construct. This collection illustrates this point exactly, with two broad categories of work; here, you'll find "traditional" scholarly articles and essays as well as oral history, poetry, visual art, and personal reflections—merging various art forms into one.

We recognize the critical importance of community and, true to a Cabo Verdean/African worldview, this is rooted in collectivist values that affirm a holistic point of view. In other words, we do not endorse the idea that academia and "community" are opposed—rather, as feminists, we affirm that we *are* the community. By selecting these particular contributions, including so-called nontraditional academics, community practitioners, artists, musicians, activists, politicians, we intend to disrupt the cannon and traditions of academia. There is a rich tradition of Cabo Verdean women's activism and social movements that have been documented only to a limited extent in Kriolu and Portuguese (Lima-Neves 2014).[3] We can point to the 1910 *Raboita di Rubon Manel* (Rubon Manel Revolt) that happened in the interior of Santiago Island. Led by Ana da Veiga (Nh'Ana Bombolon), the community organized to free local women who had been arrested and accused by local Portuguese landowners of stealing seeds from their property. This key moment in Cabo Verdean history is immortalized in the lyrics of the song *Raboita di Rubon Manel* by Orlando Pantera, renowned Cabo Verdean songwriter and recorded by singer Lura in her 2004 album, *Di Korpo Ku Alma*. Oral history is captured in much of the music known as *batuku*—perhaps most closely associated with the queen of finaçon, Nacia Gomi (1925–2011) (Lima-Neves 2012). Batukadeiras hold a rich catalog of Cabo Verdean folklore, including commentary on the culture of male-female relationships and gender mores in Santiago (and common throughout the islands) through lyrics about relationships, courting, sex, marriage, community, poverty, and hardships. Indeed, *batuku*, being largely women-led, offers us a powerful metaphor of Kriolas as keepers of the history, culture, and traditions of resistance of Cabo Verde and its people worldwide.

As previously stated, this collection has the objective of documenting the work and stories told by Cabo Verdean women, in order to educate, inspire, and empower Cabo Verdean women and girls and to add Cabo Verdean women's writings to the existing fields of African studies, Cabo Verdean Studies, Transnational Studies, Women's and Gender studies, modern African Diaspora Studies, and Black Women's Studies. It centers Cabo Verdean women's existence in fresh ways and offers testimonials in our own words. As the title, *Kriolas Poderozas* suggests, this transdisciplinary collection of essays asserts that Cabo Verdean women or Kriolas are Poderozas (empowered) beings with agency who persevere in the face of oppressive structures and are capable of contributing theoretical, critical, and practical perspectives in addressing local and global issues.

We position this analysis within the larger body of scholarship by Black and African feminist thinkers because of their preoccupation with true liberation for all Black people in Africa and across the world, regardless of sex, gender, class, sexual orientation, and abilities. This tradition is transnational in nature and recognizes the oppression of all Black people while being mindful of the specific geographic realities they face as well. Black feminist thinkers have called for solidarity among Black women on the African continent and in the diaspora as a way to better understand the oppression we live with as Black women. Although there may be particular, historical and geographic realities that impact the way Black women are marginalized in various times and spaces, it is important to recognize what Patricia Collins (2009) refers to as the "intercontinental, intersectionality of oppressions" (238). There are commonalities that exist among women of African descent that are of concern to all of us, such as sexual and domestic violence as well as media objectification, which have different meanings in local contexts. In the case of the Cabo Verdean diaspora, in general, and Cabo Verdean women, in particular, this is especially important because of the country's history of migration (a pattern that suggests it has been targeted for sex trafficking and sex tourism) and the large diaspora communities that are scattered throughout mainland Africa, the Americas, Europe, and elsewhere. To recognize this intercontinental intersectionality of oppressions (racism, sexism, classism) is to recognize the specificity of the impact of each host country on the continued marginalization and oppression of Cabo Verdean women (Collins 2009; Perry 2009).

The writing of Cabo Verdean history and our literary traditions have been historically male-centered, rendering the voice and presence of women, almost invisible. The Claridade (translated as our "light" or "awakening") Movement, the first known Cabo Verdean literary renaissance that started in the 1930s, only featured work by male writers such as Baltasar Lopes, Onesimo Silveira, and Corsino Fortes (Lobban 1995). This movement and the magazine it produced regularly was a response to the Portuguese colonial occupation of Cabo Verde and its people at the hands of the Portuguese fascist government under Antonio Salazar, speaking out against the deplorable social, political, and economic conditions of the islands.

The absence of women in the Claridade Movement doesn't mean women didn't engage in writing about topics of interest to them or in critique of the Portuguese colonial occupation. It just means it wasn't documented. In her essay for this collection, Vera Duarte writes about the Kriolas of that time period and the poems they wrote. We can also point to the groundbreaking work of historian Elisa Andrade (1974) and political scientist Crispina Gomes (2000) a few decades later (Andrade 1974; Gomes 2000). In more recent times, the research and scholarship by Cabo Verde–based Kriola scholars, Euridice Monteiro (2009, 2015) and Roselma Évora (2018), have advanced our understanding of Cabo Verdean gender politics, culture, and development. Similarly, the 2011 *Universidade de Cabo Verde* edited book on Cabo Verdean women by Carmelita Silva and Celeste Fortes offered a rich collection of scholarly essays about Cabo Verdean women in Portuguese and English written by Cabo Verdean and non-Cabo Verdeans scholars. *A Minha Passagem*, the autobiography by Paula Fortes (2013), participant in the Cabo Verdean liberation movement, and later one of the architects of the Cabo Verdean state, is perhaps the only published account of women's experiences during that time period from a first-person perspective. The work of U.S.-based Kriola writers and scholars such as Deirdre Meintel Machado (1981), Belmira Nunes Lopes (1982), Laura Pires-Hester (1994), Gina Sanchez Gibau (2008, 2009), and Claire Andrade-Watkins (2006) have been critical in laying the foundation for work on immigrant experiences, community formation, and the complexities of ethnic identity. Lastly, Clara Silva's research on the Cabo Verdean immigrant community in Italy (2015), which is predominantly female, sheds light on a very interesting and unique case study of the Cabo Verdean community in Europe.

The current digital age has helped Cabo Verdean women gain access to the world and take up space in multiple ways that weren't previously available. Cabo Verde-based scholar, Anybelle Lizardo's thesis on the impact of media in electoral politics sheds light on how everyday people learn and access information about candidates for political office and campaigns during election time (Lizardo 2019). In her published research, Sonia Melo (2008), for example, discussed the ways Cabo Verdeans use the internet to build community and create transnational networks of information and support. In our coauthored essay specifically focused on Kriolas and social media activism, we talked about how Facebook, Instagram, Twitter, Whatsapp, Viber, and other platforms are used to build transnational solidarity and coalitions for social movements, empower women and girls, share information, as well as set up entrepreneurial businesses (Lima-Neves and Pilgrim 2020). The work that happens at the grassroots level in our communities appears for the most part on social media, particularly Facebook and Instagram, because it is much easier and cost-effective to spread the word in this way and reach as many Cabo Verdeans as possible. Women-led organizations in Cabo Verde and across diaspora locations utilize these platforms to disseminate information about events, professional trainings, employment opportunities, homeland politics, cultural programs, campaigns, and fundraisers for specific causes in times of need. Yet grassroots, community organizing outside of the digital diaspora is still very much ongoing, with efforts like SABURA Youth Programs (co-founded by Aminah Fernandes Pilgrim and Anita Monteiro)—written about in this collection, Cape Verdeans of the Carolinas (founded by Terza Lima-Neves), the Cape Cod Cape Verdean Museum (founded by Barbara Burgo after years of effort), Criolas Contra Cancer, Our Children Our Future, The Cape Verdean American Museum, and the many young women's organizations that have begun, such as Kriola Professionals Association, Cape Verdean Social Workers Association, Cape Verdean Alumni Network, and more.

The river of our resistance is long and winding. It stretches from colonial times when Kriolas/Cabo Verdean women from Cabo Verde and Guinea Bissau participated in trans-Atlantic business practices as female traders of textiles, foods, and other goods to the days of enslavement when Rabeladas and Batukadeiras gave voice and body to our resistance to racial and gendered oppression and sexual violence, to active participation as militants in the armed struggle for independence from Portugal, to contemporary leadership positions in the diaspora that manifest in sustainable partnerships within their host countries for the betterment of the communities, to the digital diaspora where we use social media and technology to redefine ourselves and reclaim the image of the Kriola. Cabo Verdean women have been at the forefront of building and empowering their communities as well as creating, intervening in, and promoting Cabo Verdean development and culture. This collection is an answer to patriarchy within the diaspora and within our experiences, an answer that delivers a definitive end to the tradition of *sufri kaladu* (suffering in silence) in our mother tongue(s).

In conclusion, this anthology is divided into seven distinct parts. Part I, *Artistas* ("Artists"), features the work of the renowned Cabo Verdean human rights activist and writer, Vera Duarte exploring the literary contributions of women in the history of the patriarchal island nation. Singer-songwriter/ music educator Candida Rose writes about women who have contributed to the development of various genres of Cape Verdean American and African American music. Part II, Exploring Community, features chapters by two pioneering Kriola academics with two of the longest careers in their respective fields—Gina Sanchez Gibau and Dawna Thomas. These chapters explore various intimate aspects of community, with particular attention to gendered themes. Part III, Policy and Politics, is a combined transnational exploration of the Cabo Verdean state and its governing across sectors. Therein you will read articles by Roselma Évora, Clementina Furtado (two of the most prominent scholars in women's and gender studies in academic universities in CV), and from the United Kingdom, Aleida Borges. Part IV, *Poesias* ("Poetry"), is a section that features the work of Shauna Barbosa and Iva Brito, as well as a coauthored poem by Rosilda James, Stephanie Andrade, and Aminah Fernandes Pilgrim. Part V, *Identidadi* ("Identity") features two powerful, heartfelt essays on race and ethnicity, as well as sexuality and the experiences of coming to terms with each by Callie Watkins Liu and Idalina Pina. Part VI, Transforming Culture into Practice, is a part that includes the work of three of the best practitioners in each of their respective fields. The beloved, online curator of the CV Genealogist page, Anna "Nanie" Lima writes about the exploration of our family origins. Elizabete Andrade writes about our roots with food and cooking traditions. And Ayana Pilgrim-Brown writes about seeking our purpose in the work that we do. Part VII, Poderoza Reflections, includes four beautifully written personal reflections on attending the conference and witnessing the movement (Stephanie Andrade), working to uplift the community online and in person (Jess Evora), working as an inspired educator in SABURA Youth Programs of Brockton, Massachusetts (Ivette Monteiro), and exploring childhood, migration, and a Kriola's aspirational dreams (Edna DaCosta). Finally, part VIII, *Consedju* (or *Konseju*) which translates to "wisdom" or "advice," includes two pieces rooted in oral histories by the co-editors, both oral history practitioners.

It is our hope for readers that this volume gives birth to more and more expansive work on the Cabo Verdean diaspora and its many undiscovered stories. We offer this collection as our gift to disrupt the narrative and make the archives more inclusive. We are no longer silenced, and as coauthors of this introduction and co-editors of this collection, we emphasize the collective—the goals of feminism—the fact that there is power in this—one name not more important than the other, not one professional field more valuable than another. *Kriolas Poderozas* is making a collective step forward and letting out a collective cry of success for the decade of the Kriola that we declared and we will lead.

NOTES

1. Kriola means woman of Cabo Verdean descent, referring to the primarily Kriol/ Creole/Crioulo Cabo Verdean identity. It is often spelled in various ways, Criolas, Crioulas, and Creolas. One may also see KabuVerdianas, Cabo Verdeanas and Cabo Verdianas. The collection also features various spellings of the country's name and the people. Both Cabo Verde and Cape Verde are used here by the contributors. Cabo Verdean, Cabo Verdeana(o), Cape Verdean, Cape Verdian are all different but correct spellings of someone from or descendant of Cabo/Cape Verde.

2. For more information on Poderoza: An international conference on Cabo Verdean Women, visit www.poderozaconference.com

3. In terms of literary works that are accessible mostly in Portuguese are novels and poetry by Vera Duarte who is also an accomplished international award winning women's rights activist, poet and retired Supreme Court judge.

REFERENCES

Amado, Abel Djassi. "Cabo Verde: West Africa's Democratic 'Potemkin Village.'" https://politicalmatter.org/2015/08/03/cabo-verde-west-africas-democratic-potem-kin-village-by-abel-djassi-amado/, 2015.

Andrade, Elisa. *The Cape Verde Islands: From Slavery to Modern Times.* Eugene: Third World Students Coalition Press, 1974.

Andrade Watkins, Claire. "Some Kind of Funny Porto Rican." (Film documentary). SPIA Productions, 2006.

Blain, Keisha N. *Set the World on Fire: Black Nationalist Women and the Global Struggle for Freedom.* Philadelphia: University of Pennsylvania Press, 2018.

Busby, Margaret. *New Daughters of Africa: An International Anthology of Writing by Women of African Descent.* New York: HarperCollins Publishers, 2019.

Clark, Msia, Phiwokuhle Mnyandu, and Loy L. Azalia. *Transnational Spaces: Essays on Black Transnationalism.* Washington, D.C.: Lexington Books, 2018.

Collins, Patricia Hill. *Black Feminist Thought: Knowledge, Consciousness, and the Politics of Empowerment,* Second Edition. New York: Routledge Publisher, 2009.

Évora, Roselma. "Representação e Comportamento Politico na Perspetiva do Género em Cabo Verde." *Journal of Cape Verdean Studies* 3, no. 1, 65. https://vc.bridgew .edu/jcvs/vol3/iss1/4, 2018.

Fortes, Paula. *A Minha Passagem.* Praia: Fundacao Amilcar Cabral, 2013.

Gibau, Gina Sanchez. "Cape Verdean Diasporic Identity Formation." In *Transnational Archipelago: Perspectives on Cape Verdean Migration and Diaspora,* edited by Luis Batalha and Jorgen Carling, 13–32. Amsterdam: Amsterdam University Press, 2008.

Gibau, Gina Sanchez. "Contested Identities: Narratives of Race and Ethnicity in the Cape Verdean Diaspora." In *Community, Culture and the Makings of Identity: Portuguese-Americans Along the Eastern Seaboard,* edited by Kimberly DaCosta

Holton and Andrea Klimt, 461–495. Dartmouth: Center for Portuguese Studies and Culture, 2009.

Gomes, Crispina. "As Mulheres da Guiné e Cabo Verde na Luta de Libertacão Nacional na Perspectiva de Cabral." Paper presented at the University of Massachussets-Darmouth (Spring 2000).

Gomes, Crispina. *Mulher e Poder: O Caso de Cabo Verde*. Praia: BNL, 2011.

Jordan, June. "Poem for South African Women." *JuneJordan.net*. http://www.junejordan.net/poem-for-south-african-women.html, 1978.

Lazreg, Marnia. "Decolonizing Feminisms." In *African Gender Studies: A Reader*, edited by Oyeronke Oyewumi. London: Palgrave Macmillan, 2005.

Lima-Neves, Terza. "Nacia Gomes." In *Dictionary of African Biography*, edited by Emmanuel K. Akyeampong and Henry Louis Gates Jr. Oxford: Oxford University Press, 2012.

Lima-Neves, Terza Silva, and Aminah Fernandes Pilgrim. "Um Sabe Kem Mi Eh: Transnational Kriolas and Social Media Activism." In *Contemporary Movements Around Black/African Women's Bodies*, edited by Msia Clark and Winpuni Fatima Mohammed, forthcoming, 2020.

Lizardo, Anybelle Dos Reis. *Os Média na Formação de Preferências Eleitorais: o caso das Localidades de Manuel Lopes, Pedra de Jorge e Chã de Mato no Concelho de Porto Novo, Santo Antão*. Undergraduate Thesis, Universidade de Mindelo, 2019.

Lopes, Belmira Nunes. *A Portuguese Colonial in America: Belmira Nunes Lopes*. Ithaca: Latin American Literary Review Press, 1982.

Machado, Deirdre Meintel. "Cape Verden Americans." In *Hidden Minorities: The Persistence of Ethnicity in American Life*, edited by Joan H. Rollins, 233–256. Washington, DC: University Press of America, 1981.

Melo, Sonia. "Cape Verdean Transnationalism on the Internet." In *Transnational Archipelago: Perspectives on Cape Verdean Migration and Diaspora*, edited by Luis Batalha and Carling Jorgen. Amsterdam: Amsterdam University Press, 2008.

Mohammed, Wunpini Fatimata. "Online Activism: Centering Marginalized Voices in Activist Work." *Ada: A Journal of Gender, New Media, and Technology*, no. 15. DOI: 10.5399/uo/ada.2019.15.2. https://adanewmedia.org/2019/02/issue15-mohammed/, 2019.

Monteiro, Euridice. *Mulheres, Democracia e Desafios Pós-coloniais: Uma Análise da Participação Política das Mulheres em Cabo Verde*. Edicoes-UNI-CV, 2009.

Monteiro, Euridice. *Entre os Senhores das Ilhas e as Descontentes: Identidade, Classe e Género na Estruturação do Campo Político em Cabo Verde*. Edicoes Uni-CV, 2015.

Perry, Keisha-Khan. "The Groundings With My Sisters: Toward a Black Diasporic Feminist Agenda in the Americas." *The Scholar and Feminist Online*. http://sfonline.barnard.edu/africana/perry_01.htm, 2009.

Pilgrim, Aminah. "Tia Gen: Ms. Eugenia Fortes." In *Fandata: The Wonders and Dramas of Cabo Verde*, Winter, 2005.

Pilgrim, Aminah. "Free Men Name Themselves: U.S. Cape Verdeans & Black Identity Politics in the Era of Revolution, 1955–1975." *Journal of Cape Verdean Studies*, no. 1, April 2015.

Pires-Hester, Laura J. *A Study of Cape Verdean-American ethnic Development: The Emergence of Bilateral Diaspora Ethnicity and Its Impact in a Southeastern New England Locality.* Ph.D. Dissertation, Columbia University, 1994.

Silva, Carmelita, and Celeste Fortes, eds. *As Mulheres Em Cabo Verde: Experiencias e Perspectivas.* Santiago: Universidade de Cabo Verde, 2011.

Silva, Clara. "Immigrants from Cabo Verde in Italy: History and Paths of Socio-Educative Integration." *Journal of Cape Verdean Studies* 2, no. 1, 25–34. http://vc.bridgew.edu/jcvs/vol2/iss1/4Copyright, 2015.

Part I

ARTISTAS ("ARTISTS")

Chapter 1

I Write, Therefore I Am, from a Gendered Perspective

Vera Duarte

Cogito ergo sum, with this sentence, so simple and so deep, the French philosopher and mathematician René Descartes solidified himself as the founder of modern philosophy.[1] Descartes used the method of systematic doubt to reach his certainties during the first half of the sixteenth century, but there was no way to doubt that he was in doubt. He then had his first certainty: I doubt, therefore I am. As doubting is itself a way of thinking, swiftly, he came up with "I think, therefore I am," that is, I think, therefore I am aware of myself (*Stanford Encyclopedia of Philosophy* 2019, para. 4.1).

That is what I aim to do in this unpretentious incursion in the world of the written word of the Cape Verdean woman: *I write, therefore I exist*, with the due bow to the man to whose thought I consider myself indebted in the Cartesian strand of my legal training, because it has also been through the writing itself that women have become aware of themselves and have imposed themselves on others.

Today I am sure that it was fundamentally through writing that Cape Verdean women, similarly to other women who came from diverse latitudes, managed to overcome their traditional position of an "inferior being" that history has always reserved for them. Although the struggle for women's emancipation has had and continues to have several fronts, the writing front seems to be one of the most fundamental.

In other words, *I write, therefore I am* seems to me to be the unfinished proof of the relation between word and power in the feminine domain, perceiving this "power" in its ample sense, that is, the access to all possibilities that open up for the human being.

That is what I intend to do in the following lines: to dwell, even if briefly, on the life and work of some Cape Verdean women whose trajectory provoked the assertion *I write, therefore I am*. I understand that there is an unrelenting dialectical relation between the woman's emancipation and the writings of female authorship. Even more, I argue that the role of literature in the struggle for women's emancipation works on two levels:

First: The individual level: allowing each female writer to reach catharsis from frustrations, expand joys, manifest her own positions and feelings, advance in the process of self-knowledge, and increase her knowledge of the world and the ways in which to transform it in her favor.
Second: The collective level: allowing emancipatory messages to turn into complicity, to be socialized, to circulate, and to invade more and more "forbidden" territories, and that they are appropriated by men and women who will disseminate them, either by positively defending them or negatively contesting what will always reverse in favor of its propagation.

Paraphrasing the great Black abolitionist, a former runaway slave, Frederick Douglass, *mutatis mutandis*, when history does not omit (lie) about the participation of women in the process of construction of the universal literary building (in the struggle against slavery), we will see that they performed a great role in it.

For all of them, we use the paradigmatic example, disregarding the redundancy of the French journalist, Olympe de Gouges, who wrote in 1791 the declaration of women and female citizen rights, understanding that the Declaration of Human and Citizen Rights had been applied solely to males, while women were left forgotten.

As a consequence of this attitude and other daring writings in favor of women's rights, Olympe de Gouges was sent to the guillotine in 1793, by order of Robespierre.

Now with Arthur Rimbaud, the great prophet of libertarian mystique, we recover one of the most beautiful prophecies that we were given to read, and, we believe, it is already a reality, at least for the majority of the women in the current world.

Allow me now to a quick flight through the origins of Cape Verdean literature, to revisit some exceptional women, because even though the process of female emancipation has known anonymous heroines, many of them have been forgotten. Some do not fit the economy of this work, as it is the case of female researchers such as Dulce Almada Duarte or Fátima Fernandes, from the *repentistas* women, from the oral expression, such as *Nha Bibinha Cabral* or *Nha Násia Gomi*, and even composers such as Teté Alhinho or Lura, although everything I say can be applied to them, *mutatis mutandis*, because of the several limitations of time and space and even knowledge will not allow me to embrace them in this work.

But pay attention!

The argument I will make here does not coincide fully with many of the studies that have been done about the Cape Verdean literary system. In many of them, still following some of the historical inertia which omitted the names of women, the Cape Verdean literary building seems to be inhabited, in its infancy, almost exclusively by male voices. Although some female names have been remarked, they have occupied secondary places to that of men.

I will mention the example of Antónia Pusich, about whom I will have the opportunity to dwell: even though she was the first person born in Cape Verde to publish her writings namely in the renowned *Almanaque de Lembranças Luso-Brasileiro*, the person considered the first Cape Verdean writer is Guilherme da Cunha Dantas. Now, without demoralizing the last writer, who we quite appreciate, it is easy to verify that while the contribution made by Antónia Pusich to the *Almanaque* dates back to 1854, Guilherme Dantas' only begins in the year 1872.

It is correct that Antónia Pusich, although born in São Nicolau, lived most of her life in Portugal, and because of this, she was considered a Portuguese writer. But it is important not to forget that previously we lived under colonial times, and many other writers who were born in Cape Verde, but lived and/or died in Portugal, are considered also Cape Verdeans, as is the case of Daniel Filipe.

Guilherme da Cunha Dantas was, without a doubt, the first native writer from these islands to publish in prose, a position which, *apropos*, he almost shares with José Evaristo D'Almeida, author of the work *O Escravo*, considered the first Cape Verdean themed novel. But before them, Antónia Pusich had already revealed herself as the first woman born in Cape Verde to publish in verse. We argue that only by taking a closer look at the Cape Verdean literary building, equipped with the magnifying glass on women's rights, can we portray the picture we will present here.

Without reducing the merit of the many men who gave body to the fruitful Cape Verdean literary production, we intend to highlight the immense merit that some women had in bypassing the family stronghold of existence and project themselves outside their homes, giving voice to collective aspirations through their writing.

We believe it is possible to identify six phases in the trajectory of female writing:

First: Women do not write because they lack the conditions due to varying
   limitations, namely illiteracy.
Second: They write, but they do not publish.
Third: They write and publish, but anonymously or under a pseudonym.
Fourth: They write and publish under their own names but have no visibility.

Fifth : They write and publish, have visibility, are studied, but are subtracted
from the literary canon.
Sixth: They write and publish, have visibility, are studied, and have access to
the literary canon.

In Cape Verde, women writers have been through the first five phases only,
falling short only on the achievement of the canon. This is the challenge that
is now faced.

Let us move on then to the discussion of creole literature from the gendered perspective: With the news of writing and writers in the archipelago
since the sixteenth century—just check the writings by the immortals of the
Academia Cabo-verdiana de Letras, ACL, André Dornellas e André Alvares
de Almada, or even a certain Cristóvão Costa, African, born in the islands
in 1525 and who wrote, among others, an interesting *Tratado em louvor das
mulheres*— it is only in the middle of the nineteenth century that the corpus
which will later constitute the Cape Verdean literary system will truly begin,
with the introduction of the press in 1842.

The first great period of Cape Verdean literature known as the period
of Pioneers and Nativists, of romantic influence, begins around 1842, with
the national press; the publication of the first issue of the *Boletim oficial do
Governo Geral de Cabo Verde*, in 1842; the publication of a book of poems
by Antónia Pusich, in 1846; the collaboration of Antónia Pusich from 1854 to
the *Almanaque de Lembranças Luso-Brasileiro;* the publication of the novel
O Escravo, by José Evaristo de Almeida; the establishment of *Seminário
Liceu de São Nicolau*, in 1866, which taught a classic education, and the collaboration of Guilherme da Cunha Dantas in the *Almanaque de Lembranças
Luso-Brasileiro* from 1872.

In this period, it is possible to highlight, among several male names such
as Eugénio Tavares, Pedro Cardoso, José Lopes, the sounding names of
Antónia Pusich, already mentioned, and other two women who collaborated,
under the pseudonym of *African and Humble Peasant*, with the *Almanaque
de Lembranças Luso-Brasileiro* and the *Almanaque Luso-Africano*. They
are Maria Luiza de Senna Barcellos "Africana" and Gertrudes Ferreira Lima
"Humilde Camponesa." Of course, it is possible to find the collaboration of
names of other women, but we cannot assess their impact on Cape Verdean
writing.

This first period of Cape Verdean literature was started by men and
women of the land or born in the kingdom who, although originally from the
"metropolis," settled in the "colony" and from there they made their literary creations. Many of them collaborated on the *Almanaque de Lembranças
Luso-Brasileiro* from 1851 to 1932, and on the *Almanach Luso-Africano*,

1895, 1899, with particular emphasis to Antónia Pusich, Maria Luísa Sena Barcellos, and Gertrudes Ferreira Lima.

Let us analyze the profile of these three women more closely:

Antónia Pusich (1805–1883) was a fierce woman who married three times, had eleven children, and was the director of three literary journals. She was, without a doubt, the first woman born in Cape Verde to manifest herself publicly through her quill, having published for the first time in 1841. She was simply the first Cape Verdean presence in the *Almanaque de Lembranças Luso-Brasileiro*, in which she published between 1854 and 1859, and also collaborated on the *Almanach Luso-Africano* in 1899.

Manuel Ferreira notes that from Antónia Pusich's hands came probably the oldest literary work written by an African writer, and surely written by a Cape Verdean writer. Effectively, the elegy in memory of the unfortunate victims murdered by Francisco de Mattos Lobo, in the evening of June 25, 1841, will have been the first literary work published in Cape Verde, by a writer born in the lands of the archipelago. In a time when women were confined to the domestic space, she defended that women should also learn how to read and write and to be able to take part in the social and political life of their country. Her literary production is extensive and extremely interesting. Through her work as a journalist, she contributed to the construction of feminism and the first opening to the definition of a pioneering path in what would become the awareness of women in the struggle to alter their familiar, economic, social, political, and judicial statute.

Now, Maria Luísa de Sena Barcelos (18??–1893) is considered the first female poet who is genuinely Cape Verdean. A lady with great influence in society at her time, she would have had a strong presence in the intellectual upbringing of the great poet Eugénio Tavares.

Between the years of 1883 and 1890, she collaborated on the "Almanaque de Lembranças Luso-Brasileiro." She belonged to an illustrious family and was the sister of historian Cristiano de Sena Barcelos, author of a work of great relevance, *General History of Cape Verde*. We are happy to present a very elucidated passage written by her about her social position in the text entitled *Hunger in Brava Island*, published in the *Almanaque* in 1890.

As for Gertrude Ferreira Lima (18??–1915), she also collaborated with poetic production on the Almanaque de Lembranças Luso-brasileiro and the Almanach Luso-Africano, along with Pusich and other unknown writers. It is said that she married at sixty years to a man who was fifteen years younger than her, a fact that caused scandal and gossip in Santo Antão, her home island. She was a highly regarded teacher and had important relations with João de Deus, the author of *Cartilha Maternal*, published in 1876.

In the writings of these women, such as in the writings of men of the same time period, formal, aesthetic, and thematic aspects of Portuguese neoclassicism and romanticism prevail, but above all, it makes visible the participation of women in their instruction and subliminally their emancipation.

The second period of the Cape Verdean literary history, which begins in the 1930s, is marked by the emergence of the magazine *Claridade* in 1936, in Mindelo, and goes on until the proclamation of independence.

The texts produced in this period reflect the real Cape Verde, the social problems caused by the draughts and hunger, by the decadence of the Great Port of Mindelo, and by the people hired to work the land in São Tomé. These problems led the intellectual elite to *stick their feet to the ground*, that is to say, to become aware, or better yet, to think about the land they stepped on. This was the ideal that informed the magazine *Claridade*, whose nine issues published between 1936 and 1960 constitute, until today, the greatest historical mark in Cape Verdean literature.

In this adventure stood out the names of Baltasar Lopes, Jorge Barbosa, and Manuel Lopes, who go without introductions. As for the predominant formal and aesthetic aspects, they are the same as the ones from the Portuguese and Brazilian Modernism, with Realist themes, mainly due to the influence of northeastern Brazilian literature.

The authors of this period present a type of writing that is marked by a hybridity between the creole and spoken Portuguese, in the style developed by Guimarães Rosa in Brazil. Throughout this period, many literary generations stand out, being that in the *Claridade* generation it was not possible to identify any female collaboration.

But it is in this period, in other publications, that a significant number of women's names appear and are revealed in Cape Verdean literature. Among them, we can highlight the names of Maria Helena Spencer, Yolanda Morazzo, Orlanda Amarílis, and Maria Margarida Mascarenhas.

With Maria Helena Spencer (1911–2006), we are delighted to point out the figure of the first female Cape Verdean journalist, but who was also a fictionalist, a chronicler, and a short story writer, in whose texts her intertextuality between her journalistic writing and her literary writing can be surprising.

Now, Yolanda Morazzo (1927–2009) considered the founder of modern Cape Verdean poetry written by women was part of the *Suplemento Cultural* group (1958), the generation of the new take-off, and collaborated with the *Artes e Letras* section of the *Diário de Notícias,* in Lisbon, the newspaper *República* and Angolan journals, living in Angola as well as in Portugal. Her poem "Barcos" portrays the feeling of *saudade* ("longing"), a recurrent theme in Cape Verdean literature, mainly among the author of the diaspora, as is the case of Yolanda herself.

Orlanda Amarílis (1924–2014), who was married to the writer and scholar of Cape Verdean literature Manuel Ferreira, stood out mainly with children's literature and short stories. Amarílis belongs to a family of great writers like

Baltasar Lopes da Silva, and her father Armando Napoleão was the author of the first dictionary of Cape Verdean Creole.

We present an excerpt of the short story "The House of the Masts," which characterizes the already very developed writing of Orlanda and that represents a woman's way of letting go, with their "hair covered and downward look" that used to prevail in national literature.

Maria Margarida Mascarenhas (1938–2011) was mostly known as a short story writer. She was part of the group Seló (1962) and collaborated with Cabo Verde Boletim de propaganda e informação. After national independence, she appeared in the magazine *Raízes* and was the first coordinator of the bulletin of the Cape Verdean diaspora, in Lisbon, Presença Crioula, where she lived and passed away.

The third period of Cape Verdean literature begins fundamentally with the proclamation of national independence. The publication, in 1974, of the book of poems *Pão & Fonema*, by Corsino Fontes, tends to be identified as the starting point of this period. This postcolonial and postmodern phase is defined by several styles and tendencies by a universal character, by formal and thematic innovation, and, above all, by the assertion of female writing.

Before anything else, it is important to highlight that although the names of women had been registered in the previous period, it is only in 1974, on the verge of the proclamation of independence, that the first works authored by women were published.

Therefore, alongside the publication of *Cais do Sodré de Salamansa* (1974) by Orlanda Amarílis, *Canticos de Ferro* (1976) by Yolanda Morazzo, and *Levedando a Ilha* (1988) by Margarida Mascarenhas, there is an unnumbered amount of new female voices that emerge from the islands.

Among them, it is worth mentioning the names of Leopoldina Barreto, Dina Salústio, Fátima Bettencourt, Ondina Ferreira, and Vera Duarte, who have published works and are members of the ACL, being that Leopoldina Barreto, who passed away in 2007, is an immortal of the *Academia*. We also highlight the names of Carlota de Barros and Hermínia Ferreira, recently elected to the *Academia*.

As it has already been said, Cape Verdean literature is opening up to the world; it imbues itself with new values and new perceptions of life and things. Going along with globalization, suffering the consequences of several worldwide events, such as armed conflicts, migrations and other types of dislocation, drug escalation, alcoholism, epidemics such as AIDS, a phenomenon of acculturation and terrorists, ecological and nuclear threats, the assumption of new sexual orientations, contemporary writing impregnates itself with this new climate of life and experiences translating it into a language and style that are different from the precedent writing, both in aesthetics and themes.

A revolution and an innovation in the ways of writing, in the perception of the new Cape Verdean reality, and the ways of portraying it can be observed. And this evolution can be verified both in the literary-aesthetic aspect itself, the new images, and metaphors, and regarding the content and approach to new themes that become evident by its originality and creativity.

If it is possible to state that during the romantic and modernist period, the literary influences came essentially from Portugal and Brazil, in contemporary times there is a complete overflow of borders and styles in terms of the literary influences. From Fernando Pessoa, Rimbaud and the surrealists, including Aimé Césaire, Simone de Beauvoir, St. John Perse, T. S. Eliot, and Dostoiewsky, the intertextuality between Cape Verdean writers and writers of diverse latitudes has no limits.

The great merit of this new generation resides in its heterogeneity and universality. It is possible to state that the writers from this period excel by their diversity of style and approach to themes in a way that it is almost impossible to make an affiliation or an imperative or scanty inclusion in literary school and around dogmatic mentors.

The freedom of writing, of how and what to write about in Cape Verde, is so great that it is possible to encounter writers from the same generation with such individual and original works, as universal as they are telluric, with multiple universalist resonances, coexisting in an impressive climate of creation and publication, with themes never before approached such as madness, humor, homosexuality, pedophilia, eroticism, among others.

Some writers follow the philosophy of *art for the sake of art*, there are authors who adopt the *art for the sake of life*, there is writing of great aesthetic beauty, and there is writing of great content.

Finally, there is everything that characterizes a great literary system, rich and diversified, although, obviously, of reduced dimensions due to the country's size and population. But it is a vigorous female writing that constitutes one of the most memorable characteristics of this period of Cape Verdean literature, as José Vicente Lopes asserts. We will not dwell on them because their history is still under construction and we can apply everything that has been said so far to them.

But we will, even if briefly, highlight the names of Fátima Bettencourt, Ondina Ferreira, Dina Salústio, Vera Duarte, Hermínia Ferreira, and Carlota de Barros for being members of the *Cape Verdean Academy of Letters*, as we mentioned before.

With Fátima, Cape Verde gets one of its most accomplished chroniclers, who covers not only the universe of the islands with her point of view. Now, Ondina stands out with short stories, above all, writing about her home island, Fogo, and the diaspora in the Americas,

Dina offers Cape Verde the first novel written by a woman and that has the singularity of treating the subject of madness. Vera Duarte entered the literary universe in the islands with the prose poem since its first publication in 1993. Hermínia Ferreira embraces children's literature with enthusiasm, and Carlota de Barros covers the universe of the islands with her poetry, above all, her native island of São Nicolau.

The work of female Cape Verdean writers makes so that the historical and literary register of the islands is not exclusively masculine, be it during the long colonial night or during the postindependence period, and they prove that women have always existed and that they were the anchor of the Cape Verdean nation.

Anonymous, for sure, not recognized, even ignored, but it was them, the women, who leavened the future of the islands. They pioneered mounts, planted the plains, harvested the grain, and baked the bread with which the people of the island were fed.

More than that, they confronted the power, fought hunger, circumvented death. But they had their existence recognized when they dared to cast their spoken and written words into the wind of the islands, even facing all the fears and silencing.

Today, female writers are breaking all their ties enthusiastically, daring to open all the hatches, not silencing in the face of any challenge and accepting dismayingly the silence that closed in around them because they feel capable of breaking this silence by themselves and one more time, through words, always through words, they dare to say we are here and the word is ours as is the power.

Today, we have the word and the power. And as we said in the beginning, the stronger the word, the greater the power. And the wider the power, the stronger the word will be, in a dialectical relationship that will never deplete.

And it was like this, voice to voice, pain to pain, boldness to boldness, with tears, with blood, with love and with affection, that Cape Verdean women of all times, of all beliefs, giving body to the bullets, built this paradigm *I write, therefore I am.*

History retained these women, and they made history. And they did not do it because they could wash, cook, tidy up the house and take care of the children, treat the elderly and the sick, as it is tradition. No! History registered them because they used the spoken and written word to say I am here! *I speak, therefore I am. I write, therefore I am. I think, therefore I am!*

It was the certainty transmitted by these women that they exist and are not a subcategory or suffer from any *capitus diminutio* that, in vigorous works, has been giving women, all women, the certainty that they also exist and, after all, are capable of being. They can be everything they have traditionally been, but above all, they can be everything a human being can be—also writers.

Although female Cape Verdean writers are still subtracted from the literary canon, this is a "sweet war" that we are committed to fighting and we intend to win, whatever it takes, for as long as it lasts. We have already fulfilled all the other steps. Necessarily, the canonic step will come inevitably, for the despair of those who want to impede our walk.

Apropos, I conclude with this note of hope, there is a real elite of a new generation of female writers emerging on the horizon of the islands who we salute for their strength, for their talent and effort. For future memory, we leave the register of the names of Eileen Barborsa, Carmelinda Gonçalves, Eurídice Monteiro, and Natacha Magalhães, from the fruitful contemporaneity.

Here we are, women, in prose and verse . . .

REFERENCE

Stanford Encyclopedia of Philosophy. "Descartes Epistemology." *Plato.* https://plato.stanford.edu/entries/descartes-epistemology/, 2019.

NOTE

1. The text originally written in Portuguese was translated to English by Joyce Silva Fernandes at Brown University.

Chapter 2

Kriolas di Muzika

Not Just for Men Anymore

Candida Rose

From Morna to CaboZouk and Doo-Wop to Hip Hop, Cabo Verdean women have left their mark on the music scene around the world. However, it wasn't until the early 1990s that they began to become rightfully noticed for their contributions. Unfortunately, up until this point, the Cabo Verdean music scene, both in Cabo Verde and in the United States, was dominated by men, with women only being acknowledged for their lead singing.

Arguably, the most well-known proponent of Cabo Verdean music, male or female, is Cesaria Evora. Her ascent to world music stardom in the 1990s opened the doors for many women who would come after her. But even before her "discovery," women such as Vickie Vieira, Celina Pereira, Fantcha, and Gardenia Benros in the United States and Tete Alhinho, Titina, and Nha Nacia Gomi in Cabo Verde, to name a few, were establishing themselves within local, national, and international arenas. For example, in the 1950s, a Doo-Wop group called the Tuneweavers, with two Cabo Verdean women (Charlotte Rose and Margot Sylvia), made their way into the U.S. popular music scene.

This chapter is not intended to be a comprehensive study or listing of Cabo Verdean women in music; that has to be another project for another time. However, as an extension of my own musical performance and educational work entitled, *Exploring the Cabo Verde – United States Musical Connection and Legacy*, the primary focus here is to continue to examine the many contributions of Cabo Verdean descendant women, especially in the United States, to the Cabo Verdean and American music scenes in order to shed well-deserved light on some of their too little recognized accomplishments (Baptista 2017).

THE SEARCH FOR WOMEN IN CABO
VERDEAN MUSICAL HISTORY

My friend, mentor, and former professor, Dr. Aminah Pilgrim, helped me
to understand the importance of "saying their names" in order to keep the
memories and contributions of people, particularly women, who may otherwise be lost in the annals of history, alive[1]. However, comprehensive information on women in Cabo Verdean musical history has been a challenge
to discover. One obstacle to doing research on any aspect of Cabo Verdean
history, but especially music, is the fact that the predominant canon of Cabo
Verdean research is written in Portuguese, with very little material available
in English, and much of it published in Cabo Verde without wide distribution. For example, there is an entry about my work in the book by Dr. Glaucia
Noquiera, *Cabo Verde & A Musica: Dicionario de Personagens* (Nogueira
2016), but I had to have someone translate it to confirm whether the information was accurate.

The other obstacle to generally finding well-documented information on
Cabo Verdean American women is that online information is found mostly
on Wikipedia. Following up on the (sometimes) scant sources Wikipedia
offers presents obstacles, in that many of the live links to these bibliographic
sources have expired and are no longer live. In the case of this chapter, much
of the information has been gathered from personal contact with some of
these subjects over the years, piecing together what I know and have experienced with the bits that are retrieved from other sources. The often-stated
proposition that Cabo Verdean women, as in many other cultures, are imbued
with a cultural and social reluctance to self-promote may also help explain the
dearth of documentary materials available, despite all the amazing musical
contributions these women have made. This dilemma speaks to the gender
bias in the archives and academia in general, which leads to an overwhelming disparity in the documentation and writing of certain histories. This reinforces the critical importance of the work of the Poderoza Conference (and
this collection of essays) in documenting women's contributions, of which
my work is a part.

In a musical group that I work with, Women in World Jazz, we concentrate
our efforts on female composers from around the world. Of course, being
Cabo Verdean, I have sought to highlight Cabo Verdean women composers. I
knew of several contemporary composers such as Lura, Mayra Andrade, and
Maria DeBarros, but I was looking for women further back in history. In all
of the general inquiries that I have made with people in the music industry,
mostly musicians and vocalists, no one could readily give me a name of a
female Cabo Verdean composer, which I found to be quite disconcerting. I
finally came across the knowledge, from my friend and musical colleague,

Tete Alhinho, that she was not only a talented vocalist but also a songwriter. This information came up during my interview with her for my research in 2016 on the role of music in politics, history, and identity in Cabo Verde. This was surprising to me because although I had known of her and her vocal work for several years, I had not realized that she was a composer. One of her songs, *Dia Ki Chuva Ben* ("The Day the Rain Comes"), has since been added to the Women in World Jazz repertoire.

This is to say that to find people in Cabo Verdean musical history, and especially to find women, and even more specifically women composers, requires path-breaking and sometimes difficult research into what seems like unfamiliar territory in musical scholarship. Thanks to Dr. Nogueira, her extremely prolonged, decade-long research has birthed a book (mentioned earlier) containing over 950 entries of musical personalities and groups of Cabo Verdean and non-Cabo Verdean heritage from around the world (Nogueira 2016). Sadly, however, only slightly more than ten percent of the entries are those of women or *Batukadeiras* (women of the Batuku tradition) and their groups. This percentage is even more puzzling considering that there are always more women than men in the Cabo Verdean archipelago at any given time. It is difficult to understand why women in a nation where they typically are the majority and where music is such a central part of the culture would be so underrepresented as musical contributors.

HOLDING THE FORT IN CABO VERDE/MUSIC, WOMEN, AND CABO VERDEAN INDEPENDENCE

Although the balance of recorded musical history is skewed toward men, it's noteworthy that even a small percentage of women have been represented. Unfortunately, it stands to reason that Cabo Verde's patriarchal society, influenced by European standards, would overshadow the contributions of women to the musical islands. However, during the 1950s–1970s, as the struggle for independence began to rage, the voices of women could be heard. From the culturally accepted morna and koladera to batuku and funana, which were being brought out from the inner workings of the Island of Santiago, women were supplying the front lines of the struggle with lyrics and songs describing the cultural climate and the suffering of the people.

Leaders such as Amilcar Cabral understood the necessity of bringing forth and preserving the musical traditions, particularly those that were driven underground by the dominant colonial government. These traditions, rooted in African culture, which include batuku, and finason, thankfully have been and are still mainly propagated by women by way of the *batukadeiras* (their groups performing batuku and finançon, mainly from the Island of Santiago). With reference to preserving culture and heritage, Cabral (1973) states:

> A people who free themselves from foreign domination will be free culturally only if, without complexes and without underestimating the importance of positive accretions from the oppressor and other cultures, they return to the upward paths of their own culture which is nourished by the living reality of its environment, and which negates both harmful influences and any kind of subjection to foreign culture. Thus, it may be seen that if imperialist domination has the vital need to practice cultural oppression, national liberation is necessarily an act of culture. (43)

In her dissertation work for Brown University, *Batuko and Funana: Musical traditions of Santiago, Republic of Cabo Verde,* Dr. Susan Hurley-Glowa (1997) describes the importance of *batuku* to the community in a section entitled, "Batukadeiras Role in Cabo Verdean Society." The following is a partial excerpt:

> Batuko provides a sense of belonging to a community of women on their own and reinforces a sense of ethnic pride in their African roots.

> Batuko allows women who are in a powerless position to feel good about themselves and openly express their defiance and contempt for Portuguese authority and morality.

> Batuko's function in establishing and solidifying mutual assistant ties cannot be underestimated. The women who do batik together care about each other and assist each other in a variety of ways. (254–256)

Nha Nacia Gomie (Batuku and Finançon Vocalist/Storyteller)

With the importance of *batuku* in mind, there are several women figures known for their performances of *batuku* and *finançon*, however, one name stands out, that of Nha Nacia Gomi. She will be remembered as the "Queen of Finançon." She was the epitome of what it means to be a culture bearer. According to online sources, she was born in 1924 and began singing for weddings and baptisms at the age of twelve. She is described as a "woman of batuku" and a "storyteller," as well as being known as "one of the voices of Cabo Verdean resistance." In her later years, she was invited to participate in festivals in Cabo Verde and took part in several recording projects. Among them is an album entitled *Cu Se Moçinhos*, which was originally released in 2005 and re-released by Sons D'Africa recording company in 2016.

Gomi passed away on February 3, 2011, at the age of eighty-six, and the Government of Cabo Verde declared the following February 5 as a national day of mourning (CaboVerde-infoa 2019; SapoNoticias 2011).

It is significant to trace the history of pioneering women such as Nha Nacia Gomi through particular islands and genres. Another example then, from the island of San Vicente, is the aforementioned Alhinho, as well as Saozinha, from the island of Brava.

Tete Alhinho (Vocalist and Composer)

Born on the Island of San Vicente, Tete Alhinho was a teenager when the independence movement was in full swing. She remembers being a part of the marches and protests during the mid-1970s (Alinho 2016). Later, in the 1990s, she became the lead singer of the famed group Simentera, which represented Cabo Verde throughout the world performing traditional, folkloric, roots-oriented Cabo Verdean music, some of which were composed by her.

Saozinha (Vocalist)

Saozinha Fonseca was born and raised on the island of Brava, Cabo Verde, and grew up in a musical and religious family. As a result, her musical style has been influenced by her church participation and the songs of her island, most notably, the *mornas* penned by famed poet Eugenio Tavares. In 1986, after immigrating to Boston, Massachusetts, she won a singing contest "The Whole World Sings" representing the Cabo Verdean community in the United States. She has since gone on to record several CDs, focusing mainly on *mornas* from Brava, including one dedicated solely to Mr. Tavares entitled *"Saozinha canta Eugenio Tavares"* ("Saozinha sings Eugenio Tavares"). She continues to grace the stages of Cabo Verdean events and festivals around New England and beyond (Nogueira 2016; Caboverdeb 2019).

Titina (Vocalist)

Considered to be "one of the most authentic voices in Cabo Verde," Titina (Albertina Almeida Rodrigues) has been singing since the age of six and recorded her first single at the age of fifteen. She studied under the tutelage of the famed Caboverdian composer B. Leza. Her first album *Titina Canta B.Leza* was recorded in 1993. She was honored in 2006 by the Government of Cabo Verde for her contributions to the preservation of the traditional genres of *morna* and *koladera* (CaboVerde-info 2019).

WORLDWIDE RECOGNITION: CESARIA EVORA

The primary recent proponent of Cabo Verdean music worldwide, as confirmed by Billboard (Verna 1995) was Cesaria Evora, who came to the forefront of Cabo Verdean music in the 1990s, although she had been performing in Cabo Verde for much of her life. She was discovered in Cabo Verde but then moved to France to produce her first album, Miss Perfumado. She maintained a home in Cabo Verde but was based in France. Her most noted song is *"Sodade,"* which was written in the 1940s, and it strikes a chord with Cabo Verdeans and others all over the world. It was this song that allowed Cesaria to put Cabo Verdean music on the world music map.

"Sodade," a deep longing for a land or loved one left behind, is a theme resonant with Cabo Verde's history and culture and continues to resonate with Cabo Verdean descendants in the diaspora in the United States and other locations. It is a concept that captures the heart of a country whose history has been built on the premise of colonial domination, where much of its population has had to emigrate in order to find a better life elsewhere. As Frantz Fanon (1963) writes in *Wretched of the Earth*, "A national culture is the whole body of efforts made by a people in the sphere of thought to describe, justify, and praise the action through which that people has created itself and keeps itself in existence" (233). It is this legacy of longing and "body of effort" translated through music and culture that continues to unify the transnational community scattered in diaspora across the globe. Furthermore, researchers of diverse diasporas note the persistence as well as the transformation of heritage culture, particularly as conveyed through music, in supporting the immigration experiences of diverse groups while conveying cultural and political values from both sending and receiving communities (Martin 2010).

I had the honor and privilege of meeting Cesaria Evora after one of her concerts, because I was completing an assignment for my World Music Class at the University of Massachusetts, Dartmouth, in my second semester (2001) as an undergraduate student. The assignment was to review the concert and give my impressions of the performer and the performance. It was a great concert and she was very gracious, despite a slight language barrier (my Kriolu was not very fluent at the time). Her global ascent as the "Barefoot Diva" and "Queen of Morna" is a testament to the viability of Cabo Verdean music worldwide (Martin 2010).

CARRYING THE CABO VERDEAN MUSIC
BATON IN THE UNITED STATES

As early as the 1940s, Cabo Verdean women began carrying the baton of cultural heritage in the United States. Up until the 1970s or 1980s, Vickie

Vieira was the sole American-born, Cabo Verdean voice of women in a sea of Cabo Verdean men in the United States who were passing on Cabo Verdean musical heritage. As U.S. immigration opened in 1965, other vocalists from Cabo Verde reached the United States and proceeded to keep its culture alive through music.

Vickie Vieira (Vocalist) and Amor di Mai

Born and raised in the Fox Point neighborhood of Providence, RI to parents from San Nicolau and Santiago islands, Cabo Verde, "Aunt Vickie," as she was affectionately known by many, and her brother, "Flash" Tavares were a Cabo Verdean musical team. Aunt Vickie and her brother were among the first generation of Cabo Verdean-Americans who played Cabo Verdean music all across New England from the early 1940s. However, as a solo artist, she also performed with local bands infusing jazz with Cabo Verdean music. She performed with big bands, such as The Skyliners and the Duke Oliver Orchestra, which were both led by Cabo Verdeans. She became known for her "beautiful voice and mastery of Cabo Verdean music" (Discogs 2019, para. 1). She, along with the Creole Sextet, represented Cabo Verdean culture in the United States at the Smithsonian Folk Life Festival in Washington, DC, in 1995, along with several other bands from the New England area (So Sabi 1999). In 2006, the Rhode Island Historical Preservation and Heritage Commission inducted her into the Cabo Verdean Hall of Fame (Mason and Morrin 2020). Aunt Vickie was also the actual aunt of the famous R&B group "Tavares," and "Flash" was the father of this famed group of brothers. Indeed, my own musical genealogy and connection to this history is both personally and professionally strong—clearly a driving force for both my performing and writing this musical legacy.

Songs about women, and particularly mothers, are quite prevalent in the Cabo Verdean repertoire. This phenomenon is no different in the United States. One such song was written by Joaquim do Livramento, Jr., born in Sao Nicolau, Cabo Verde Islands on January 25, 1891. The song *Amor di Mai* (A Mother's Love) was inspired by his son, Arthur. While he was doing U.S. military service in World War II, he wrote to his father and requested that he write a song telling a story of the profound love of his mother.

This song became a staple in the United States Cabo Verdean music repertoire. It also became one of the songs that Aunt Vickie was known for. "Amor di Mai" helped to solidify her place as a Cabo Verdean culture bearer. The English translation of the first lines of the song says it all, "There is no one in this world who has a love as deep as is a mother's love." With her vocal interpretations of traditional Cabo Verdean songs, she, along with her brother, touched the hearts of many. Ms. Vieira's rendition can be found on the CD entitled "SoSabi: Cape Verdean Music from New England" (Rounder Records 1999). A contemporary version is featured on my CD "KabuMerikana: The Sum of ME" (Baptista 2006).

Gardenia Benros (Vocalist, Composer, Producer, Educator)

Gardenia Benros, born in Praia, Santiago, is a vocalist, composer, producer, and educator. She made her way onto the music scene in the 1980s being the first Cabo Verdean woman to be signed to a major U.S. record label, Polygram Records. Gardenia also went on to graduate from Berklee College of Music in Boston, again being the first accomplishment of its kind for a Cabo Verdean woman. During her career, she also represented Cabo Verde in the United States as the winner of "Miss Cabo Verde/USA Beauty Pageant." Gardenia has traveled the United States and other countries carrying on the musical traditions of Cabo Verde through her voice and compositions (CaboVerde 2019).

Belinda Lima (Vocalist)

Belinda Lima is a first-generation American-born Cabo Verdean whose parents were born in Cabo Verde on the islands of São Vicente and Brava. According to her personal biography, she began her experiences with Cabo Verdean cultural endeavors "before the age of ten" performing in Batuku and Koladera dance groups. In addition, by the age of eighteen, she was crowned Miss Black Rhode Island and Miss Black New England.

As early as 1987, Belinda started performing at festivals in Cabo Verde, the first being Baia das Gatas in San Vicente, at the tender age of fourteen. While there she met members of the group Expedition, who were based in Connecticut and she began performing with them. She subsequently joined other United States–based Cabo Verdean bands, including Jamm Band, from Rhode Island. She went on to record her first CD entitled *Realidade d'Amor* (Reality of Love) in 1999 and subsequently recorded *Un Momento* (One Moment) in 2000, which led her to success at the Festival di Santa Maria on the Island of Sal with the song *Santa Maria*.

In 2007, Belinda was invited by the Cabo Verde Embassy in Angola to perform in Luanda. In 2010, Belinda moved to Cabo Verde where she lived for six years, developing a musical apprenticeship program called the "DoReMi" Music School, located in Mindelo on the island of São Vicente.

Currently residing in Rhode Island, in addition to pursuing her Cabo Verdean cultural endeavors, Belinda also has a love for gospel music and is also an accomplished gospel vocalist. She is currently working on fusing her gospel influences with the Cabo Verdean traditional genres of morna and koladera with a new solo project. In her words, "Stay Tuned!" (Lima 2019).

Celina Perreira (Vocalist, Composer, Educator)

Among the many vocalists gracing United States stages in the 1990s was Celina Pereira. After traveling, performing, and recording all over the world, during this time, she settled in Boston, Massachuttes, working in the Boston Public Schools as a storyteller. She later joined the representation of Cabo Verdean culture at the Smithsonian Folklife Festival in Washington, DC, in 1995 and later appeared with Ivo Pires and his band in 1996 at the Boston Center for the Arts' New England Cabo Verdean Folk Life Festival, *"So Sabi."* Born on the Island of Boa Vista, she recorded her first single in 1978 and has continued with a long list of credits that includes albums (CDs), concerts, children's books, awards, and so on. She now lives in Portugal where she has distinguished herself as a premier proponent of Cabo Verdean history and culture as a performer and educator. In 2014, Ms. Pereira was presented with a Career Award at the Cabo Verdean Music Awards (Pinto 2018).

Fantcha (Vocalist, Composer)

Another defining Cabo Verdean voice of the 1990s was that of Fantcha. Born in San Vicente, she started singing at a very young age. According to her biography, at the age of 10, she joined a carnival group called *Flores do Mindelo* ("Flowers of Mindelo"). She was soon discovered by a well-known composer, Gregorio Gonsalves, better known as Ti Goy. He later introduced her to Cesaria Evora who took her under her wing, and the rest, as they say, is history. She joined Cesaria in concert in the United States in 1988 and decided to stay, residing in New York. By the late 1990s, she had established herself as a culture bearer in her own right. She continues to record and has several albums/CDs under her belt (Fantcha 2019).

CABO VERDEAN WOMEN IN AMERICAN MUSIC

Not only have Cabo Verdean and Cabo Verde-descended women demonstrated proficiency in Cabo Verdean music in the United States, but they have also incorporated themselves into the musical mainstream of American music.

Margo Sylvia, Charlotte Rose-Davis, Alice Fernandes (The Tuneweavers)

With the 1950s came the rise of the Doo-Wop era. As Cabo Verdeans continued to acculturate to U.S. society, they also began to display the musical talent that comes from within. This can be seen in the example of The

Tuneweavers that emerged during this period. This group was made up of four individuals who were Cabo Verdean.

The Tuneweavers became a very popular Doo-Wop group from 1956 to 1964. A little-known fact about them is that one of the singers, Margo Sylvia, co-wrote the song that sold a million copies "Happy, Happy Birthday Baby" with her brother, Gilbert Lopes, who was also part of the group. Margo was the first Cabo Verdean American woman to ever write a very successful and well-received song, which reached no. 4 on the Billboard charts. Two of the four members, John Sylvia and Charlotte Davis-Rose received a Lifetime Achievement Award and were inducted into the Doo Wop Hall of Fame in 2003. In order to perform for the award ceremony, Mr. Sylvia added two new Cabo Verdean descended members to the group, Dr. Burt Pina and Alice Fernandes. They currently travel the country performing with other Doo-Wop groups from the 1950s (Sylvia 2016; Walker 2019).

Shawnn Monteiro (Jazz Vocalist, Educator)

Shawnn Monteiro is a Cabo Verdean American jazz vocalist well known not only in the United States but also in Europe, especially Italy where she was noted in *Verve Magazine, Italy* as the best jazz vocalist. She has been conducting jazz workshops in Italy since 1995. She was "discovered" in California by jazz great Mango Santamaria but has spent most of her time based in Rhode Island. She is the daughter of the late legendary jazz bassist Jimmy Woode, who was a veteran of the Duke Ellington band (the band that also housed Paul Gonsalves for over twenty-five years). Her biography reads as a virtual who's who of jazz with all of the personalities that she has performed with. She is also an educator of jazz music and performance teaching at Rhode Island College and Hart School of Music in Connecticut (Monteiro 2019).

In an online article by Burt Jagolinzer of *Motif Magazine*, Rhode Island, Shawnn is described as "one of the top female jazz singers in America" (Jagolinzer 2019). Why she hasn't yet been invited to sing at the Kriol Jazz Festival in Cabo Verde is still a mystery to me. If anyone should be representing Cabo Verdean/American Jazz artists, it should be Shawnn Monteiro. However, this is an example of the information gap between the "powers that be" who are organizing these festivals in Cabo Verde, who happen to be mainly men, and their lack of knowledge of the amazing talent that resides in the United States among women musicians who are of Cabo Verdean descent.

Lisa "Left Eye" Lopes (R&B/Hip Hop Artist/ Rapper/Producer, Member of TLC)

Probably the most generally well known of all American-born Cabo Verdean women musical artists is Lisa "Left Eye" Lopes of the group TLC, although most people do not realize that she is of Cabo Verdean descent. According to an article by Ethnicelabs (2019), "Lisa was the daughter of Wanda Denise Coleman and Ronald Eugene Lopes" (who was Cabo Verdean) (para. 1). She was born in Philadelphia, Pennsylvania, and died tragically in a car accident in Honduras at the age of thirty.

Lisa Lopes (Left Eye), Rozonda Thomas (Chilli), and Tionne Watkin (T-Boz) formed the group TLC in 1991 and by 1994 had gone on to sell eleven million copies of their recordings in the United States with their second album "Crazy Sexy Cool" becoming the largest selling hip-hop recording by a female group. The album's success led them to two Grammy Awards. Lisa was the rapper of the group, and according to an article in biography.com, "Left Eye" was "known for her brash, uncompromising demeanor" and "engineered the group's brand of empowered womanhood that vaulted the trio to the top of the charts" (Biography.com 2019, para. 1).

Lisa took several trips to Honduras and involved herself in projects to help victims of Hurricane Mitch, a devastating storm that hit Central America in 1997, and eventually owned a condominium there. She was also working on finding her own peace after what has been said to be a difficult childhood (Imdb 2019). In 2000, she began work on her debut solo project entitled "SuperNova" which was released internationally but not in the United States. Soon after, she was beginning a project to release another album, signing a deal with Suge Knight. However, the project never happened. Sadly, according to her biography, she was the only fatality in a vehicle containing seven passengers on their way back to her home in Roma, Honduras. She passed away on April 25, 2002, a month before her thirty-first birthday (Ethnic 2019).

Mikelyn (Lynn) Roderick (R&B Vocalist)

Mikelyn Roderick, who was recently featured in a program about Cabo Verdean women called "Coffee with Kriolas" produced by Rashad Roulac, is a second-generation, American-born Cabo Verdean. Her parents are from Brava and Fogo, as well as Senegal and Sicily. She grew up in the Cabo Verdean community of Onset, Massachusetts. Her paternal grandmother was also a singer and told stories about singing to passengers on "The Ernestina" traveling from Cabo Verde to the United States (Roderick 2019).

According to her biography on last.fm, Mikelyn started in the music industry when she was nineteen years old recording a version of the ballad by the legendary R&B group Blue Magic entitled "Sideshow." This recording led her to work with writer/producer Jon Lind as a demo vocalist. As a result, she became a background singer for well-known R&B and Gospel artists such as Stevie Wonder, Quincy Jones, Bill Withers, Barry White, and Kirk Franklin, to name a few.

She went on to become a member of the group "By All Means" which experienced wide acclaim not only in the United States but also in Europe and Japan. In addition, she had the privilege of working with Halle Berry as a singer in the HBO movie *The Dorothy Dandridge Story*, as well as being featured in a double role as actress and singer in the Netflix film *Wonderland* (Roderick 2019).

Mikelyn recently finished her first solo project entitled "Copasetic is" which was recorded on Dome Records and can be found online. She is also assisting with the career of her daughter, Elle Varner, who is finding a level of success in the music industry following in her mother's and grandmother's footsteps. That's what legacy is all about (Last.fm 2019)

Danielle Andrews (R&B Vocalist, composer, educator)

Danielle Andrews is a talented and dynamic vocalist currently residing in New Bedford. She is also a second-generation American born of Cabo Verdean descent. She grew up in the Cabo Verdean community of Wareham, Massachusetts. She, along with several other Cabo Verdean female vocalists, was featured on an episode of the online program "Coffee with Kriolas."

Danielle began her ascent to stardom as a young girl singing in, and winning, many New England area talent shows. According to her biography, she joined a group of three other local women named "Shades." They went on to be signed by Motown Records in 1997 and earned a hit single "Tell Me I'll Be Around" (Almeida 1997).

After the group disbanded, Danielle enjoyed a successful solo career touring as a backup vocalist for Enrique Iglesias who gave her the opportunity to travel worldwide. She also toured with Whitney Houston and Destiny's Child among others. After touring, she returned to New Bedford to raise a family. However, she currently performs in New England and Rhode Island as a soloist and with various groups. In 2018, Danielle released her first solo single "Your Body's Callin" and is working on a full album. In addition, according to internet sources, she and other members of the group Shades are planning a revival tour (New Bedford Guide 2018).

SOME CURRENT CABO VERDEAN MUSIC CULTURE BEARERS RESIDING IN THE UNITED STATES

With Cesaria Evora opening doors for Cabo Verdeans, other talented musicians and vocalists have been able to expose themselves to a wider musical world audience. Unsurprisingly, most of them are women.

In the United States, the most noted Cabo Verdean singer happens to be the goddaughter of Cesaria Evora, Maria DeBarros. Her parents were born in Cabo Verde, but she was born in Senegal and raised in Mauritania, as expressed in the song and title track of her first album *"Nha Mundo"* ("My World"). She spent much of her early life in Providence, Rhode Island, where she became part of the Jamm Band, a group made up of Cabo Verdean musicians playing contemporary Cabo Verdean songs as well as American top-40 standards. She also enjoyed a career as a Mexican singer performing Spanish language songs in California, and she is still based in Los Angeles, California. However, as she also relays in the song, her blood and soul are with Cabo Verde. As a result of her deep love for the country of her cultural upbringing, she now travels to many other countries spreading the music of Cabo Verde (DeBarros 2003).

Other important Cabo Verdean female musical figures are included. Lutchinha, a Cabo Verdean–born vocalist living in Brockton, Massachusetts, travels frequently to and from Cabo Verde to perform and promote her music. Gutty Duarte, who also immigrated to the United States at the age of 20, presents the music of her native island, Santiago, in the forms of batuku and funana. Ingrid Monteiro, born in Cabo Verde but immigrated to the United States as a young girl, is the voice behind many of the solo artists recording and performing live in the United States. She is a well sought-after background vocalist who is also working toward a solo project.

Among the contemporary crop of New England Cabo Verdean vocalists are Lisa Lopes also from Brockton (not to be confused with Lisa Lopes of TLC) and Sarah Barbosa from Rhode Island. Both Lisa and Sarah are talented cabo-zouk/pop artists as well as contemporary R&B/hip hop artists. Lisa Lopes was recently nominated for a CVMA (Cabo Verdean Music Award). In addition, Emmanuela "Nadia" Alves is a Cabo Verdean vocal artist and recent graduate of Berklee College of Music who is also mixing her Cabo Verdean musical roots with various African American genres such as neo-soul, jazz, and gospel to add to the exchange and continuance of cultural heritage. Lori Gomes, the daughter of well-known R&B Cabo Verdean American vocalist Kevin Gomes, is also an R&B/Neo Soul vocalist who is exploring her Cabo Verdean musical heritage and incorporating more of this into her performances. Michelle Cruz is a Cabo Verdean/American jazz artist based in Rhode Island who is also incorporating Cabo Verdean–inflected music into her American jazz repertoire. Kristen Perry-Speller is also a second-generation Cabo Verdean. Her father, Leo Perry, was also a well-known Cabo Verdean musician who played with several Cabo Verdean bands in and around New England. Kristen is a singer/songwriter and Taunton native, whose song "Phoenix Rising Up" won a Grammy Award in the category of "Global Peace Song" in 2018 (Perry-Speller 2019).

All of these artists represent the myriad ways in which Cabo Verdeans women in the United States are helping to keep cultural legacies alive by pursuing their passions for music and heritage in all of its various forms and genres while keeping their connections to Cabo Verde. It should also be noted that in addition to these artists, over the last several years, there has also been a new crop of talented women rising in Cabo Verde. They include singer/songwriter Melisse Andrade, Cabo Verdean Hip-Hop Artist; Blacka, Vocalist and Composer, Elida Almeida; and Traditional Vocalists Cremilda Medina and Assol Garcia, just to name a few. Therefore, it is clear to see that the legacy of Cabo Verdean women carrying and passing along the cultural baton both in and out of Cabo Verde is alive and well.

CONCLUSION

There are far too many Cabo Verdean women musicians and vocalists to mention who are continuing the legacy in the United States left by people such as Vickie Vieira. However, I am proud to confess that I feel as though "Aunt Vickie" passed her torch on to me in order to assist in keeping the musical culture and heritage alive. By this, I mean that since Spring of 2001, when I entered (at the age of forty) the University of Massachusetts, Dartmouth, to earn a bachelor of arts degree in music; I have also been studying, performing, and promoting Cabo Verdean and Cabo Verdean American music and culture.

As an undergraduate, I received permission from my professors to focus all of my scholarly research (when appropriate) on Cabo Verdean music, culture, and history. I was in a Jazz/World Music Studies program; therefore, I also continued the exploration and performance of jazz, gospel, and rhythm and blues (In some respects, much like Ms. Vieira). In 2006, a year after graduating, I released a CD entitled "KabuMerikana: The Sum of ME," which included versions of *"Amor di Mai"* and *"Sodade,"* as well as jazz standards such as "Afro Blue" and "That's All." The CD also included several original compositions in English and Kriolu. I termed my music "KabuJazz" honoring both sides of my musical heritage. Later that year, I made my first trip to Cabo Verde to sing backup with Ms. Vieira's nephew, "Tiny" Tavares. From 2007 to 2009, I traveled the United States with a Performing Arts Festival troupe, educating people about Cabo Verdean culture and music, as well as Native American, Alaskan, and Hawaiian cultures. However, because of my work as a Life Enrichment Entertainer, singing for nursing homes, assisted living, and adult daycare facilities in the New England area since 2007, I had the pleasure and blessing of singing for "Aunt Vickie" while she was at a nursing home in East Providence, Rhode Island. Subsequently, I was asked to sing *"Amor di Mai"* for her funeral in January 2013. In my heart, I could feel her presence, and this honor remains as one of the most precious memories and highlights of my career.

In 2014, I made my fourth trip to Cabo Verde to sing at the internationally known Kriol Jazz Festival. In 2016, I was awarded a grant to assist me in researching Cabo Verde while working to earn a master's degree in science in transnational, cultural, and community studies (University of Massachusetts, Boston 2017). My research and capstone project was concentrated on the Cabo Verdean/American musical connection and legacy, of which Ms. Vieira and her brother "Flash" played a huge role. In 2019, I was asked to be included in a national television program on an episode focusing on the Portuguese connection between Azorean, Brazilian, and Cabo Verdean food and cultures in the Boston area. The episode, which aired in March of 2020 on PBS entitled "No Passport Required/Boston," hosted by Marcus Samuelson, featured some of my singing as well as discussion surrounding Cabo Verdean history and my experience as a Cabo Verdean American performer.

This chapter is part of my continuing attempt to bridge the gap of information and educate the different sides of the Cabo Verdean diaspora as well as the general public about the accomplishments left by those who came before us and those who continue to unapologetically honor our cultural heritage through song, dance, and other forms of artistic expression. We are a people whose music lies deep within and it is time for the contributions of Cabo Verdean women in the musical realm to be acknowledged and honored.

NOTE

1.   Pilgrim lecture based on the often-quoted African American proverb which stated that if the names of elders who had contributed to our liberation were spoken, they would never die nor would their legacies disappear. The statement has become most widely associated with the struggles of women and is an example of black feminist politics.

REFERENCES

Alinho, Tete. Personal Interview, June 2016.

Almeida, Diane. "Local Girls Rise to Fame in Music Industry; Perform July 13." *American Magazine (The Providence American)*, July 3, 1997.

Baptista, Candida Rose. "KabuMerikanus-The Sum of US: Exploring the Cabo Verde-United States Musical Connection and Legacy." *MS-TCCS Capstone Presentation*. UMASS Boston, 2017.

Biography.com. "Lisa "Left Eye" Lopes Biography." Accessed March 2019. https://www.biography.com/people/lisa-left-eye-lopes-9542471.

CaboVerdea. "Gardenia: The Voice of Cabo-Verdean Soul." http://www.caboverde.com/music/gardenie.htm, 2019.

Cabo Verdean Heritage Awards. "Joaquim Livramento." Accessed March 2019. http://www.Caboverdeanmuseum.org/2007halloffame.html, 2007.

CaboVerdeb. "Saozinha: Biography." http://www.caboverde.com/music2/saozi.htm, 2019.

CaboVerde-infoa. "Maria Inácia Gomes Correia (Nácia Gomi)." http://www.caboverde-info.com/esp/Identidade/Personalidades/Maria-Inacia-Gomes-Correia-Nacia Gomi&prev=search, 2019.

CaboVerde-infob."Albertina Rodrigues Almeida (Titina)." http://www.caboverde-info.com/esp/Identidade/Personalidades/Albertina-Rodrigues-Almeida-Titina&prev=search, 2019.

Cabral, Amilcar. *Return to the Source: Selected Speeches of Amilcar Cabral.* Edited by African Information Services. New York: Monthly Review Press, 1973.

DeBarros, Maria. *Nha Mundo (My World): Music of Cabo Verde*, produced by Djim Job and Carlos "Kalu"Monteiro, 2003, compact disc.

Discogs. "Vickie Vieira, Profile." Accessed March 2019. https://www.discogs.com/artist/5660418-Vicki-Vierra.

Ethnic. "Lisa Lopes." Accessed March 2019. https://ethnicelebs.com/lisa-lopes.

Fanon, Frantz. *The Wretched of the Earth.* New York: Grove, 1963.

Fantcha. Accessed March 2019. https://fantcha.com/bio.

Hurley-Glowa, Susan. "Batuko and Funana: Musical Traditions of Santiago, Republic of Cabo Verde." Dissertation, Brown University, 1997.

Imdb. "Lisa 'Left Eye' Lopes: Biography." Accessed March 2019. https://www.imdb.com/name/nm0519912/bio?ref_=nm_ov_bio_sm.

Jagolinzer, Burt. "Jazz Insights: Shawnn Monteiro." Accessed March 2019. http:/motifri.com/shawnnmonteiro.

Last.fm. "Mikelyn Roderick: Biography." Accessed March 2019. https://www.last.fm/music/Mikelyn+Roderick/+wiki.

Lima, Belinda. "Personal Biography and Phone Conversations." March 2019.

Martin, Carla. "Cesaria Evora: The Barefoot Diva and Other Stories." *Transition* 103: 82–97. Indiana: Indiana University Press, 2010.

Mason, Jeanine, and Cheyenne Morrin. "Vickie Tavares Vieira." Accessed March 2019. http://mappingartsproject.org/providence/artists/vickie-tavares-vieira-2/, 2020.

Monteiro, Shawnn. "Biography." Accessed March 2019. http://www.shawnnmonteiro.com/biography.

New Bedford Guide. "Faces of New Bedford #166: Danielle Andrews." Accessed March 2019. https://www.newbedfordguide.com/faces-of-new-bedford-166-danielleandrews/2018/08/10, 2018.

Nogueira, Glaucia. *Cabo Verde & A Musica: Dicionario de Personagens.* Lisbon: Campo da Comunicação, 2016.

Perry-Speller, Kristen. "Personal Biography and Conversations." April 2019.

Pinto, Domingos. "Celina Pereira: Promotora Da Cultura e do Dialogo Intercultural." https://www.vaticannews.va/pt/africa/news/2018-11/celina-pereira-promotora-da-cultura-e-do-dialogo-intecultural.html, 2018.

Roderick, Mikelyn. "Personal Biography and Phone Conversations." April 2019.

SapoNoticias. "Died Nha Nacia Gomi, Queen of Finason." https://noticias.sapo.cv/actualidade/artigos/morreu-nha-nacia-gomi-rainha-do-finason&prev=search, 2011.

So Sabi: Cabo Verdean Music from New England. Rounder Records, 1999. Compact disc.

Sylvia, John. "Personal Interview." May 10, 2016.

Verna, Paul. "Cabo Verde in World Beat Spotlight: Tiny Nation Has Rich Musical Heritage." November 18, 1995. Billboard, 1995.

Walker, Toby. "The Tune Weavers, Soulwalking." Accessed March 2019. http://www.soulwalking.co.uk/Tune%20Weavers.html.

Part II

EXPLORING COMMUNITY

Chapter 3

On Fieldwork and Family

Gina Sánchez Gibau

I

As I walked tenuously up the inclined, stone-paved road in the darkness, clutching the hands of two young Cape Verdean girls, my "adopted daughters" aged eight and ten, a wave of emotion settled in. I swayed our clasped hands to the rhythm of the *tambores* and marveled at the throngs of people in front of us. This night was one of several in the days ahead culminating the tireless work that I had witnessed in preparation for the *festa di San Djon*. As I fought back tears, I breathed in the electricity stimulated by the call and response of *kola*, the piercing sounds of whistles, and the *foguetes* lighting up the starry sky with color and sound. At that moment, I contemplated the miracle of our ancestors, mine, and my husband's, who made their way across the Atlantic and were responsible for our very existence and presence in Brava and for the spectacle of cultural performance of which we were a part of.

This was our second trip to the islands, this time as a married couple and accompanied by our eleven-year-old son. On the first trip in June of 2001, I joined the ranks of a precious few third-generation Cape Verdean Americans with the desire and the opportunity to travel to the homeland of our ancestors, Cabo Verde. The trip was both personal and professional, with the former outweighing the latter. As I attempted to engage in an exploratory study of gender relations in Brava, the weight of my husband's grief as he encountered friends and relatives who offered their condolences on the passing of his grandmother, who raised him, became the focus of my attention. Despite this overarching agenda, we were able to witness some components of *San Djon*, the annual celebration of Brava's patron saint, *Sao Joao Batista*, or St. John the Baptist.

As I returned to Brava sixteen years later, in 2017, my encounter with the *festa di San Djon* was markedly different. During this trip, the anthropological endeavor, though unplanned to a certain extent, figured prominently in my experiences. Specifically, during my two weeks of "fieldwork," I gained a deeper understanding of *San Djon* not only through participant observation but also by being embedded within the social contexts undergirding the planning and execution of the event. As a result of being a part of the creative process of *San Djon*—the doing and making of *San Djon*—I was not learning *about* this tradition, but rather I was learning *from* it.

This phenomenological approach to discovery—of learning *from* the environments in which we interact—has been conceptualized by Ingold (2013) and is used here as a theoretical framework to understand the "making" of *San Djon* as a cultural site of experiential learning and how this type of transformational learning occurs during anthropological fieldwork. Marchand (2010) describes the concept of making as an interpretation of knowledge production that involves "a dialogical and constructive engagement between people, and between people, things, and environment" (xii). By invoking this concept, I acknowledge the paradox presented here as I attempt to translate this deeper, embodied knowledge I now have of *San Djon* in written form for the reader, without my experiences becoming fixed and otherwise lost in translation once they are described.

Ingold (2013) privileges experiential learning over (ethnographic) documentation and participation observation, as he argues for the "ultimate objective" of anthropological transformation (13). My more recent experience in Brava was distinctly anthropological and not ethnographic, by Ingold's definition, given the fact that I did not make a conscious effort to document the events in writing nor did I make an explicit attempt to record the events in any systematic way. I did document the event visually, through photographs and some video, which was initiated more so to capture auditory moments (e.g., video shot at night with little to no additional lighting). Although this last trip was staged more as a vacation than fieldwork, I could not ignore my anthropological impulses—of seeing, feeling, and knowing. Yet, I had no idea that this experience would provide me with a fresh perspective on the practice of anthropology, one that accommodates an element of freedom from the ethnographic enterprise.

II

Doing and making as an "art of inquiry" (Ingold 2013, 6) affords one the ability to follow a flow of knowledge production, where learning is revealed with each new activity. Knowledge becomes an outgrowth of our engagements with our environment and the people therein. There is not necessarily an impulse to hypothesize or predict the next logical step. The art of inquiry requires us to surrender to the present moment, to let learning unfold through our engagements. In doing so, other questions naturally arise: What can we learn from our own experiences and how will those experiences move us forward, as a person or a researcher?

Given my experiences, perhaps this is not a novel idea but rather an example of coming full circle. My initial foray into anthropological fieldwork began when I was a graduate intern at the Smithsonian Institution's Folklife Festival in 1995. That was the year in which people of Cape Verdean ancestry were one of the many groups featured at this annual summer spectacle of cultural heritage. There, I was placed in a position of learning by doing, having to manage a stage on which performances and demonstrations of Cape Verdeans from the various islands as well as Cape Verdean Americans occurred. This unprecedented event, entitled "The Cape Verdean Connection," represented the largest gathering of individuals from Cabo Verde and its global diaspora for ten days on the National Mall in Washington, DC.

It was there, under sweltering tents during that momentous last week of June, that I first learned about the rhythms, cadences, movements, and melodies of Cape Verdean culture embodied in *txabeta, finason, kola, batuku,* and *mazurka.* Women figured prominently in my transformative learning process that summer. I bore witness to the power of Nha Nacia Gomi leading a circle of *batukaderas,* Vicky Viera alongside her brother, "Flash" (Feliciano, father of the Tavares brothers), belting out tunes with their Cape Verdean American band, and Celina Pereira and Titina Rodrigues singing *morna.* My grandmother, who was 83 years old at the time, reveled in being at the festival. She traversed the expansive graveled grounds being pushed by my aunt in a wheelchair. Every day at around 4 or 5 o'clock, she was parked right at the very front of the Music Stage, so she could be up close and personal with the various Cape Verdean musicians taking the stage and the crowd of people dancing on trampled grass.

While shuttling people on and off the Narrative Stage, I interacted with familial strangers, as a member of the Cape Verdean diaspora, as I encountered a multitude of Cape Verdean nationals, speaking an array of variants of *Kriolu,* thus enacting a type of dynamic intercultural exchange that was foreign to my upbringing. Learning by doing provided me with additional knowledge that consumed my thoughts, infiltrated my pores, and enveloped my senses, with spontaneity and simultaneity, all at once. This experience would be replicated many times over, once I began my fieldwork in Dorchester and Roxbury, Massachusetts, the following year.

III

Native anthropological research is often a transformative and performative exercise of legitimization undertaken by the researcher who is both an insider by affiliation and an outsider by training (Jacobs-Huey 2002). Research conducted by people of African ancestry in their own communities may also employ the method of auto/ethnography, whereby the subject-object dichotomy of research is purposefully blurred, with the researcher often including him/herself as an observable object of study (McClaurin 2001). This approach, which emphasizes critical self-reflexivity, acknowledges the power relationships inherent in the anthropologist-informant interaction and includes the authentic experiences of the anthropologist as valid informational sources.

My research in Boston in the 1990s focused on Cape Verdean diasporic identity formation and was contextualized through the praxis of native anthropology by virtue of my cultural heritage and political connections to the community. The findings from this study were many and are still applicable to a large extent to the current Cape Verdean cultural experience. Cape Verdeans in Boston, as a Black diaspora population, construct and negotiate their identities in contrast to other neighboring sociocultural groups of African, Latin American, Caribbean, and European descent. Since Boston is a city that is still characterized by de facto residential segregation, Cape Verdeans reside alongside other minoritized communities of color. Therefore, Cape Verdeans assert their identities in relation to how their neighbors perceive them as well as how they wish to be distinguished from these neighbors. In addition, Cape Verdeans are interpellated as racial subjects through the U.S. Census and other institutionalized methods of documentation and surveillance employed by federal, state, and local governments.

In the midst of this identity management, Cape Verdeans engage in self-identification practices, through which the label "Cape Verdean" is appropriated, utilized, and disputed. As Lopes and Lundy (2014) indicate, nowadays, Cape Verdeans in the diaspora may identify as "American, Cape Verdean, Cape Verdean American, African American, African, Creole, Lusophone, and Patriots fans" (78) or any combination of these identities. For many people of African ancestry who relocate to the United States—Cape Verdeans included—the utilization (though not always in name) of an understanding of diaspora as both a process and a mode of becoming crucial to their physical, social, and emotional survival.

Given the ways in which Cape Verdeans continue to assert multiple constituted diasporic identities within global contexts, I am compelled to place my own negotiations at the center of any inquiry, in order to understand how Cape Verdean identity formation is a situational exercise. For example, prior to my going to the Cape Verde Islands for the first time in 2001, I discussed my research intentions with several of my Boston colleagues. One woman in particular discussed with me the concept of female respectability. This captured my attention and subsequently influenced my own preparations. As a Cape Verdean American young woman, about to "go home" for the first time, and acutely aware of how my U.S. cultural upbringing marks me off and thus separates me from Cape Verdean nationals, I was thrust yet again into the position of researcher and research subject; everything about me (e.g., behavioral expectations) became the test case for what I would observe and experience with respect to gender relations in the islands.

In this instance, I became aware of the matter of accountability and representation in native anthropological research. The added dimension of the woman mentioned above being nearly a sister-in-law (and eventually becoming just that) and the fact that I was traveling with her brother confounded the malleability of my positionality. In short, my accountability to the Cape Verdean community became one in which I was mandated to conduct myself in particular ways, as a respectable woman: wearing clothing that expressed a prescribed feminine modesty (e.g., limiting skin exposure), requesting soft drinks instead of alcoholic beverages when offered, and engaging in gendered exchanges in aggregated spaces where men's socialization practices were privileged. To do otherwise would not only reflect poorly on me but would be a personal affront to the family to whom I had become connected. It is only in hindsight that I am able to see the ways in which my packing, though not wearing, pantyhose, for example, for use in this sub-Saharan climate, signified the immense amount of agency and influence that is wielded by the community among whom the native anthropologist works.

After having built a national reputation in a particular field, one can develop a feeling that there is not much more to learn. However, when taking the perspective of what Ingold (2013) refers to as "convert(ing) every certainty into a question," one discovers how much there is yet to be learned (2). Although I had familiarity with the culture, from personal and fieldwork experiences, I discovered that there was not only much more to learn but new ways of doing so.

IV

In my study of Cape Verdean diasporic identity formation in Boston, the use of historical memory figured prominently in the stories of Cape Verdean immigrants. The ways in which *nha terra* was frequently invoked as a tool of authenticating their contemporary definitions of Cape Verdeanness signified, for me, a distinct strategy used to legitimize their current positionality as a diasporic community in the United States. For me, going back to the "old country," as my grandmother called it, for the first time in 2001, was a momentous occasion, to say the least. I was struck by the juxtaposition of old and new. I was also amazed by the similarities between cultural practices in the islands and in Boston.

The islands (and Brava in particular) that I encountered in 2001 and in 2017 were not the ones that were described in my grandmother's stories: a desolate place, brown and dusty, with people traveling on *burros*, a place of famine and hardship. Rather, I encountered a Cabo Verde that was vibrant, filled with people of all ages, some from other countries like Senegal and China. Other people appeared to be dislocated, uprooted from the United States, and artificially transplanted through processes of deportation. The landscape was lush with fruit trees and vegetation, and random animals roaming around—dogs, cats, cows, goats, roosters. And most importantly, it was a place where I witnessed people going about their everyday lives, engaged in regular, mundane activities like construction, child-rearing, shop-keeping, education, worship, and the like. The demystifying experience of observing Cape Verdean immigrant life that I witnessed in Boston and visiting the islands was an experience in which the dreams of the past stood in stark contrast to the realities of the present.

When we received a long-distance call from Cabo Verde from my *kunhada*, my sister-in-law, in 2016, telling us that she "took the flag" (*toma bandeira*) for the *festa di San Djon* for the following year, I was elated for her. I knew from my previous visit to Cabo Verde that carrying the flag of St. John the Baptist during the various public processions was considered a privilege usually reserved for *emigrantes*. A few weeks later, I became aware of the fact that the honor does not come without a cost. The designated flag-bearer and her family are tasked with organizing and raising the funds to make the three-day event happen. In my naiveté, I thought that the emigrante simply had to show up and carry the flag. With my newfound knowledge, I was thrust into the reality of the social life of festival making that is otherwise hidden from the casual tourists who simply observe, witness, and literally consume the resultant cultural pageantry as part of their heritage vacations.

According to Ingold (2013), engagement with materials is needed in order to "understand how things are made" (22). My engagement with the practice of *San Djon* was instrumental to my understanding in more depth the importance and significance of this annual event—to the organizers, to the community, to the emigrantes, and ultimately to myself, in terms of my ability to later reflect upon and feel the ramifications of this event on my very being and that of my family. This experience with *San Djon* was of a strikingly different scale than the one in 2001.

As a participant by virtue of my familial connection to the flag-bearer, I was able to witness the more intricate details involved in the planning and execution of *San Djon*. No longer simply a spectator, I actively participated in the preparations that occurred in the domestic sphere: purchasing items, unpacking goods, balloon blowing, house cleaning and clearing, coordinating food distribution, and decorating. I attended formal social events leading up to the celebration. I participated in the procession that culminated in the receipt of the bandeira from the home of relatives where the flag resided a year in advance. I paraded with my family and the newly acquired bandeira through the streets of Vila Nova Sintra, en route to my kunhada's family home, occasionally stopping along the way for people who ran up to pin money on the bandeira. I clapped and chanted to the kola songs with what appeared to be the entire town congregating outside of the home the night before the main celebration, as others hoisted oversized trays of sliced cake over their heads, to carry down from the house and into the crowd. My image was captured among the crowd of participants in a local video recording of the event, produced for distribution as a DVD for purchase for $5 a week later.

The more I participated rather than simply observed, the more I realized how much more knowledge I was acquiring, beyond what I could have read about in texts or from prior knowledge acquired through fieldwork. I was getting closer to the ways of "knowing and being" (Ingold 2013, 5) that constituted this event, and how it is not a static phenomenon but one that takes on a distinct characteristic, depending upon whom/which family is involved. Engaging as a member of a family charged with implementing *San Djon*, I gained new knowledge on the experiences of the emigrantes, whose return to the islands is awaited by many with much anticipation and whose presence at *San Djon* is given much attention, particularly by media outlets.

For example, I discovered that there is a degree of orchestration in their participation in *San Djon*. There were specific events, dubbed the "immigrant gala" and the "immigrant mass," facilitating ample time for emigrantes and locals to co-mingle, reconnect, and otherwise have a good time. I also saw the same group of emigrantes circulating among various events leading up to and following *San Djon*. I was of course implicated in this orchestration too, which was in a way an orchestration of signification, by virtue of my connection to the sponsors of the event, my family. Preparation for public presentation was coordinated, down to our matching colored outfits and customized t-shirts, marking off our special status.

At *San Djon*, I also became more aware of how children acted as co-participants in the *festa di San Djon*. They not only participated in the processions alongside their family members, but they figured prominently in the mass associated with the celebration, as members of the choir and with their own distinction as being the first group of participants called forward for the procession of the Sao Joao statue from the church to the *praça* and back again. Prior to the church celebration of *San Djon*, these children also participated in the previous nights' processions to the home of the bandeira, where they assisted in distributing food and beverages to the throngs of adults in the street, as well as to the performers assisting the *koladeras*. With every passing year, I hear concern from adults about whether or not these same children will eventually assume responsibility for the continuation of this cultural tradition. Barros' (2012) study of *kola san jon* serves to quell these fears. She describes the practice of the koladeras as the literal and figurative transmitters of Cape Verdean cultural literacy in the stylized ways in which the crowd receives the information—impromptu chants of storytelling, cupped from the mouth of the singer, and then moved outward from their palms (Barros 2012, 104). She contends that this transmission of Cape Verdean cultural literacy to younger generations occurs through the years from the shared experiences, forms of expression, and other behaviors embodied by the koladeras during *San Djon* (Barros 2012, 99).

My most vivid experience that encapsulates my learning by doing at *San Djon* was my participation in an early morning ritual, on the main day of the event, which spoke volumes to me on the communal effort involved in the making of *San Djon*. The *presenti di mastru* entailed the votive "gifting" of the *mastro* with flowers, toys, gourds, specially baked bread, tree branches, and fruits. Rows of volunteers lined up with trays of these items on their heads, while others held multi-hand bunches of bananas against the backs of their necks, swaying and chanting with the koladeras in procession. Some balanced the tray perfectly without assistance, moving in perfect rhythm, while others, like myself, used one hand to hold the tray on their heads. The procession ran from the church, around the *praça,* and on to the site of the mastro. Once there, the items were delivered to males waiting to string up the items on the mastro as situated on the ground, which was then hoisted as any other mainsail on a mast would be, high onto a concrete pole structure stretching upward, about three stories high.

The social context in which *San Djon* took place situated me interstitially between categories of foreigner, relative, emigrante, heritage tourist, wife/ mother, and global traveler. In familial and affinal relationships, there is a level of expectation that supersedes individual activity. In this space, I could not operate as a mere emigrante, with the freedom to either engage in activities or stay at home. I was an active participant because there was a clearly articulated expectation of the role that I had to play. Being summoned to assist when needed—in this case, with the presenti di mastro—was prefaced with a statement that presumed my desire to bear witness to the practice, whereas the real intent was to make sure that I could assist with yet another integral component of this complex festival,

Being in the midst of the festival, and not merely a spectator of it, was truly transformational in the sense of transforming the anthropological mode of knowledge acquisition. This experiential mode of collecting data provided me with a less romanticized understanding of an event which functions as: (1) a mechanism through which a community comes together in collective effort to ensure its successful execution; (2) a reaffirmation of a cultural practice that binds a community together in solidarity; and (3) a means through which a community can demonstrate collective care for one another, through socialization, communal worship, and the redistribution of food, drink and *amizadi*.

Marchand (2010) contends that "knowledge is explored both in its various modes of articulation (i.e., motor, sensory, and propositional) and in its range of social, cultural, and material manifestations" (xii). As a person living and interacting with fellow cultural actors, *San Djon* became a familiar practice and not a tourist experience for me. Witnessing each component of the festival—the lead up, the implementation, and the aftermath—imbued it with new and deeper meanings. While the festival itself is a fleeting, temporal activity, the practices lead to a level of sustainability that promises to continue, amid those feelings expressed by the older generations about its survival.

The act of being in Cabo Verde for a personal endeavor became anthropological, because I became ensconced in the culture unfolding all around me. I could not ignore the cultural information coming my way. My enactment of *San Djon* rituals and activities provided me with a new way of acquiring knowledge that went beyond the exercise of qualitative data collection. It was a way to be conversant with the cultural phenomenon of *San Djon* enveloping all around me. Using a lens of inquiry based on experiential learning propelled me to dig deeper into my understandings of this tradition. How was *San Djon* lived by its participants? How did the role and status of the emigrantes add to the legitimacy of the celebration? What lived experiences occurred during the times in between the communal activities? What sacrifices were made by the participants for the good of the whole?

Through this inquiry process, I discovered the reality of *San Djon*, which is that it occurred in the foreground of a real life that was always the backdrop. The *festa di San Djon* calls for many sacrifices, of time, talent, and treasure. It takes a good year of fundraising, planning, and organization on both sides of the Atlantic for an event that ends up costing an average $15–20,000. This includes the management of volunteers from the town in the month leading up to the event, securing contracts with vendors, and soliciting donations, both monetary and in-kind. I witnessed women who not only mixed, baked, and frosted an impressive amount of pound cakes to be consumed during the festivities but also hauled into the house the small ovens in which to bake them.

In between preparing for the event and its implementation, we had to engage in the customary visiting of relatives that must occur when people return to Cabo Verde, regardless of a major celebration occurring simultaneously. I had the added responsibility of caring for my son, which provided me with heightened awareness as I had to navigate my own movement as well as his, many times among crowds, in darkness, at times with the real danger of *foguetes* lurching toward him, scrambling away to avoid any injury and managing his fears afterward.

Then, there was the everyday life of my kunhada taking care of a business, her boutique, that did not relate back directly to *San Djon*, though sales may have offset any additional costs of the celebration. Preparations for *San Djon* intertwined with the everyday life of her business, even when in Boston, given her need to take advantage of the limited time she would have in the islands for both activities. The life of the boutique was ongoing. It did not end with the preparations leading up to *San Djon*. Someone still had to physically open and close the shop. Someone had to describe the utility of items and convince people to purchase them. The boutique was even taken "on the road." The owner had her employee accompany her to a popular coastal area of the island, at which the emigrantes and locals continued an extension of the *San Djon* celebration. This employee was charged with selling various products that could be used by those at this location, where people tended to swim. So, there were bathing suits, sunscreen, floating devices, flip flops, and snack items for sale, placed strategically over the balcony of a relative's home, so as to be visual to the casual strollers along the *caminho* parallel to the ocean.

The boutique became an alternative space where the semblance of everyday life intertwined with the celebration. Additional plans and tasks were set in motion by the assistant-relative, who came to check on the festival preparations while the owner was at the store. Additional tasks were assigned to those who stopped by the store; one must accompany the assistant to talk with someone else about the established plans for the days ahead. The day did not end with the closing of the boutique, as the owner attended to additional preparations at home. Leaving the boutique and walking a few streets over to attend to additional cleaning of the host home occurred as well as the organization of items, shipped to and stored in the same home, to be sold at the boutique the following day.

I met the woman who would become my friend and later my kunhada long before I ever met her brother who would become my husband of now 18 years. I met her through a key informant who was connected to a privileged group of Cape Verdean professionals in Boston, engaged in community work, primarily through the arts. This group was composed of artists, activists, musicians, educators, filmmakers, and the like. This was a foray into the Cape Verdean community that would forever change any perceptions that I had of Cape Verdean culture that had previously been fomented by my small slice of Cape Verdean American life on the south shore.

During my ten-day stay in Brava, my kunhada maintained a mantra of "*mudjer poderosa*" as a symbol of her fortitude in serving in the role of flag-bearer and one that espouses her overall feminist valuation of Cape Verdean women. A major media outlet even touted her advocacy in a news story the year before, in which she was featured, by highlighting that an "*um grupo de mulheres tomou a bandeira.*" While women have taken the bandeira in the past, most often they have done so in the shadow of the men with whom they were affiliated. In reflecting on her conscious decision to assert this name of her group, *mudjeres poderosas*, she later told me that she did so to empower Cape Verdean women, to publicly validate their voices and contributions to society, and to highlight the fact that the majority of her network that would be tapped to put on the *festa di San Djon* were indeed women. In fact, she identified only one male cousin as a major contributor to the fundraising effort, with the rest being women. As a single mother of two, she nearly single-handedly willed this successful event into existence; whereas other organizers in the past may have received financial support from government entities, she received none. She is and remains for me a model and embodiment of mudjer poderosa. Through this experience, I have come to realize how much of my life has been shaped by many powerful women. The first one being my grandmother.

V

On my desk at home and at work, I have two different pictures of my grandmother. The one at home, at which I was staring at the time this was written, is a 4×6 restored photograph reprinted on Kodak paper when she was apparently twenty-five years old in 1937, as written in her large cursive handwriting on the back. This restoration is rose-tinted, which foregrounds her smiling and brightly painted lips, bumper bangs, and a floral necklace on top of a white sweater, posed in front of an artificial painting backdrop. In her eyes, I can see every single one of my relatives.

My grandmother is the foundational source of my Capeverdeanness. She was the person with whom I attended Cape Verdean American dances at a very early age. I remember drinking Shirley Temples and watching my grandmother in awe, as she sashayed up to the dancefloor of a local hall to partners, sometimes males but most often other females, dancing to music from a live band, singing songs in a language I could not understand. It was a feast for the eyes and enchanting, even during the times when I had much rather been somewhere else.

It was from my grandmother that I acquired any semblance of Kriolu as a child. Like many other second- and third-generation immigrant children, I learned the "bad words" and expressions only. I would later learn from my grandmother that during her generation, the elders often "shooed" the children out of the room when speaking. So, my mother never grew up knowing or using Kriolu, and thus she could not pass that on to her children. So, I always relished when my grandmother would let those expressions fly, mostly when gossiping about others or watching TV: "*kufiad*"; "*koitad*"; "*diab!*" At that time, I had no idea how this cultural upbringing would fuel my intellectual curiosity for Cape Verdean culture as an adult.

My grandmother always told me stories about "the old country," but like many Cape Verdean Americans I had encountered as a youth growing up in southeastern Massachusetts, many of them had no desire to return. My grandmother and her contemporaries were quite content and perhaps relieved to be living on this side of the Atlantic. But that did not stop them from creating a sense of community in an environment that mapped racial and ethnic identities and meanings onto their everyday lives. And it did not prevent future generations, of which I am a part of, from dreaming of a return to the islands as a result of this cultural upbringing.

Perhaps it was because I spent countless hours with my grandmother at her senior living apartment complex during my formative years as a teenager that I could envision myself actually going to the islands when I had the chance to do so. None of my other four siblings had this same desire. Indeed, were it not for the presence of my son, I believe I would have been the only member of my immediate family to have gone to Cabo Verde in my lifetime. Fortunately for him, his experience was not clouded by preconceived notions, and he took a liking to the islands right away, now longing to return.

How else could I have embarked on the journey of motherhood as a tenure track professor were it not for the examples of strong Cape Verdean womanhood in the landscape of my social and intellectual upbringing? Only in adulthood have I come to understand my own mother's example, as a woman who brought five individuals into the world and raised them in a housing project environment that was a tight-knit and joyful community while rife with crime, drugs, and violence. There is also the case of my sister and aunt, who traveled 3,000 miles from California to Massachusetts to convince me and my mother around a kitchen table that I, a nearly straight-A student, could succeed in pursuing a four-year college degree. It took these strong women to help me see my own potential. Over the years, I have come to realize the obvious: I, like many others, come from a long line of *mudjeres poderosas*.

VI

I have come to understand native anthropological praxis as having more to do with the individuals with whom I interact than my actual "nativeness" or any politicized tendencies on my part. Through this experiential learning of *San Djon*, I am more mindful than ever of the importance of critical self-reflection while in the field, to understand how we conceive of our accountability to our communities as well as how we are situated into various social and political fields by these communities (Zavella 1996). I have come to terms with the ways in which I have been rendered an activist or advocate by the community. It is not a matter of me coming to this activist stance on my own; it is imperative that I follow the lead of the community that mandates my advocacy at any given time. My ongoing contributions to Cape Verdean scholarship are perceived by the community as a demonstration of my ongoing social and political commitment as an engaged researcher. My positionality, vis-à-vis the community is assumed, and my participation becomes required to maintain legitimacy. This type of contribution is, indeed, characteristic of the tradition of native anthropology and applied practice in general (Garcia 2000, 90).

Ingold speaks of how knowledge is embodied and experienced in non-verbal ways. Ultimately, the way to capture and harness the power of transformational engagements with people is to recognize how these interactions change us irrevocably. For me, my ongoing experiences with Cape Verdeans continue to situate me as a lifelong learner and never truly an expert. The question is how to stay disciplined to turn every experience into a question through which a future can be discovered. How can we place ourselves in contexts in which we are able to take that from which we are learning and apply it to solve critical issues occurring in our communities? To me, this challenge is best understood methodologically, as a means of utilizing anthropological inquiry as one's own personal sensibility, a method of knowing and being in the world. Similar to Trajano Filho's (2009) reference to coevalness in his experience with *tabanka*. The engagements that we have with other people speak to our interrelationship and interdependency in the world. The challenge is bringing this perspective on methodology, of "learning from," into every aspect of one's daily life.

REFERENCES

Barros, Jessica. "*Koladeras*, Literacy Educators of the Cape Verdean Diaspora: A Cape Verdean African Centered Call and Response Methodology." *Community Literacy Journal* 6, no. 2: 97–113. http://doi.org/10.1353/clj.2012.0024, 2012.

Garcia, Maria Elena. "Ethnographic Responsibility and the Anthropological Endeavor: Beyond Identity Discourse." *Anthropology Quarterly* 73, no. 2: 89–101, 2002.

Ingold, Tim. *Making: Anthropology, Archaeology, Art and Architecture*. New York: Routledge, 2013.

Jacobs-Huey, Lanita. "The Natives are Gazing and Talking Back: Reviewing the Problematics of Positionality, Voice and Accountability Among 'Native' Anthropologists." *American Anthropologist* 104, no. 3: 791–804, 2002.

Lopes, Jessica, and Brandon Lundy. "Secondary Diaspora: Cape Verdean Immigration to the Southeastern United States." *Southern Anthropologist* 36, no. 2: 70–102. http://digitalcommons.kennesaw.edu/facpubs/4103, 2014.

Marchand, Trevor H. J., ed. *Making Knowledge: Explorations of the Indissoluble Relation between Mind, Body and Environment*. Oxford: Wiley-Blackwell, 2010.

McClaurin, Irma. "Theorizing a Black Feminist Self in Anthropology: Toward an Autoethnographic Approach." In *Black Feminist Anthropology: Theory, Politics, Praxis and Poetics*, edited by Irma McClaurin, 49–76. New Brunswick: Rutgers University Press, 2001.

Trajano Filho, Wilson. "The Conservative Aspects of a Centripetal Diaspora: The Case of the Cape Verdean Tabancas." *Africa: Journal of the International African Institute* 79, no. 4: 520–542, 2009.

Zavella, Patricia. "Feminist Insider Dilemmas: Constructing Ethnic Identity with Chicana Informants." In *Feminist Dilemma in Fieldwork*, edited by Diane L. Wolf, 138–159. Boulder: Westview Press, 1996.

Chapter 4

The Cabo Verdean Women's Project

Reporting on Gender-Based Violence

Dawna Marie Thomas

Early[1] feminist movements in the United States brought about a wide range of social changes to confront violence against women, creating new legislation, shelters, and recognition of the pervasive and persistent power of violence against women. Yet, to this day, Cabo Verdeanas in the United States are underserved, misunderstood, and often misidentified—leaving them at greater risk of living with violence in their homes. Multicultural and transnational feminist analysis offers a foundation to examine how race, gender, class, and women's oppressive histories intersect with gender-based violence. A multicultural and transnational perspective shows how gender-based violence in the Cabo Verdean community is a complex phenomenon, centered around the community's history of Portuguese colonialism, immigration, cultural patriarchy, and social invisibility in the United States. Moreover, the lack of awareness and understanding of Cabo Verdean culture continues to create barriers to effective intervention and prevention services and reinforces a code of silence. The Cabo Verdean Women's Project (CWVP)[2] was a qualitative study to explore Cabo Verdeanas' experiences with gender-based violence. This chapter reports the research findings of the study, offering insight into Cabo Verdeanas' experiences with gender-based violence, as well as recommendations for intervention and prevention strategies. The intention of this chapter is not to generalize to all Cape Verdeanas but to hear from them, to share the participants' experiences, and to provide a starting place or foundation for future activism and advocacy to foster social change. Understanding Cabo Verdeans' history, migration to the United States, spoken languages, and family dynamics are important to developing culturally relevant strategies for combating gender-based violence.

CABO VERDEANS' JOURNEY TO THE UNITED STATES

Despite the Cabo Verdean community's long history in the United States, which dates back to the middle 1800s, I am frequently asked, "Where is Cabo Verde?" and "Who are Cabo Verdeans?" While there is some debate about whether Cabo Verde was an uninhabited set of islands before the Portuguese arrived, the archipelago's history is deeply rooted in Portuguese colonialism and people from West African cultures. Cabo Verde is a nation of ten islands off the coast of West Africa that was colonized by the Portuguese in the 1400s (Appiah and Gates 1999; Lobban 1995; Lobban and Saucier 2007). The Cabo Verde islands are divided into two regions: the Barlavento/ Windward Islands, Antão, São Vicente, Santa Luzia, São Nicolau, Sal, and Boa Vista, and the Ilhas do Sotavento/Leeward Islands of Maio, Santiago, Fogo, and Brava. Portuguese continues to be the language of Cabo Verde, alongside Creole/Kriolu—a mixture of Portuguese and African dialects—is spoken at home. Creole/Kriolu is also the language of resistance against the colonial power that repressed much of Cabo Verdeans' African cultures and languages. As Lima (2002) suggests, "The term Creole embodies the Cabo Verdean identity and defines Cabo Verdean people" (9), demonstrating how culture, history, and language are all essential to understanding the community (Thomas et al. 2010; Thomas 2018).

Historically, harsh colonial rule and socioeconomic and cultural oppression caused many Cabo Verdeans to emigrate from Cabo Verde to a variety of places around the world. Today, southeastern New England has the largest community of Cabo Verdeans in the United States, and the shores of Massachusetts and Rhode Island have historically been the gateways to Cabo Verdeans seeking economic opportunity (Appiah and Gates 1999; Carling 2003; Lobban 1995; Lobban and Saucier 2007). Cabo Verdean migration history is best understood in three major eras: (1) whaling era; (2) postcolonial era; and (3) post-9/11 era.

During the first era—the middle 1800s—Cabo Verdeans came to the United States on whaling vessels and were considered some of the earliest laborers in southeastern New England. Men came first, followed by women, with both groups working in the blueberry fields, cranberry bogs, factories, and as housekeepers. However, as with other communities of color, immigration policies of the early twentieth century stalled much of Cabo Verdeans' emigration to the United States (López 1996; Omi and Winant 1994; Sánchez 1998). Next, the postcolonial era began in the middle 1970s, increasing when Cabo Verde gained its independence from Portugal in 1975. This phase came to an end with the response to 9/11, when the United States moved to restrict immigration to the United States for many, including Cabo Verdeans. The third era is characterized by these post-9/11 laws and, more recently, the Trump

Administration's increasingly restrictive immigration policy, which has created greater challenges for Cabo Verdeans wishing to enter the United States.

The three immigration phases have unique social and political histories that influence Cabo Verdeans' acculturation experiences in the United States, relationship to Cabo Verde, individual identities, and spoken languages. For example, Cabo Verdeans who immigrated in the first wave (i.e., whaling era) under Portuguese colonial rule was identified as Portuguese. In contrast, those who have entered the country since Cabo Verde's independence identify more strongly as Cabo Verdean and/or African. Moreover, despite this shift, Cabo Verdeans continue to struggle with the binary racial classification of black and white, which is also centered around skin color (Halter 1998; Lima 2012; Sánchez-Gibau 2005a, 2005b; Thomas 2014).

Racial identity in the United States is influenced by a black/white dynamic that is rooted in a racist ideology in which whites are superior and all non-whites are inferior (López 1996; Hacker 1992; Omi and Winant 1994). Not only does this black/white dynamic play a role in racial identity, but it is also a major determinant of group membership, social mobility, success, and discrimination (DeAndrade 1997; Lima 2012; Thomas 2014). However, in reality, Cabo Verdeans' physical features are diverse, and many Cabo Verdeans experiences "the harsh reality of racialization in American society when they try to fit into a system where race is a prominent factor in identity development and socioeconomic process" (Thomas 1992, 2014). For example, CWVP study participants reported their frustrations with being racially and culturally misunderstood and misidentified, and this misunderstanding was seen as a significant barrier to any effective intervention or prevention strategies to combat violence against women and children. As one participant noted, "We are always challenged to be a race. When I say I am black, they say no, you're not; look at your hair, it is straight, you're too light. But why can't I be Cabo Verdean and black? Who says I have to choose?" The participants highlighted this long struggle between the Cabo Verdean community and mainstream America, suggesting that the experience has left them marginalized and socially invisible. Furthermore, despite mainstream social service agencies' cultural competency training, federal guidelines, and an increased understanding of the importance of collecting ethnicity data alongside traditional racial data, Cabo Verdeans continue to be underserved, misidentified, culturally misunderstood, and lumped with other racial groups (Thomas et al. 2010; Thomas 2014). In order to properly address gender-based violence, service providers and law enforcement alike must understand both the differences between Cabo Verdeans who recently immigrated with limited English abilities and those whose ancestors have been here for generations, and the fact that Cabo Verdeans might identify themselves in various ways (e.g., Cabo Verdean, black, African, and other).

Understanding the family is another important feature of any service delivery program. Unlike the American nuclear family model, the Cabo Verdean
family is characterized in broad terms that include not only blood relatives
but also extended family members (i.e., grandparents, godparents, aunts/
uncles, and non-blood relatives). Moreover, due to Cabo Verdeans' migration
history, many families were separated for long periods of time, and family
ties often extended across the geographical borders of Cabo Verde and the
United States.

Although Cabo Verdeanas are disproportionately responsible for the well-
being of the family, they are also revered in the community. As many participants in the CVWP study suggested, "Cape Verdean women take care of their
families" and "she does so with pride." In more recent times, Cabo Verdeanas
in both Cabo Verde and the United States have advanced socially, politically,
and educationally. However, in both communities, traditional patriarchal values are prominent. Thus, while Cabo Verdeanas may be revered and highly
respected in the community, they still defer to male authority. The importance
of the family and traditional gender roles plays a significant role in how, and
why, Cabo Verdeanas' silence about the violence they experience persists
(Thomas 2014; Carter and Aulette 2009; Challinor 2015).

FROM A SOCIAL CONDITION TO A SOCIAL PROBLEM

Understanding gender-based violence requires casting a wide net and considering disciplines, organizations, advocacy groups, definitions, and theories.
The literature on gender-based violence is expansive—reaching across countries and cultures, offering many definitions, and laying a foundation to build
upon. It is important to understand that intimate partner violence (IPV) is a
complex social phenomenon that, while difficult to accept and comprehend,
has existed in all times across all geographies; socioeconomic statuses (SES);
racial, ethnic, and cultural groups; and genders (Barnett et al. 2011; Gelles
1997; Gosselin 2000; Miller-Perrin et al. 2018). As such, an understanding
of gender-based violence requires an understanding of how gender-based
violence was, and is, socially perceived, accepted, and defined.

DEFINING GENDER-BASED VIOLENCE

To begin, it is important to review the continually evolving definitions of
gender-based violence. Over the last several decades, terms to describe violence against women have included "domestic violence," "domestic abuse,"
"IPV," and more recently, "gender-based violence." Both in the United States

and internationally, these terms are often used interchangeably, reflecting an inclusive foundation regarding gender, sex, and culture (Barnett et al. 2011; Breiding et al. 2015; Wallace 2005). The terms to describe those who are abused are also diverse, such as "battered women," "abused women," "victims," and survivors. The term "survivor" is often preferred over "victims," as it reflects a social justice paradigm that gives those who were abused (women, men, and children) a sense of control and empowerment. In the CVWP study, participants used the terms "domestic violence," "IPV," and "survivor" when discussing abuse. Thus, in this chapter, I will use the terms "IPV," "gender-based violence," and "domestic violence" as the study participants did.

There is no single definition of gender-based violence; definitions of gender-based violence are extremely diverse across different states in the United States and countries around the globe. The Centers for Disease Control and Prevention (CDC)[3] defines IPV as "physical violence, sexual violence, stalking, and psychological aggression (including coercive tactics) by a current or former intimate partner (i.e., spouse, boyfriend/girlfriend, dating partner, or ongoing sexual partner)" (Breiding 2013, para. 1). Some forms of IPV can be perpetrated electronically through mobile devices and social media sites as well as in person. IPV happens in all types of intimate relationships, including heterosexual relationships and relationships among sexual minority populations. Moreover, the term "family violence" is even broader, referring to the range of violence that can occur in families, including IPV, child abuse, and elder abuse.

Definitions of gender-based violence, IPV, and family violence are grounded in ideology and have evolved as a result of social change. For example, until recently, IPV was not recognized as a significant issue—it was merely considered part of everyday life for women. One of the problems with recognizing IPV is the perception of the idealized family as a safe place, the safest place to be (Barnett et al. 2011; Gelles 1997; Wallace 2005). Sociologists were some of the first scholars to question the idealized notion of the family as a place where one is loved and feels safe and supported. Gelles (1997) noted that "people are more likely to be killed, physically assaulted, hit, beat up, slapped or spanked in their own homes by other family members than anywhere else, or by anyone else" (1). While men may experience abuse, they do so at a lower rate than women and children. In fact, as of this writing, the world has been stricken with the coronavirus—requiring people to stay at home and social distance—which has put more women and children at higher risk for abuse while giving them little recourse to reach out for help and/or escape their abusers. Furthermore, the literature shows that violence begins when one starts dating and is not exclusive to cohabitating couples. For example, teen couples experience similar levels of dating violence, stalking, and sexual assault as adult couples (Barnett et al. 2011; Miller-Perrin et al. 2018).

UN Women reports an estimated 35 percent of women worldwide have experienced physical and/or sexual IPV or sexual violence by a non-partner at some point in their lives. They also estimated that of the 87,000 women who were intentionally killed in 2017 across the globe, more than half were killed by an intimate partner or family member. These figures are similar in the United States; the National Coalition Against Domestic Violence estimates that, on average, twenty people experience intimate partner physical violence every minute—a figure that equates to more than 10 million abuse victims annually. Moreover, over their lifetimes, one in four women and one in nine men will experience severe IPV, sexual assault, intimate partner stalking that results in physical injury, fearfulness, posttraumatic stress disorder, the use of victim services, and/or the contraction of sexually transmitted diseases. It is difficult to know whether the rate of gender-based violence in the Cabo Verdean community mirrors these global trends because, for many reasons, there is limited data on gender-based violence in the community—both in the United States and in Cabo Verde.

One reason for this limited data is a culture of silence. Sociologists suggest that "social conditions only become recognized as social problems as a result of successful advocacy by those concerned about the social issue" (Miller-Perrin et al. 2018, 4). Those who raise public attention to social problems are called claims makers or trouble makers. Claims makers include a wide variety of people, such as advocates, survivors, policymakers, and other stakeholders interested in social justice. As the CVWP participants suggested, female survivors who bravely come forward to challenge the cultural norm of silence not only bring awareness about gender-based violence, but they may also precipitate an opportunity for social change and justice.

Social/cultural factors are another explanation for why it has taken so long for gender-based violence to be recognized and studied as a social problem. Social/cultural theory notes that violence has historically been, and continues to be, deeply embedded in our society. Some levels of violence are not only accepted by society but encouraged. For example, spanking children continues to be an accepted, and often expected form of discipline—hence the saying, *spare the rod spoil the child.* Similarly, the spousal exemption legal principle historically stated, "husbands were exempt from charges of raping their wives even if they used considerable force because upon marriage, women give their husbands irrevocable consent to having sex with them" (Miller-Perrin et al. 2018, 32). It wasn't until the mid-1970s that marital rape first became illegal, and even then, it took until the 1990s for marital rape to be outlawed in all states.

Nonetheless, some men around the globe still believe that a marriage license gives them absolute control and access to their wives' bodies. While more and more zero-tolerance policies regarding gender-based violence are employed in the workplace and professional sports organizations, there is little attention paid to education, training, and discussions to counteract the social and cultural norms that glorify violence in our society. For example, there is an ongoing debate about whether there is a correlation between pop culture (e.g., movies, video games, music) and increasing hyper-sexualized violence that glorifies violence against women. Although there is no conclusive evidence that watching violence and/or sexualized violence in videos or movies leads to real-life violence, many theorists suggest that, at the very least, media makes society desensitized to these issues, causes many people to have distorted images of sexual relationships, and makes individuals less empathetic to victims of violence (Barnet et al. 2011; Gelles 1997). Furthermore, these images and ever-evolving social media portrayals also establish a skewed sense of masculinity, where male—and especially white male—aggressiveness is normalized (which many men of color emulate), while females are seen as weak and easily abused. These types of attitudes continue to create barriers to the kind of social change that would allow women and children to be safe.

Feminist Understanding of Gender-Based Violence

Feminists, advocates, and the feminist movement brought about a recognition that interpersonal violence is a social problem rather than a normal social condition. While the CVWP study participants did not have a clear definition or explanation of feminism or feminist theories, they did have ideas of what feminism meant. For many participants, feminism meant that women were strong and resilient amid the hard work and gender-based violence they experience in their daily lives. For example, when I asked study participants how they would define feminism, they responded, "we don't need to define feminism we just do feminism." Hence, a feminist theoretical framework offers an important lens to understanding Cabo Verdeanas' experiences with gender-based violence and how these experiences initiated legislation both in the United States and in Cabo Verde.

A feminist theoretical framework is centered along similar lines as a structural/cultural explanation of violence against women, blending theory with social activism. Early feminists, the feminist movement, and survivors were at the forefront of changing social perceptions about gender-based violence in the United States and around the globe. Such claims makers noted that violence against women is rooted in a "patriarchal culture where women are subordinate to men and men hold power and privilege" (Barnett et al. 2011, 47). This approach brings an understanding that gender-based violence is not a social condition, a private matter of the home or within couples, nor a normalized part of being a woman. Conceptualizing this social condition as a social problem demonstrates how traditional patriarchal and hierarchical structures sanction men's use of violence to maintain power and control over women (Barnett et al. 2011; Bograd 1990; Childress 2013; Kelly 2011). Women were—and continue to be—culturally and politically socialized to be subordinate to male authority, superiority, and dominance. As a result, women are often powerless and experience violence at the hands of men with little or no recourse.

Contemporary scholars recognize that the feminist perspective espoused by first and second-wave feminists reflected a Western middle-class ideal that did not consider the oppressive conditions faced by women of color (Cho et al. 2013; Carbado et al. 2013; Patil 2013). Third-wave feminism grew in response to the lack of attention paid by earlier feminists to women of color, marginalized people of both genders, and those in the Lesbian, Gay, Bisexual, and Trans* (LGBT*) communities (George and Stith 2014). Crenshaw (1991) suggested that the concept of intersectionality brings a greater understanding of women of color's experience with interlocking systems of oppression, domination, and racism, and to the ways in which women of color's experiences differ from the experiences of white women. Sokoloff and Dupont (2005) noted, "We exist in a social context created by the intersections of systems of power (e.g., race, class, gender, and sexual orientation) and oppression (e.g., prejudice, class stratification, gender inequality, and heterosexist bias)" (44). Effective strategies must consider how women of color experience gender-based violence simultaneously with other structural forms of oppression and dominance (Carbado et al. 2013; Crenshaw 1991; Kelly 2011; Sokoloff 2008). Racism and other structural forms of oppression impact both men and women of color simultaneously (Cho et al. 2013; Kelly 2011; Parker and Hefner 2013). For example, the realities of police brutality and racism persist and are a major reason why many women of color stay in abusive relationships and do not report IPV/gender-based violence (Bent-Goodley 2001, 2004; Pitt 2008). Cabo Verdeanas and other women of color are often put in a position where they have to decide between their safety, loyalty to their culture, and the safety of their partner. Many women in the CVWP study suggested that gender-based violence continues to be a well-kept secret, because they do not want to bring shame to their culture—especially in a society where their culture is already misunderstood and marginalized.

The transnational feminist perspective is an important feature of third-wave feminism and provides an opportunity to better understand how IPV/gender-based violence intersects with the experiences of women of color. Transnational feminism is concerned with women across cultures and borders and considers how imperialist, colonialist, economic, and political powers have exploited, abused, and shaped women's lives around the globe (Mohanty 2013; Patil 2013; Shaw and Lee 2012). For example, Cabo Verdeanas experience IPV in a way that embodies their complex history of colonialism, immigration, cultural patriarchy, and social invisibility. Transnational feminism recognizes women's differing cultures, socioeconomic, classes, and sexual orientations, while simultaneously building international alliances and networks to promote women's equality and safety worldwide. It works toward political and legal rights for women to combat violence in the home and those violent acts used as weapons during war. Transnational feminism draws on the principles of the Convention on the Elimination of All Forms of Discrimination Against Women (CEDAW), which was adopted by the United Nations General Assembly in 1979 and ratified by Cabo Verde in 1980. These principles are considered in international Bill of Rights that protects the human rights of women. CEDAW strives for the elimination of discrimination against women, stereotyping of women as inferior, trafficking women, prostitution, and violence toward women.

In addition to CEDAW, Cabo Verde has implemented other protocols to combat gender-based violence. The Protocol of the African Charter on Human People's Rights on the Rights of Women in Africa (Maputo Protocol) and Africa 4 Women's Rights (2015) website report a series of legislative reforms that brought Cabo Verdean laws into compliance with international obligations. For example, the nation's 2004 Criminal Code increased sentences for perpetrators of sexual violence and introduced provisions to criminalize domestic violence, the 62/2005 Proclamation of Decree established legal centers to promote access to justice, the National Gender Equality and Equity Plan (2005–2009) and the National Action Plan (2009–2011) were aimed at raising awareness about gender-based violence and women's rights, and the Gender-Based Violence Act (No. 84/VII/2011) was adopted and implemented by Cabo Verde with assistance from the Institute for Gender Equality and Equity (ICIEG) and support from the Network of Women of Parliamentarians. These laws' objectives were to offer greater protection to victims, increase penalties for perpetrators, and raise public awareness of gender-based violence. More importantly, the laws also challenge the expectation that gender-based violence is a social condition—reframing it as a social problem by defining and prosecuting gender-based violence as a crime. Finally, the laws instituted a network of civil society organizations called "SOL," ensuring the collaboration and coordination between nongovernmental organizations (NGOs), community law centers, national policies, hospitals, and health centers (U.S. Department of the State 2012). Many political and grassroots groups have also organized, including the Association in Support of Women's Self Promotion and Development, the Cape Verdean Women's Organization, and the Women's Jurists Association. These groups offer a range of services—many of which are free—to address violence, abuse, and discrimination.

Nonetheless, the Cape Verde 2019 Human Rights Report notes that actually implementing these laws by creating care centers with financial and management autonomy has lagged as a result of inadequate staffing and financial resources. Although the National Police accompanied victims of violence to locations that they believed would be safe, victim rights organizations found that officers were sometimes not fully supportive or sensitive to the problems that victims face. Very often, victims return to their abusers due to economic and social pressures. As of September 2019, when the Human Rights Report was drafted, the Cape Verdean Institute for Equality and Equity had received information on 325 cases of gender-based violence. The National Statistics Institute states that, since 2017, 89 percent of victims of gender-based violence were girls or women, with individuals between the ages of twenty-two and thirty representing 34.7 percent of the total and those between the ages of thirty-one and forty-five representing another 30 percent of the total. At the same time, 89.5 percent of perpetrators of gender-based violence were men between the ages of twenty-two and forty-five. We must remember, however, that this data is four years old and that there is still a lack of reporting among victims of abuse. Furthermore, the report also shows that NGOs have found a lack of social and psychological care for survivors and perpetrators alike and that the government has not effectively enforced the laws against rape and domestic violence.

In Cabo Verde, awareness of gender-based violence has increased. As Carter and Aulette's (2009) research shows, women are taking action against gender-based violence in two ways: (1) a private approach and (2) a public approach. A private approach involves women taking subtle steps to avoid violence while also protecting the family and empowering themselves. A public approach involves outreach through NGOs, social networks, and clubs to combat violence and sexual assault against women and girls. Cabo Verdeanas have also taken to the streets in public to protest against the violence and the ultimate death of women at the hands of the partners showing progress against gender-based violence.

Although the United States has not ratified CEDAW, it has passed the Violence Against Women Act of 1994 (VAWA) and its subsequent reauthorizations in 2000, 2005, 2013, and 2019. Led by years of grassroots campaigning, VAWA is a landmark legislation designed to end gender-based violence (Wallace 2005). Its impact has been significant—creating new and mandatory punishments for offenders and broadening services to help survivors. The Act has also helped coordinate services between federal and state agencies, across communities, and across borders. Another major objective of the Act is to engage in better outreach in underserved communities, such as the Cabo

Verdean community. At the same time, the Act created 24-hour hotlines, training for law enforcement, and better response procedures for healthcare providers to protect survivors. Through these initiatives and through the passing of the Act itself, VAWA raised public awareness nationwide about the complex issues and the dangers women face from gender-based violence. Gender-based violence is no longer hidden behind closed doors or seen as a normalized part of being a woman—it is recognized as a public health problem having socio-economic, health, political problems with far-reaching consequences for those in immediate danger, future generations, and society in general.

THE CABO VERDEAN WOMEN'S PROJECT

Although data on gender-based violence in the Cabo Verdean community is still limited in both the United States and Cabo Verde, we know that there is a history of violence and sexual assault against women and children that persists to this day. The CVWP grew out of both my advocacy work and my previous research. The CVWP provided an opportunity for conversations on the intersection of gender race and violence against women and children in the Cabo Verdean community. My research findings included: (1) the perception of violence against women, (2) culture and violence, (3) the code of silence, and (4) Cape Verdeanas'[4] strength and resilience. The participants closed each interview and focus group with recommendations for the future.

Research Procedures

The CVWP included fifty women from Southeastern Massachusetts[5] recruited through a convenience sampling procedure (Creswell 2009; Hammersley 1990). Study participants represented four generations of Cabo Verdeana with the full spectrum of life experiences; the youngest participant was eighteen years old and the oldest was eight-two years old. The participants' educational backgrounds ranged from high school, GED, and some college to doctoral degrees. The women were married, divorced, single, and never married. Half of the women had children—both male and female—and two participants had grandchildren. The wide spectrum of participants offered varied acculturation and immigration experiences, all of which are related to the various phases of Cabo Verdeans' migration history. For example, half of the women's families migrated to the United States during the whaling era. All other participants came to the United States during or after the 1970s and have maintained strong ties to their families in Cabo Verde. All of the study participants were fluent in English, and more than half also spoke Creole/Kirolu and Portuguese. Other participants spoke Spanish and French. A total of three focus groups were conducted, each with seven to eleven participants, and all other participants were interviewed individually. The principal investigator consulted with many scholars and community advocates in the Cabo Verdean community, who were familiar with the research topic to ensure data reliability and reduce research bias, and conducted an extensive literature review with scholarly articles, social media, and websites. Finally, it must be noted that the principal investigator is Cabo Verdean and took great strides to maintain objectivity.

Study Limitations

The CVWP was exploratory—its goal was to learn about the lives of Cabo Verdeanas in the United States. As such, the study did not focus exclusively on gender-based violence. Nevertheless, throughout all of the interviews and focus groups, gender-based violence emerged as a major recurring theme, even though only half of the women shared their personal experiences with violence. Moreover, all of the women in the study spoke either of their personal experiences with violence or of violence that they had seen against others in their family, illustrating its importance. While the majority of women spoke of violence against women, study participants did suggest that men were also abused, though the consensus was that men were abused at a much lower rate than women. This consensus also corresponds with the literature on violence against men (Barnett et al. 2011). Thus, despite the study's limitations, the CVWP offered an opportunity for Cabo Verdeanas to share their voices about a topic that is a well-known secret in their community. Sharing life experiences and narratives is a fundamental element in the feminist theoretical framework and presents a chance to transform a social condition into a social problem and foster change.

RESEARCH FINDINGS

The participants in the Cabo Verdean Women's Project were open, generous, compassionate about sharing their experiences with abuse and offered recommendations for social change. The findings included: (1) the perception of violence among families, (2) culture and violence, (3) the code of silence, and (4) Cabo Verdeanias' strength and resilience. The study also offered lessons for us all to learn.

The Perception of Violence among Families

Study participants did not offer definitions of IPV, gender-based violence, or family violence, yet the concepts were clearly understood by all. As one participant suggested: "Every Cape Verdean woman knows what her boyfriend/

husband does to a woman, we all know, he hurts her. We don't have to say it out loud and sometimes we can't say it but we know." The lack of a clear and concise definition or the ability to articulate violence that one knows about or has experienced oneself is not unusual. The definition and details of gender-based violence in the Cabo Verdean community continued to evolve with each group and interview. Participants suggested that the patriarchy, male control, and male womanizing were viewed as remnants of Portuguese colonialism. In fact, much of the violence that women experience was connected to the harsh and abusive conditions of Portuguese colonialism, which was seen to have trickled down into family violence and to have served as the root of Cabo Verdeana suffering. When participants were asked to be more specific in describing their experiences with violence, their responses included "you know, all kinds, every time," and "we are beaten, raped, and abused mentally." They also stated, "It happens when you are a young girl, a woman, and to boys but you hear less about boys." Participants made it very clear that it was hard to describe and talk about violence publicly, especially when the norm is to be silent.

In general, the consensus among participants was that Cabo Verdeanas suffer in many ways in both Cabo Verde and the United States. This suffering manifests itself in the grueling amount of work that Cabo Verdeanas do in the home with little help from men, the responsibility of taking care of family members of all ages, the responsibility of taking care of the sick, and the responsibility for taking care of men. As one participant suggested, "Men do not help, and if they do women are lucky." Participants also suggested that Cabo Verdeanas' responsibility for caring for the family was extensive, overwhelming, and a form of oppression that kept them from challenging male privilege and control. At the same time, however, participants stated that Cabo Verdeanas take on this challenge with pride and privilege. As another participant noted, "how do we Cape Verdean women suffer, let me count the ways, there are too many"—a phrase which became the project's mantra.

How Culture and Violence Intersect

Exploring potential causes of violence in the Cabo Verdean community, study participants overwhelmingly suggested that violence and sexual assault on women and children are part of the culture. When I explored the theme of violence as part of the culture and community, I asked all participants, "Where does violence come from?" The same response was repeated throughout the study—participants overwhelmingly stated that violence was "in our culture," "part of our culture," and "may not be our culture itself but feels that way." Furthermore, violence and sexual assault transcend geopolitical boundaries and exist both in Cabo Verdean and the United States. As one participant suggested, "I sent my daughter to the US so she would be safe and she was not the abuser, and abuse is here as well." Another participant who came to the United States as a teenager reported how surprised she was to have men she admired, loved, and cared for treat her inappropriately. Although she did not report any abuse herself, she knew of many women who were abused both sexually and physically. Participants suggested that violence felt a part of the culture because it was so prevalent and they had so few resources and so little knowledge of how to stop it. Participants' perceptions and experiences also suggest that there is a lack of protection by the government and the police in both Cabo Verde and the United States. Again, they believed that Cabo Verde's history with colonial power, violence, and oppressive conditions was a major factor in the problem. Many recounted stories of the strict code of conduct imposed by Portuguese rulers and the long-term side effects of this code on their culture, family, and the dynamics between women and men. Participants further suggested that they were afraid that the police in Cabo Verde and the United States would not help them, and instead would hurt them and their culture; thus, women are forced to take care of themselves in their own way.

Another topic discussed by participants was the impact of violence on children. Specifically, participants suggested the increase of youth violence was related to violence in the home. More importantly, the use of violence was perceived to be an American cultural phenomenon that did not occur in Cabo Verde until many American-raised teens were deported back to the islands. All participants agreed that gender-based violence had harmed the family in general. Participants who were close to families in Cabo Verde noted that there was more understanding of gender-based violence in Cabo Verde than in the United States due to the work done by NGOs, social workers, recent legislation, and others. Activism in Cabo Verde has raised awareness and, as one participant suggested, "more women especially young women are talking about equality, education, violence, and all sorts of things." Yet, there was also a difference across generations, with older participants suggesting "if a man does not respect you, then he may hurt you, and don't stay with him."

Despite laws and the increase in public awareness, however, women still did not trust the system to report abuse because the word would get out in the community. Again fear, the code of silence, and a belief in protecting the community deter women from reporting abuse to police both in Cabo Verde and in the United States, as reporting incidents not only go against their culture but also bring shame.

The Code of Silence

There is a strict code of silence about most things in the Cabo Verdean community, and especially about gender-based violence. As one participant noted, "we Cape Verdeans are private people." The participants again suggested the strict code of silence, along with gender-based violence, rape, and other forms of abuse, were a byproduct of colonial rule, deep religious beliefs, and cultural practices that are centered around the patriarchy. In fact, in almost every interview and focus group I was told that the study was risky for both the participants and me because it constituted breaking the code of silence. Breaking the code of silence was connected to a range of experiences, including shame, embarrassment, and hopelessness. The code of silence was imposed by all, on all, and applied to both women and men alike.

If women did talk about the violence they experienced or saw, the discussion occurred with someone they could trust and who would not judge them, and the conversation was held in strict confidence in private. Issues related to gender-based violence or any other type of unkind acts were never discussed publicly, and especially not with outsiders—meaning anyone outside of the family—because "we are proud people and don't want that to change." Participants believed that discussing any issues pertaining to violence in the family would bring tremendous shame, not only to their family but also to Cabo Verdean culture in general. Moreover, the idea that talking about family problems would also elicit disapproval from women themselves, family, and friends was prominent. When exploring how disapproval was expressed, participants gave no direct or clear answer, but many said everyone would know, especially those with close ties to families in Cabo Verde. As one participant stated, "My family in Cape Verde and in the United States would all know." For many, knowing about violence in their family caused unbearable embarrassment and shame. On this issue, several participants suggested similar responses, with one stating that in many ways, "you just know that your family would talk about you, and what did you do wrong to make your husband hurt you." Another participant suggested, "when I complained to other women I was shushed. I didn't know they kept this awful secret." Again, the sentiment was that violence is a well-known secret. Another participant said, "abuse exists and everybody knows about it, do nothing, say nothing, no reporting, you just deal with it and stay with it." Others implied keeping this secret hurts all women and all suggested the community knows gender-based violence and child abuse exist but that victims generally suffer in silence. For example, as one participant noted, "You see a woman hard and tough you know why she hurts and keeps this secret, but it can't stay hidden, it can't stay in here, it comes out somehow. It comes out in how you see the world, view others, and then you get tough and sometimes mean." She added, "Be kind to women like this and do not judge them because you don't know what they have been through."

Cabo Verdeanas' Strength and Resilience

One of the major sources of pride among the CVWP participants was Cabo Verdeanas' strength and resilience. This pride is also noted in the literature on the subject (López-Fuentes 2007). Women continue to be held in high esteem, revered, and respected within the culture because of how they embrace and display their strength. For Cabo Verdeanas, strength is a virtue amid ongoing social and economic hardships, including Portuguese colonialism, long separation from family members, and hard work both inside and outside the home. Study participants noted that women endured hardship with honor and pride and that this hardship was part of being a Cabo Verdeana. At the same time, however, many women in the study suggested that such hardship "takes a toll on [women]." Nonetheless, Cabo Verdeanas' strength was seen as a mechanism that helps them to endure all of the hardships that they face, including gender-based violence.

Strength and resilience were seen as a part of a woman's role across all generations included in the study. Cabo Verdeanas' identity is embraced with pride, giving birth to the term "A Good Cape Verdean Woman," which was repeated throughout the study by all participants. A Good Cape Verdean Woman was defined as a woman who is strong, resilient, and keeps the house clean. She is a woman who takes care of her family and the community while preserving her culture. She is a wonder-woman who does it all.

Even so, there was some variation in the definition of a Good Cape Verdean Woman across generations. Younger participants reported,

> Today's generation women are strong as their mothers and grandmothers but she is also educated whereas many women in the past did not have the opportunity to go to school. Today a Good Cape Verdean Woman is described as strong like her mother and grandmother but she also has a master's degree or is a doctor and now her strength can make a change for the future and still clean her house.

Another participant added that today, "it's up to the young people to fight for the change but it is difficult to challenge the status quo. We may be older and maybe there is no threat to us but we women have the strength and we must stand together." Yet some of the younger participants offered a still different perspective, suggesting that "no woman can live up to this ideal of the Good Cape Verdean Woman and it hurts all women because if she is criticized for not being like her mothers and grandmothers." Many of the younger participants felt burdened and overwhelmed by this ideal—especially those who were pursuing career goals in the absence of having a family. Others suggested that their families thought they had become Americanized and that this caused Cabo Verdean culture to suffer.

DISCUSSION

Conducting the CVWP and presenting its findings both within and outside the Cabo Verdean community has been by far the most challenging, rewarding, and instructive experience I've had, both as a researcher and as a community member. As a Cabo Verdeana/Black woman myself, I was honored to be among these women and hear their stories. They are today's claims makers— displaying the courage to speak out about gender-based violence. There are many lessons for all of us to learn about community outreach and awareness to help women and children have safer lives.

Two major themes that continue to resonate with study participants, audience members at conferences, and in classroom discussions are (1) the code of silence and (2) how violence intersects with culture. These two themes intersect with each other in ways that both protect women and put them at risk for violence. Reactions to both themes demonstrate the complexity of gender-based violence and the important work that still needs to be done in order for Cabo Verdean families to be safe.

As I presented the study findings in the Cabo Verdean community, in university settings, and in community-based events, I received a combination of silence, support, and resentment. Question and answer sections at conferences were very quiet, if not eerie with silence. However, in more private, out-of-the-way spaces, women and men would come up to me and share stories about the violence they experienced or saw. Silence is a recurring theme and a common concept among the domestic violence literature (Kalunata-Crumpton 2005; Kasturirangan et al. 2004; Moe 2007). Like many women, the participants in the study truly believed that their silence was protecting themselves and their family members while maintaining family honor and preserving their culture (Gulizar and Tabassum 2013; Bonomi 2006; Moe 2007). Most of the participants experienced gender-based violence in ways that were too difficult to voice out loud. However, silence has also been described as a tool of protection, power, and resistance by victims (Gulizar and Tabassum 2013; Jeremiah et al. 2017; Moe 2007; Owusu 2016). Several oppressed groups have historically used silence to their advantage, such as slaves, Native Americans, and women. In fact, in certain instances, silence is the only tool that a victim has to protect themselves or their children against more extreme violence. Silence can also be empowering—taking away the abuser's control or satisfaction.

Cabo Verdeans used this strategy against the Portuguese colonizers who abused them in order to exercise power in the islands. In this context, silence became a coping strategy for survival—reinforced by the Cabo Verdean community's cultural norm of privacy. For Cabo Verdeana in particular, silence embodies the virtue of strength to endure the hardships that they live with. More importantly, for those undocumented Cabo Verdeans living in the

United States, silence is a necessary means of protection from deportation and separation from their families, and to avoid the shame and scrutiny that may come from others in their community.

Silence is a part of the cultural script in a society that determines what can be said and who can challenge the status quo, especially when the status quo is based on cultural norms of hegemonic, masculine, and oppressive control. Silence is a patriarchal tool of oppression where males assume power and control—a fundamental feature of gender-based violence (Jeremiah et al. 2017; O'Brien et al. 2013; Warrior 2005). Furthermore, the code of silence also keeps men silent, extinguishing the voices of those who might want to speak out against gender-based violence for women and/or about the violence they personally have experienced. For example, at one presentation, a young man spoke out about the pain he felt seeing his father hurt his mother, asking, "How do I not become an abuser?" as if it was a natural feature of being a man. At this event, we all rallied around the young man and assured him he was on the right path to be a strong, loving man because he was already doing the work to ensure that he was not going to become an abuser. This young man is also a claims maker, and his actions represent a social change. Thus, while silence is often misinterpreted as cooperation, in practice, its power can help both victims and abusers.

The second theme, culture, and violence broke much of the silence among audiences and even sparked anger in some instances. While the theme of culture and violence originated from the study participants themselves, it was strongly contested at events. At a Cabo Verdean conference, a prominent male scholar challenged this theme, suggesting that I was demonizing my own culture. He stated that he would "teach me how to analyze the data properly.[6]" His reaction is not surprising, especially in the context of talking about black and brown communities (e.g., the Cabo Verdean community) who have been marginalized in society. Moreover, black and brown people have not only been marginalized, but they have also been viewed as inherently violent and dangerous, suggesting that this violence is part of their "nature." No one example of this could be clearer than the historical and ongoing shooting of black and brown women and men, which spawned the contemporary Black Lives Matter movement. We have gone from lynching black and brown women and men to shooting them—showing how Black women and men are scrutinized in their daily lives because they are perceived to be inherently criminal and untrustworthy. As of the writing of this chapter, as the country is facing a global pandemic, people in the United States are risking their lives to protest for George Floyd, a black man who was killed by a white police officer. George Floyd's death marks another unnecessary killing of Blacks at the hands of those who are supposed to protect us—illustrating how complex and contentious the question of violence and culture can be within the Black community.

In contrast to the prominent male scholar's reaction, other audience members were very understanding and supportive when I presented the CVWP. As one viewer suggested, "we need to bring this topic out into the open, however painful it is to do so." The combination of resistance and support makes sense for a community that has been marginalized and rendered socially invisible in American society. Given the Cabo Verdean community's history of racism, colonialism, and social invisibility, it is understandable that they might deny that gender-based violence exists in their culture and be protective of their community. It is also difficult for any community to comprehend, understand, and then express the unimaginable existence of gender-based violence. The very thought that someone who loves you can also hurt you can be difficult to imagine, proving that "violence and love co-exist in twisted ways" (Thomas 2020).

Crucially, the theme of culture and violence is not suggesting that Cabo Verdeans are inherently violent, but instead exploring how cultural norms play a significant role in how, and why, gender-based violence persists. The social and cultural acceptance of violence is broadly socialized in most, if not all, societies around the world. As described earlier in this chapter, many types of violent behaviors are both socially and culturally acceptable (Barnett et al. 2011; Gelles 1997). For example, bullying was once thought to be a natural part of growing up and learning how to deal with conflict, and children were told that the best way to deal with a bully is to fight back—perpetuating violence. Today, most schools have a zero-tolerance policy for bullying, and many social workers and scholars now suggest that bullying is learned behavior that is more than likely related to issues in a child's home.

WHERE DO WE GO FROM HERE?

Gender-based violence has been recognized as a serious and complex problem that impacts individuals and their families—creating both long and short-term consequences for generations. Intervention and prevention strategies in the Cabo Verdean community must include collaborations between the grassroots groups, families, service providers, and law enforcement—all of whom must be dedicated to learning from each other to make social change.

Working at the Grassroots

We must recognize that many community organizations in both the United States and Cabo Verde have been working on these issues for some time. Community-based organizations in the United States (i.e., formal and informal) and NGOs in Cabo Verde are essential. These organizations collaborate with providers across a variety of networks—family, community, state, federal, county, and country. Community groups evolved out of need and a lack of support from mainstream organizations and offer a wide range of information and services, including college scholarships, immigration assistance, economic development, entrepreneurship, and housing. NGOs in Cabo Verde provide important links between women and the government in the face of economic and social constraints. Providers who work in the Cabo Verdean community must be willing to collaborate across networks—community, family, and nation—to provide education and resources and foster social change for women and men.

From Victims to Survivors

CVWP participants suggested that education must be a central tenet of working toward ending gender-based violence. Such education should include a multilevel and cultural approach with both intervention and prevention strategies. Education has the potential to teach individuals about the difference between an unhealthy and healthy relationship. This is especially important as many study participants noted that they didn't know their relationship could be different—a phenomenon that the literature notes are not uncommon.

There are many educational resources that are used to help prevent domestic violence, including models that highlight the differences between healthy and unhealthy relationships. One such model is the Cycle of Abuse, which shows how a relationship cycles between abusive and controlling behavior and loving behavior (see figure 4.1).[7] At the center of the cycle are denial, hope, and love, where both the abused and abuser deny the abuse, hope for change, and believe in the love they once had or thought they had. The abuser will blame anyone and anything for the abuse, including the victim, instead of taking responsibility for their actions. The victim may even believe that she did something wrong or that she can end the abuse by changing herself, further absolving the abuser of his abuse.

Throughout the domestic violence field, power and control are recognized as major principles, helping to explain the dynamics in an abusive relationship. Historically, abusive behavior has often been normalized due to social factors such as culture, family history, and patriarchy. Not only must we show women who have been abused what abuse looks like, but we must also show how abuse works and how the cultural norms of the abuser and others in their community can be controlling.

Changing one's perception of oneself from a "victim" to a "survivor" entails bravery and understanding from one's community. A major complexity of gender-based violence is that it is embedded in the universal

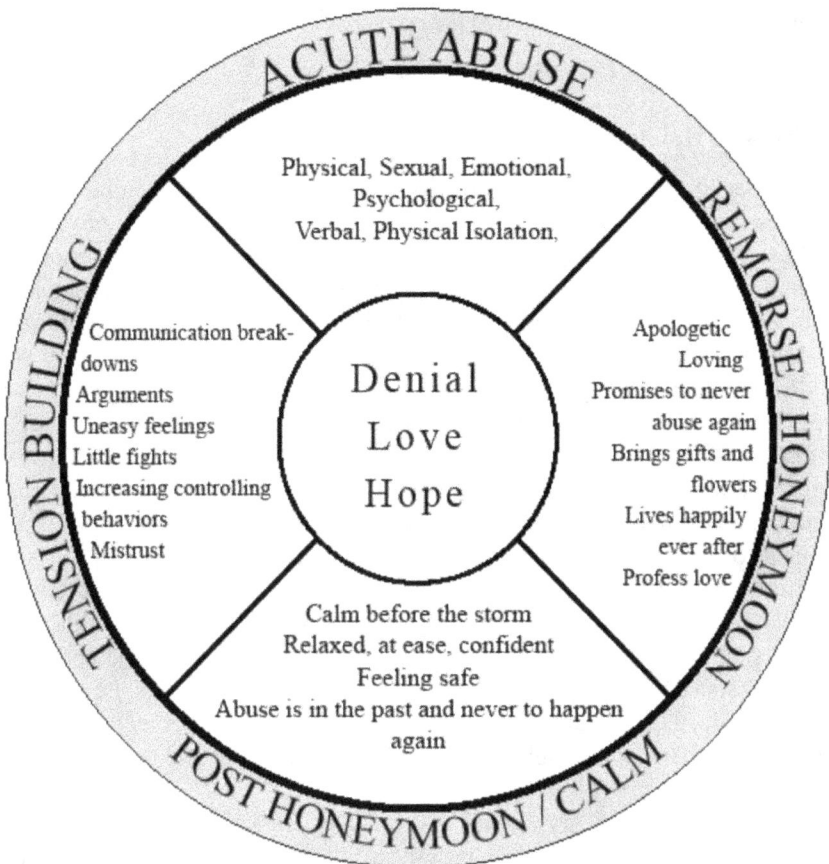

Figure 4.1 Cycle of Violence. Dr. Lenore Walker, a psychologist, was well-known for developing the Cycle of Abuse in the 1970s, which included four phases: tension-building phase, violent episodes phase, remorseful/honeymoon phase, and calm. Her Cycle of Abuse has been transformed into many variations and used throughout the Domestic Violence community. I modified the Cycle of Abuse by developing this wheel to include discussions from the classroom, advocates, and research participants.

emotional desire to be loved. Breaking the cycle of abuse involves knowing that a healthy and loving relationship includes respect, fairness, embracing positive cultural features, and trust. CVWP participants suggested that the most difficult aspect of dealing with abuse is the fear that reporting abuse will cause the victim to lose her family, her culture, and her community. The thought of being ostracized by the community was too painful for many participants. Thus, intervention/prevention should be thought of in a holistic way—including not only victims but also families and the community. As such, raising community awareness in the Cabo Verdean community and including both men and women in the conversation has the potential to reduce gender-based violence.

Culturally Relevant Outreach

Today, legislation across state and federal agencies mandates cultural competency training for law enforcement, court officers, and service providers. Cultural competency has been defined in many ways, but its principles include appropriate linguistic services, professional development, community outreach, and culturally diverse staff (Jackson 2002; Thomas 2014; Office of Minority Health 2020). Traditional cultural competency models have not addressed the inherent power imbalances between providers and clients, however, which remain a feature of American individualism's competitive culture. Traditional models have also failed to consider the aspects of historical oppression, systematic racism, and sexism that have contributed to mistrust and silence in many communities of color. In addition, providers are often trained to be "experts," using jargon that is unique to their profession and reinforcing an inherent power differential between the provider and client. Finally, cultural competency protocols are most times developed with a one-size-fits-all approach, acting as if all women of color are the same and have identical social, political, and cultural histories. As a result, despite genuine efforts to develop cultural competency protocols, disparities persist within the Cabo Verdean community and among women of color and undocumented women.

The "cultural humility model" is a direct contrast to many cultural competency models. It requires providers to "engage in self-reflection and self-critique as lifelong learners and reflective practitioners" (Tervalon and Murray-Garcia 1998, 203). The "golden rule" of the cultural humility model is that "those who participate in cultural competency training gain knowledge; however, there are no experts in this process" (Thomas 2014, 203).

In addition, historical trauma (HT) and informed care approaches used among Native American cultures offer tools for many communities, including Cabo Verdeans, whose histories are shaped by generational violence, oppression, and hardship (Brave Heart et al. 2016; Walters et al. 2011). HT is defined as acts of violence that suppress one's culture, liberty, and freedom; massive, cumulative, and intergenerational trauma that many communities have experienced at the hands of their oppressors (Brave Heart et al. 2016; Brunett 2015; Walters et al. 2011). HT considers how unresolved grief and pain are internalized and can linger in a community's present-day in many forms, such as violence and other destructive behaviors. Participants in the CVWP study often spoke of the Portuguese colonial rule's extreme violence as if they had experienced it themselves and viewed this HT as a significant factor in the violence perpetrated in their homes. Both women and men are victims of HT, even if it is the men who are often the present-day perpetrators of violence.

Informed care approaches used by mental health providers have several distinctions, addressing cultural trauma, HT, intergenerational trauma, and current trauma. Informed care approaches also consider how HT and other environmental factors contribute to an individual's development of feelings of insecurity, uncertainty, and emotional distress. These feelings can lead to the person using violence as a way to maintain a sense of control and confidence. Based on the principles of HT, informed care, and cultural humility, intervention and prevention programs should consider working with Cabo Verdeanas' history of oppression and the current environment of oppression, racism, and sexism. Doing so would bring a deeper understanding of the Cabo Verdean community's diversity, culture, and family dynamics and help to prevent or reduce the violence in the community.

CONCLUSION

There are ongoing challenges for Cabo Verdeana who are dealing with abuse. Not only is there a lack of knowledge about the community itself, but there is also dismissiveness among mainstream systems about Cabo Verdeanas' roles and devotion to their community and family. As a result, major barriers and a lack of trust continue to exist between Cabo Verdeanas and the very systems from which they need help. In addition, while research sources are always problematic, this is even more true for the Cabo Verdean community, as they are a small group or considered a subgroup, a designation that sees them as inferior, which consciously or unconsciously systematically reinforces oppression; therefore, there are limited funds available for research on Cabo Verdeans. The goal of this chapter was not only to share the research findings from the Cabo Verdean Women's Project but also to share the women's stories, to increase awareness about their community and how to better help them. A multidisciplinary and leveled approach to intervention and prevention strategies should include the Cabo Verdean community's HT, experiences with immigration, and the oppression they currently experience. These histories and experiences are linked in multiple ways and are significant to abuse in the community. Future research should involve law enforcement, court officers, agencies, and the Cabo Verdean community, as real change must emanate from both inside and outside of the community.[8]

NOTES

1. Originally the project was titled The Cape Verdean Women's Project. In 2013 Cabo Verde name change signifies how the Cabo Verdean language and country continue to evolve and be empowered beyond the English Portuguese spelling. My work over 20 years has also changed as with early works of the 1990s the use of Capeverdean, later Cape Verdean, now to Cabo Verdean. This is a positive evolution as a community both in Cabo Verde and in the United States representing our self-confidence, culture, and independence.

2. A special thank you to all the women who participated in the study and helped along the way.

3. Intimate Partner Violence Surveillance: Uniform Definitions and Recommended Data Elements, National Center for Injury Prevention and Control, Division of Violence Prevention at the Center of Disease.

4. Again, both Cape Verdean women, Cabo Verdeana will be used throughout the chapter showing how language has progressed, but also many people continue to use both going back and forth.

5. Interviews and focus groups took place in Boston, Brockton, Hyannis, Taunton and New Bedford Massachusetts.

6. Follow-up meeting by the Pedro Pires Institute for Cape Verdean Studies at Bridgewater State University organized the Community Health Through Individual Empowerment, Partner/Domestic

7. The Cycle of Abuse was modified and adapted from many versions of this cycle.

8. This chapter and all my work are dedicated to Elizabeth, Deborah, and Tiffany—the women who love and support me.

REFERENCES

Africa4 Women Rights. "African Women's Rights: Ratify & Respect." [Online forum comment]. Accessed January 5, 2015. http://www.africa4womenrights .org.

Appiah, Kwame A., and Henry Louis Gates Jr. 1999. *Africana: The Encyclopedia of African and African American Experience*. New York: Basic Books.

Barnett, Ola W., Cindy L. Miller-Perrin, and Robin D. Perrin. 2011. *Family Violence Across the Lifespan: An Introduction* (3rd ed.). Thousand Oaks: SAGE.

Bent-Goodley, Tricia B. 2001. "Eradicating Domestic Violence in the African American Community: A Literature Review and Action Agenda." *Trauma, Violence & Abuse* 2, no. 4 (October): 316–330.

Bent-Goodley, Tricia B. 2004. "Perceptions of Domestic Violence: A Dialogue with African American Women." *Health and Social Work* 29, no. 4 (November): 307–316.

Berg, Bruce L. 1989. *Qualitative Research Methods for Social Sciences*. Newbury Park: SAGE.

Bonomi, Amy E., David G. Allen, and Victoria L. Holt. 2006. "Conversational Silence, Coercion, Equality: The Role of Language in Influencing Who Gets Identified as Abused." *Social Science & Medicine* 62: 2258–226.

Brave, Heart, Maria Yellow Horse, Josephine Chase, Jennnifer Elkin, Jennifer martin, Jennifer S. Nanez, and Jennifer J. Mootz. 2016. "Women Finding the Way: American Indian Leading Intervention Research in Native Communities." In *Women's Health: Readings on Social Economic, and Political, Issues* (7th ed.), edited by Dawna Marie Thomas, 154–167. Dubuque: Kendall Hunt.

Breiding, Mathew J., Kathleen C. Basile, Sharon G. Smith, Michelle C. Black, and Reshma R. Mahendra. 2015. *Intimate Partner Violence Surveillance: Uniform Definitions and Recommended Data Elements, Version 2.0.* Atlanta, GA: National Center for Injury Prevention and Control, Centers for Disease Control and Prevention.

Carbado, Devon W., Kimberlé Williams Crenshaw, Vickie M. Mays, and Barbara Tomlinson. 2013. "Intersectionality: Mapping the Movements of a Theory." *DuBois Review* 10, no. 2: 303–312.

Carling, Jørgen S. 2003. "Cartography of Cape Verdean Transnationalism." *Global Networks* 3, no. 4: 533–539.

Carter, Katherine, and Judy Aulette. 2009. *Cape Verdean Women and Globalization: The Politics of Gender, Culture, and Resistance.* New York: Palgrave Macmillan.

Challinor, Elizabeth. 2015. "Caught Between Changing Tides: Gender and Kinship in Cape Verde." *Ethnos: Journal of Anthropology* 82, no. 1: 1–26.

Cho, Sumi, Kimberlé Williams Crenshaw, and Leslie McCall. 2013. "Toward a Field of Intersectionality Studies: Theory, Applications, and Praxis." *Journal of Women in Culture and Society* 38, no. 4: 785–810.

Crenshaw, Kimberlé. 1991. "Mapping the Margins: Intersectionality, Identity Politics, and Violence Against Women of Color." *Stanford Law Review* 43, no. 6: 1241–1299.

Creswell, John W. 2009. *Research Design: Qualitative, Quantitative, and Mixed Methods Approaches* (4th ed.). Thousand Oaks: SAGE.

Creswell, John W., and David J. Creswell. 2018. *Research Design: Qualitative, Quantitative, and Mixed Methods Approaches* (5th ed.). Thousand Oaks: SAGE.

De Andrade, Lelia L. 1997. "The Question of Race: Cape Verdean Americans Talk About Their Race and Identity." *Cimboa: A Journal of Letters, Arts and Studies* 4, no. 2: 23–25.

Gelles, Richard J. 1997. *Intimate Violence in Families* (3rd ed.). Thousand Oaks, CA: SAGE.

George, Jayashree, and Sandra M. Stith. 2014. "Updated Feminist View of Intimate Partner Violence." *Family Process* 53, no. 2: 179–193.

Gosselin, Dense K. 2000. *Heavy Hands: An Introduction to the Crimes of Domestic Violence.* Upper Saddle River: Prentice-Hall.

Gulizar, Saleema A., and Nishat Tabassum. 2013. "Under the Veil of Silence: Violence Against Women." *Journal of Nursing* 3, no. 2: 29–33.

Hacker, Andrew. 1992. *Two Nations: Black and White, Separate, Hostile, Unequal.* New York: Charles Scribner's Sons.

Halter, Marilyn. 1998. "Identity Matters: The Immigrant Children." In *The Social Construction of Race and Ethnicity in the United States*, edited by Joan Ferrante and Prince Brown Jr, 77–97. New York: Addison-Wesley Educational.

Hammersley, Martyn. 1990. *Reading Ethnographic Research: A Critical Guide.* New York: Longman.

Jackson, V. H. 2002. "Cultural Competency: The Challenges Posed by a Culturally Diverse Society and Steps Toward Meeting Them." *Behavioral Health Management* 22, no. 2: 20–26.

Jeremiah, Rohan D., Camille R. Quinn, and Jicinta J. Alexis. 2017. "Exposing the Culture of Silence: Inhibiting Factors in Prevention, Treatment, and Mitigation of Sexual Abuse in Eastern Caribbean." *Child Abuse & Neglect* 66: 53–63.

Kalunta-Crumpton, Anita. 2015. "Intersections of Patriarchy, National Origin and Immigrant Nigerian Women's Experiences of Intimate Partner Violence in the United States." *International Journal of Sociology of the Family* 41, no. 1 (Spring): 1–29.

Kasturirangan, Aarati, Sandhya Krishanan, and Stephanie Riger. 2004. "The Impact of Culture and Minority Status on Women's Experience of Domestic Violence." *Trauma, Violence & Abuse* 5, no. 4 (October): 318–332.

Kelly, Ursula A. 2011. "Theories of Intimate Partner Violence: From Blaming the Victim to Acting Against Injustice, Intersectionality as an Analytic Framework." *Advances in Nursing Science* 34, no. 3: 29–51.

Krueger, Richard, A., and MaryAnn Casey. 2015. *Focus Groups: A Practical Guide* (5th ed.). Thousand Oaks: SAGE.

Lima, Ambrizeth. 2012. *Cape Verdean Immigrants in America: The Socialization of Young Men in Urban Environment.* El Paso: LFB Scholarly Publishing LLC.

Lobban, Richard. 1995. *Cape Verde: Crioulo Colony to Independent Nation.* Boulder: Westview Press.

Lobban, Richard, and Paul K. Saucier. 2007. *Historical Dictionary of the Republic of Cape Verde* (4th ed.). Lanham: Scarecrow Press.

López-Fuentes, I., and E. Calvete. 2015. "Building Resilience: A Qualitative Study of Spanish Women Who Have Suffered Intimate Partner Violence." *American Journal of Orthopsychiatry* 85, no. 4: 339–351.

López, Ian H. 1996. *White by Law: The Legal Construction of Race.* New York: University Press.

Miller-Perrin, Cindy L., Robin D. Perrin, and Claire M. Renzetti. 2018. *Violence and Maltreatment in Intimate Relationships.* Thousand Oaks: SAGE.

Moe, Angela M., 2007. "Silenced Voices and Structured Survival: Battered Women's Help Seeking." *Violence Against Women* 13, no. 7 (July): 676–699.

Mohanty, Chandra T. 2013. "Transnational Feminist Crossing: On Neoliberalism and Radical Critique." *Journal of Women in Culture and Society* 38, no. 40: 967–991.

Morgan, David L., and Richard A. Krueger. 1993. "When to Use Focus Groups and Why." In *Successful Focus Groups: Advancing the State of the Art*, edited by David L. Morgan, 3–19. Newbury Park: SAGE Publications.

Nichols, Andrea J. 2013. "Meaning-Making and Domestic Violence Victim Advocacy: An Examination of Feminist Identities, Ideologies, and Practices." *Feminist Criminology* 8, no. 3: 177–201.

O'Brien, Kristy K., Lynne Cohen, Julie A. Pooley, and Myra F. Taylor. 2013. "Lifting the Domestic Violence Cloak of Silence: Resilient Australian Women's Reflected Memories of Their Childhood Experiences of Witnessing Domestic Violence." *Journal of Family Violence* 28: 95–108.

Office of Minority Health. *Assuring Cultural Competence in Health Care: Recommendations for National Standards and an Outcomes-Focused Research Agenda.* Accessed June 1, 2020. http://www.minorityhealth.hhs.gov/templates/browse.aspx?lvl=2&lvlID=15.

Omi, Michael, and Howard Winant. 1994. *Racial Formation in the United States: From the 1960s to the 1990s.* New York: Routledge.

Owusu, Dora A. 2016. "Mute Pain: The Power of Silence in Triggering Domestic Violence in Ghana." *Social Alternatives* 35, no. 1: 26–32.

Parker, Karen F., and Kristen M. Hefner. 2013. "Intersections of Race, Gender, Disadvantage, and Violence: Applying Intersectionality to the Macro-Level Study of Female Homicide." *Justice Quarterly* 32, no. 20: 223–254.

Patil, Vrushal. 2013. "From Patriarchy to Intersectionality: A Transnational Feminist Assessment of How Far We've Really Come." *Signs: Journal of Women in Culture and Society* 38, no. 4: 847–867.

Perilla, Julia L., Josephine Vasquez Serrata, Joanna Weinberg, and Caroline A. Lippy. 2012. "Integrating Women's Voices and Theory: A Comprehensive Domestic Violence Intervention for Latinas." *Women & Therapy* 35: 93–105.

Pitt, Karen A. 2008. "Intersectionality, Gender and Race in Women's Experience of Domestic Violence: Applications to Postcolonial Trinidad." *The Caribbean Journal of Social Work* 6 (December): 58–82.

Sánchez, Gina E. 1998. "Between Kriolu and Mercano: Cape Verdean Diaspora Identities." *Cimboa: A Journal of Letters, Arts, and Studies* 5, no. 5: 22–25.

Sánchez-Gibau, Gina. 2005a. "Diasporic Identity Formation Among Cape Verdeans in Boston." *The Western Journal of Black Studies* 29, no. 2 (Summer): 532–539.

Sánchez-Gibau, Gina. 2005b. "Contested Identities: Narratives of Race and Ethnicity in the Cape Verdean Diaspora." *Identities: Global Studies in Culture and Power* 12: 405–438.

Shaw, Susan M., and Janet Lee, eds. 2012. *Women's Voices, Feminist Visions: Classic and Contemporary Readings* (5th ed.). New York: McGraw Hill Companies.

Sokoloff, Natalie J. 2008. "Expanding the Intersectional Paradigm to Better Understand Domestic Violence in Immigrant Communities." *Critical Criminology* 16, no. 4 (December): 229–255.

Sokoloff, Natalie J., and Ida Dupont. 2005. "Domestic Violence at the Intersections of Race, Class, and Gender." *Violence Against Women* 11, no. 1 (January): 38–64.

Tervalon, Melanie, and Jann Murray-Garcia. 1998. "Cultural Humility Versus Cultural Competence: A Critical Distinction in Defining Physician Training

Outcomes in Multicultural Education." *Journal of Health Care for the Poor and Underserved* 9, no. 2: 117–125.

Thomas, Dawna M. 2014. "Cape Verdean Perspective on Disability: An Invisible Minority in New England." *Women, Gender and Families of Color* 2, no. 2 (Fall): 185–210.

Thomas, Dawna M. 2018. "Breaking Their Silence on Intimate Partner Violence: Discussions with Cape Verdean Women." *Journal of Cape Verdean Studies* 3, no. 1: 66–91.

Thomas, Dawna M., William Sanchez, and Joanne M. Maniche. 2010. "Providing Culturally Relevant Vocational Services to Cape Verdeans with Disabilities." *Journal of Applied Vocational Rehabilitation Counseling* 41, no. 4: 11–20.

UN Women United Nations Entity for Gender Equality and the Empowerment of Women. 2016. *Ending Violence Against Women: Passing and Implementing Effective Law and Policies.* Accessed June 6, 2020. http://www.unwomen.org/en/ what-we-do/ending-violence-against-women/facts-and-figures.

United Nations Entity for Gender Equality and the Empowerment of Women Convention on the Elimination of All Forms of Discrimination Against Women. 2013. "Concluding Observations on the Combined Seventh and Eighth Periodic Reports of Cape Verde." Accessed April 5, 2013. https://www.un.org/women-watch/daw/cedaw/.

United States Department of State, Bureau of Democracy, Human Rights and Labor. 2019. "Country Reports on Human Rights Practices for 2019." Accessed June 5, 2020. https://www.state.gov/wp-content/uploads/2020/02/CABO-VERDE-2019 -HUMAN-RIGHTS-REPORT.pdf.

Wallace, Harvey. 2005. *Family Violence: Legal, Medical, and Social Perspectives* (4th ed.). Boston: Pearson.

Walters, Karina, Selma A. Mohammed, Teresa Evans-Campbell, Ramana E. Beltrán, David H. Cae, and Bonnie Duran. 2011. "Bodies Don't Just Tell Stories, They Tell Histories: Embodiment Historical Trauma Among America Indian and Alaska Natives." *DuBois Review* 8, no. 1 (April): 179–189.

Warrior, Sujata. 2008. "'It's in Their Culture": Fairness and Cultural Considerations in Domestic Violence." *Family Court Review* 46, no. 3 (July): 537–542.

Part III

POLICIES AND POLITICS

Chapter 5

The Effects of the Closed List on Representation by Gender, Political Participation, and Civil Society in Cape Verde's Democratic Regime

Roselma Évora

The political systems of the twenty-first century, although with different degrees of consolidation of democracy, are increasingly challenging to stabilize a pluralistic institutional design capable of integrating historically marginalized minorities from the spheres of representation of political power. It is in this sense that the issue of equality and equity between the sexes in the decision-making process is at the center of the debate and stands out on the global agenda. In this debate, several approaches and numerous variables have been considered to explain the profile of the decision and representation spheres of several countries.

This chapter is divided into three sections. In the first section, our intention is to present the panorama of representation by sex in the two main political decision-making bodies in Cape Verde: national legislative power and political decision-making bodies at the local level (executive and legislative). Our interest is to focus, in particular, on the role of institutional variables, particularly to verify the impact of the electoral and party system on the gender profile in the archipelago with respect to representation in national and local elected positions. We also propose in the second section to look at the trend of political participation in Cape Verde over the two decades of democracy, leaving for the final a brief reflection on the dynamics of civil society in the democratic regime.

Years ago, Cape Verde was referred to as an exemplary case of democracy with gender parity in its governing cast. In fact, in 2001, there was a significant increase in the presence of women in the government cast in the archipelago, reflecting a greater visibility brought by the democratic regime to the presence of women in the public sphere. There was even a period in which the country's governing composition was practically equal between the sexes, with a significant number of women holding ministerial positions. If we take, for example, the months that preceded the beginning of the 2011 legislative campaigns, Cape Verde had, at that time, nine women with positions of minister in a governmental group of sixteen people.

This encouraging panorama, despite being symbolically positive, however, as Costa (2011) warns us, a sociologically misleading reality since it is a portrait with little statistical weight in the national sociopolitical reality. The author points out that our enthusiasm does not rest on evidence that is anchored in fragile assumptions, since we must take into account that being part of the cast of a government does not require in the case of Cape Verde to be elected by popular vote. The practice of government formation in the country is based on the choices of people who are recruited by political appointment, and it is not mandatory to integrate the party lists that win elections.

The recent visibility of the presence of women in the public space in Cape Verde hides a reality of profound inequality of power distribution between the sexes in the country's decision-making spheres. This reality is justified by historical and socio-cultural reasons. Some Cape Verdean authors call attention to the weight and strength of the Portuguese colonial legacy in Cape Verde, whose relations between the sexes resulted in the founding of a patriarchal society, with direct consequence in the role assumed by both sexes. To man, as the naturally shaped being for space and the public sphere, and women, a role that is bound to the private sphere and a position of invisibility in various areas but more markedly in the political and representation spheres (Costa 2011; Coutinho 2011; Gomes 2011; Monteiro 2013).

Despite the undeniable role of the socio-cultural aspects in explaining the gender profile in the scenario of representation in Cape Verde, our interest here will be to focus on the institutional dimensions, in this case, to verify the effects of the electoral and partisan system, as institutional variables, as factors determinants that directly impact the representation by sex in that archipelago.

Cape Verde will soon complete three decades of implementation of the democratic regime. We have until now seen signs of consolidation of some procedural dimensions of the democratic regime. Specifically to the party system, the country presents evidence indicating the consolidation of a bipartisan party system. Since the political opening in 1991, disputes and election results have been divided by the two largest political parties in the archipelago, PAICV (African Party of Independence of Cape Verde) and MPD (Movement for Democracy). Both have obtained electoral results that

Table 5.1   Percentage of Seats per Party in the National Assembly, 1991–2016

Year	MPD	PAICV	Other Parties
1991	62.5	31.6	—
1995	61.29	29.75	9.77*
2001	30.19	47.85	9.16*
2006	29.1	41.2	3.67*
2011	42.27	52.68	4.3
2016	53.58	37.53	7.24**

Source: Created by author with figures from the Cabo Verdean National Statistics Institute.
* Sum of three party votes.
** Sum of four party votes.

indicate the control of more than 80 percent of the seats of the National Assembly, as shown in table 5.1.

The consolidation of the bipartisan system stems from some factors that are relevant here. At the time of the democratic transition, the ruling political class opted for the proportional electoral system and the D'Hondt method to choose the members of the national parliament. This option also meant preserving the size of the electoral circles, with most of them in Cape Verde should be considered circles of low magnitude, where the great majority of them elect only two deputies. The revision of the Electoral Code in 2010 did not mean at all to be a structural change in our view, rather, we perceive a continuity, and there are not many possibilities to encourage within the political parties, the entry of a profile of a certain category, as women, for example, in electoral disputes.

According to Silva (2007), the maintenance of the size of the electoral circles in the democratic period reflects a legacy of the authoritarian regime. The author states that the electoral law of the authoritarian regime established that in each electoral circle there would be 1 deputy for every 3,000 registered voters or with more than 1,500 registered voters when the value did not reach 3,000. That rule determined a minimum of two members per round. Without the change of the electoral rules in the process of democratic transition, when Cape Verde already had a new demographic configuration, naturally, it would have reflected in the configuration of the party system that emerges in the democratic regime with an impact on the profile of the configuration of the representation of the archipelago.

Cape Verdean electoral legislation also establishes the rule for the election of national deputies by a closed and blocked party list. This means that the party first makes its selection so that the elector can later choose the candidates, and the voter cannot change the candidate's position in the list and the mandates are obtained based on the D'Hondt formula. The closed and blocked list election has, according to the literature, an impact on political representation by gender. An extensive bibliography maintains that the closed and blocked list electoral system does not favor the election of women in decision-making positions (Rule 1997; Osório 2010; Matland 1993), considering their place in the lists and dimension of the constituency.

At the time of selecting the names for the lists, how did the parties decide? According to Gomes (2011), the structures of the decision-making bodies of political parties in Cape Verde, reflections of patriarchal society, are hegemonically controlled and dominated by men and for years, women have occupied a minority position. Because they are in disadvantageous positions in the top-level party spheres, they are less likely to emerge as real leaders who could later position themselves in the competition for eligible seats at the time of doing the lists, with the aggravating factor in Cape Verde, where there are small electoral circles.

Recently, it is possible to perceive a growing participation of women in the leading positions of political parties in Cape Verde, however, Monteiro's studies (2008, 2013, 2014) point out that, despite the timid advancement of women's leaders in the structures of political party leadership, it is important to see in what way women do politics. There are leaders that emerged and affirmed themselves in a context of masculine habitus because males are dominant in the structures of power. The Cape Verdean woman who leads in party organizations and politics in general plays this role with strong masculine characteristics, particularly in speeches (Monteiro 2013, 434).

What persists in the democratic regime in Cape Verde according to Monteiro (2013) in relation to the political representation of women is evidence that in fact indicates a marginal presence in politics because they continue to be under-represented in the electoral lists. This underrepresentation occurs in a context where the size of the electoral circles is small and the positions that women occupy on the electoral lists are not favorable to them. Both factors have a role in the representation profile, and we understand that they contribute to reinforce the inequality of representation by sex in the structures of power, although recent evidence indicates a timid advance. In these two decades of democracy, women represent only one-fifth of the seats in the national parliament according to the data in graph 1.

Gender inequality is even more pronounced when we look at the gender profile in the local municipal power. Here we consider the municipal legislative power (Municipal Assemblies) and the local executive power (Municipal Councils). Both spheres indicate a high level of underrepresentation and a low presence of women in decision-making powers at the local level.

It is very frequent in Cape Verde, speeches that promote substantial advancement of the presence of women in the spheres of power. However, the evidence above points to a reality in which the slow and timid presence of women in the main decision-making spheres is visible. There has been an increase, but it is not very expressive, considering the social and

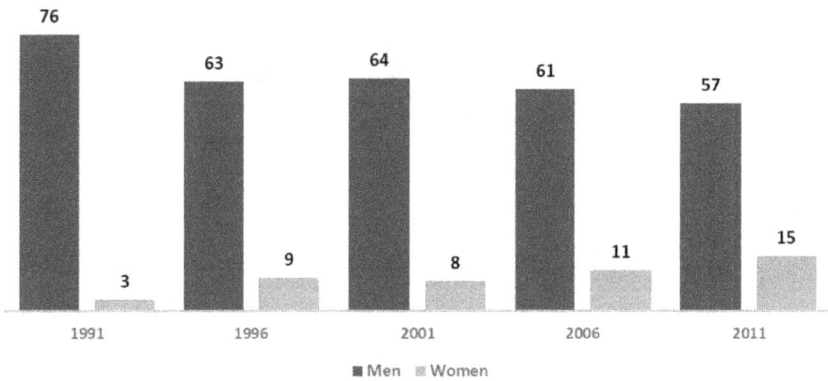

Figure 5.1 **Number of Members of Parliament (MP) at National Level by Gender, 1991/2011**
Source: Évora, R., and Ramos, N: "Relatório Preliminar Comportamento Eleitoral na Perspectiva Género." Programa das Nações Unidas para o Desenvolvimento. Praia, Cabo Verde, 2013.

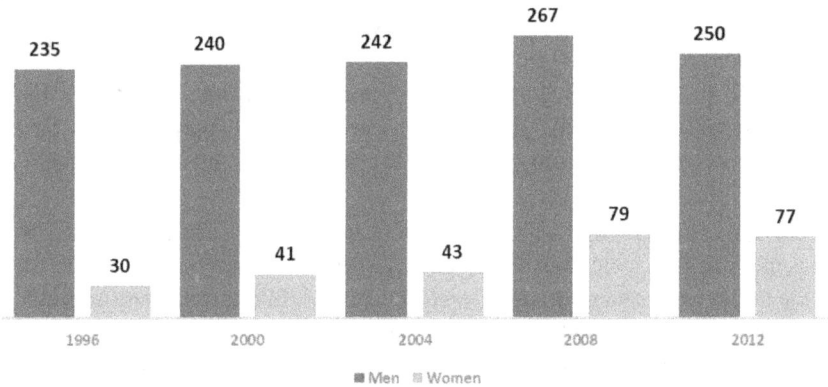

Figure 5.2 **Number of Deputies by Gender in the Municipal Assemblies, (1996/2012)**
Source: Évora, R., and Ramos, N. "Relatório Preliminar Comportamento Eleitoral na Perspectiva Género." Programa das Nações Unidas para o Desenvolvimento. Praia, Cabo Verde, 2013.

demographic reality of Cape Verde. The picture of the low participation and weak presence of women in decision-making positions in the main spheres of power in Cape Verde raises a set of equally relevant questions. In her analysis, Monteiro (2008, 2013, 2016) presents evidence that allows for deconstructing the discourse of emancipation and increasing women's leadership in the public sphere in Cape Verde. In addition, according to the author mentioned above, this increase must be followed by an important question that is, to know who are the women that are in politics and live from politics in Cape Verde?

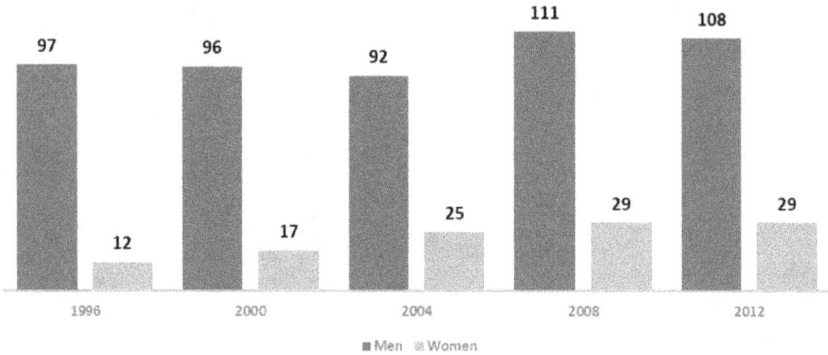

Figure 5.3 Number of Municipal Councilors by Gender, 1996/2012
Source: Évora, R., and Ramos, N. "Relatório Preliminar Comportamento Eleitoral na Perspectiva Género." Programa das Nações Unidas para o Desenvolvimento. Praia, Cabo Verde, 2013.

When we look at traces of a biographical analysis of women who entered the spheres of power in the archipelago, Monteiro (2013) presents evidence, which indicates that they come mainly from a privileged social category, coming from a favorable class condition and naturally facilitated by a family environment—a profile that is a typical picture of representation based on top-down logic, far from being a button-up portrait, thus far from reality.

> In social terms, it is effectively verified that women-ministers come from, as much as men or a little more than them, from privileged social background. Relative to the family environment of origin, some of them manifest a greater inheritance of the middle class, having familiar ties with the old agrarian bourgeoisie, the commercial bourgeoisie, the generation of the struggle for national independence and the political-administrative bourgeoisie of the post-independence era. Therefore, some of them appear as a second generation of the Cape Verdean elite in the context of post-independence. In this way, the favored character of the family environment of origin is verified. In this sense, gender parity leads to the symbolic realization of the social reproduction of the political elite, rather than broadening the bases of recruitment or subversion of the technocratic selection model of government members. In a certain way, women-ministers in very little or nothing reflect the image of Cape Verdean women in their diversity. (Monteiro 2013, 443)

Therefore, the challenge to promoting equal representation in the decision-making spheres in the archipelago should also mean broadening the more fragile social strata, which is particularly significant in Cape Verde's socio-economic context in the way that the country could have a picture of representation that shows the social diversity, and that could be a plural representation.

POLITICAL PARTICIPATION IN THE
DEMOCRATIC REGIME IN CAPE VERDE

The crisis of representative democracy is at the center of the debate in almost every country in the world. It reaches countries with different levels of democratic consolidation, including, in some cases, countries with a long democratic life. Part of this crisis is manifested particularly and especially in the reduction of electoral participation. In the new democracies, it is possible to find evidence indicating a great dissatisfaction with the functioning of democracy. When we talk about electoral participation, what has been the trend of electoral behavior in Cape Verde over the two decades of democratic rule?

The Cape Verdean constitution determines the election by universal and direct suffrage of three levels of power: to the legislative, president of the republic, and to elect the executive and legislative of local government. With almost three decades of democracy, twenty elections have been held since 1991: six legislative elections, six municipal elections, and eight presidential elections. The regularity and normality of the elections in Cape Verde have contributed to the reinforcement of a crucial aspect of procedural democracy, particularly since political openness is an environment of governance stability.

Voting in Cape Verde is not mandatory. In an attempt to answer the initial question, our objective in this section is to present the trend of electoral participation over two decades of democracy through evidence of electoral participation in the three levels of power mentioned earlier. We will present the average voting over a period of twenty-one years from the elections held from 1991 to 2012 in national electoral circles and in the diaspora electoral circles.

Diaspora electoral circles were created in the democratic period, allowing Cape Verdeans living on three continents (Africa, Europe, the Americas) to participate in the political life of Cape Verde. However, for diaspora circles, the right of voting only includes participation in the legislative and presidential elections.

Regarding electoral participation in national electoral circles, the evidence in table 5.2 indicates different levels of electoral participation among the three types of election, with a tendency of selective behavior of the Cape Verdean elector in the three levels of power. Assuming that the system of government in Cape Verde is parliamentary, the overall average of the total votes of the legislative national electoral circles indicates that it is the election that Cape Verdeans most participate in, with a voting average of 71 percent in more than two decades of holding elections. Participation in local elections follows legislative elections, with a global participation rate of 65 percent, and presidential elections are the least voted, with an overall participation average of 57.4 percent.

Table 5.2   Average Electoral Participation in National Electoral Circles by Island, 1991–2012

	Global	Legislative	Presidential	Municipal
Total National	63.5	70.6	57.4	64.7
São Vicente	57.8	69.2	51.2	56.2
São Nicolau	63.9	70.9	57.0	66.2
Sal	60.7	66.6	51.5	66.4
Boavista	68.7	78.2	60.0	70.8
Maio	72.7	78.6	64.3	77.8
Santiago North	62.6	67.4	56.9	64.3
Santiago South	62.8	70.8	58.7	61.0
Fogo	69.5	73.7	61.1	75.9
Brava	67.4	72.9	58.2	73.5

Source: Évora, R., and Ramos, N. "Relatório Preliminar Comportamento Eleitoral na Perspectiva Género." *Programa das Nações Unidas para o Desenvolvimento,* Praia: Cabo Verde, 2013.

This differentiated participation can be explained by some factors. First, we must consider the impact of each election and each power in the life of the voter. As in other democracies, and according to the literature, depending on the interest of the voter and the type of election, the symbolic weight assigned by the voter to each power will be different, resulting in a higher or lower level of electoral participation.

The Cape Verdean constitution assigns powers and levels of competencies quite differently between the powers. Each of them has a very different degree of impact and can be very important or insignificant depending on the power. In the concrete case of the legislative elections, the result of the elections leads to the formation of a government that will have a budget with more resources than the other powers. This allows it to assume a broad agenda of public policies, which, when implemented, will have an impact on people's lives. The national government agenda resulting from the legislative elections is what we believe will better reflect the expectations of voters, because they have the best material conditions to respond to the demands and interests of voters, in many different areas, particularly, for example, education, health, employment, security, sanitation, housing, and so on.

For the election of members of local power (local executive and municipal assembly), the financial and technical resources are smaller, have fewer powers compared to the central power, but is the power that is closed as it is inserted in the same locality and on daily life which gives it a considerable degree of importance for the voter. The spheres of local power and local politics thus have a great relevance and considerable impact on the life of the voter and their interests in the local sphere.

In relation to the election of the president of the Republic, also elected by direct and universal vote, we consider that in the case of Cape Verde, its power and its attributions are exclusive of a symbolic nature, particularly with regards to the representation of the State at an external level. With the lack of power to make laws, an essential condition for the materialization of public policy, nor having a budget that allows to materialize the demands of the voters, the president's importance in the people's life is much smaller when compared with the two other powers.

Regarding electoral participation in the diaspora in the three electoral circles where Cape Verdean emigrant communities exist, throughout the almost three decades of democracy, there have been significantly low turnouts when compared to the participation rates of national electoral circles. In the case of the electoral circles in the diaspora, there are high levels of abstention.

The overall average of electoral participation in the diaspora varies between the two elections. We consider a period of analysis about two decades of elections held in the diaspora electoral circles, about five legislative elections, and six presidential elections. The overall average participation of legislative elections in the diaspora in the period from 1991 to 2011 is about 39 percent. In the presidential elections, considering the period from 1991 to 2012, the overall participation average is 30 percent.

Cape Verde has an expressive diaspora, especially considering that this diaspora exceeds the population residing in the archipelago. Despite this, however, the participation of this diaspora in the two elections that allows the vote is insignificant. Several factors may explain the weak electoral participation of the Cape Verde diaspora. Although a small part of the Cape Verdean diaspora has electoral capacity, which means the right to vote, the data indicates that only a small group participates in the national elections.

The low voter turnout of the diaspora can be explained by a variety of factors. We particularly highlight two factors that we consider extremely relevant. A first aspect is related to operational and organizational aspects that influence the functioning of electoral institutions in diaspora circles. There is a recognition by the Cape Verdean electoral authorities (PNUD 2013), that there is a set of constraints that reflects on their operational capacity in overseas circles. They believe that such limitations affect their institutional capacity and their institutional efficiency in those circles, which may be an aspect with a possible reflection on the level of participation in the elections.

Among the constraints, there are institutional deficiencies in knowing and mastering the geographical and demographic aspects of diaspora circles. This limitation dictates that electoral institutions rely on information from others, which reduces their ability to control central aspects of the electoral process. They admit that they cannot respond satisfactorily and efficiently both in the run-up to the elections and during the election period. These limitations

Table 5.3   Average Abstention of the Diaspora Electoral Circles by Election, 1991/2012

	Global	*Legislative*	*Presidential*
Total Diáspora	66.4	60.8	70.4
Electoral Circles			
Africa	48.8	45.2	51.4
Americas	57.5	49.7	63.0
Europe	77.0	72.0	80.5

Source: Évora, R., and Ramos, N. "Relatório Preliminar Comportamento Eleitoral na Perspectiva Género." *Programa das Nações Unidas para o Desenvolvimento.* Praia, Cabo Verde, 2013.

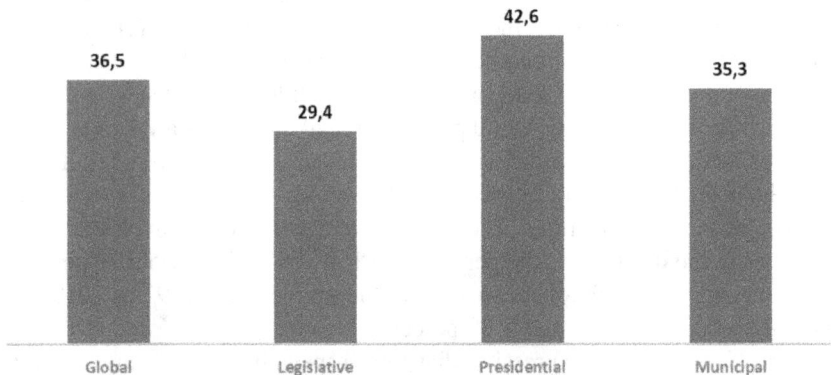

Figure 5.4   Electoral Abstention by Election, 1991/2012
Source: Évora, R., and Ramos, N. "Relatório Preliminar Comportamento Eleitoral na Perspectiva Género." Programa das Nações Unidas para o Desenvolvimento. Praia, Cabo Verde, 2013.

should be considered in our point of view as factors that have an impact on voter participation.

The main Cape Verdean political actors, on the other hand, understand the low voter turnout of diaspora circles as a reflection of voters' low interest in national politics in Cape Verde. They believe that the diaspora voter sees politics in Cape Verde as having a secondary impact on their lives and therefore have little interest in participating. The Cape Verdean voter residing in foreign countries, in the opinion of some party leaders, is more interested in the domestic politics of the host country, because this directly affects them.

What is noteworthy in the analysis of the trend of diaspora electoral participation is the high levels of abstention of foreign electoral circles, with considerable abstention rates compared to national electoral circles. Table 5.3 and figure 5.4 show the overall abstention rates in diaspora and national electoral circles, indicating a large gap between the two circles in electoral participation.

STRENGTHENING CIVIL SOCIETY FOR A
REAL DEMOCRACY IN CAPE VERDE

The election of a government by popular vote is considered an essential requirement of a democratic regime (Bobbio 2000; Bratton 1998). In this sense, electoral participation in the choice of a democratic government is crucial to the foundations of democracy. A large literature, however, advocates that it is not enough for a country to hold elections and choose a government by complying with the procedural principles of democracy that guarantees a solid and quality democratic regime.

The existence of a strong and active civil society is recognized by several authors, from classics like Toqueville (1999) to contemporaries like Atwood (1992), Linz and Stepan (1999), Putnam (1996) as an important and indispensable dimension for the consolidation of democracy. A strong and vibrant civil society is recognized as a sign of the exercise of a genuine democratic practice. Civil society is the element that gives meaning to the democratic process. With regards to the role of civil society in the democratic regime in Cape Verde, successive Afrobarometer surveys carried out in the archipelago regularly indicate that this is one of the most fragile dimensions of the country's democratic regime. The evidence indicates a weak and very apathetic civil society.

Paradoxically, this weakness of civil society manifests with a high support to the democratic system. In Cape Verdean society, evidence shows a growing tendency to support democracy as a preferred political regime to any other political regime. Cape Verdeans show increasing support for the democratic regime as we can see in figure 5.3 and that support is more than the average of the African continent, that is, 67 percent.

If this support for democracy is encouraging, it is paradoxical when we look for evidence that characterizes the type of civil society in Cape Verdean democracy. The successive results of the Afrobarometer (2002, 2016), present us with evidence that indicates what we can call a deep apathy of the civil society with signs more evident in the low level of participation of Cape

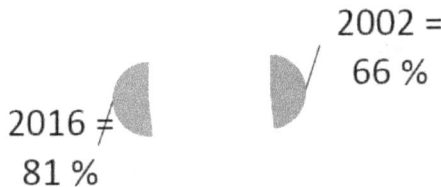

2002 = 66 %

2016 ≠ 81 %

Figure 5.5   Popular Support for Democracy in Cape Verde
Source: Afrosondagem/Afrobarometer. "Qualidade da Democracia e da Governação." Praia, Cabo Verde, 2002/2016.

Verdeans in civic activities. The data indicate that more than 80 percent of Cape Verdeans do not participate in activities of civic and political engagement, such as participation in marches and protests, participation and activism in associations, unions, and so on.

Civic fragility is, in our view, a symptom of an anemic democracy, and some factors justify it. Some authors attribute the causes of the weakness of Cape Verdean civil society, partly because it is the result of a legacy of an authoritarian political culture, a legacy of non-participation in public affairs. On the other hand, some authors advocate that there is still a strongly paternalistic view of political power in the archipelago, which constitutes an obstacle to development, autonomy, and emancipation of civil society. Such legacy contributes to the persistence of political practice with a strong centralization of power, which favors the autonomy of civil society, rather, which conditions its strengthening and development.

The challenge of affirming a strong and autonomous civil society may be the answer to the dissatisfaction that Cape Verdeans have demonstrated in how democracy is conducted in that archipelago. Although Cape Verde has one of the largest African averages of democracy support, 81 percent in a continental average of 67 percent, however, when asked about their satisfaction with democracy, Cape Verdeans show a below-average African result, 23 percent while the continental average is 35 percent (Bratton and Mattes 2016).

In conclusion, we believe that the quality of Cape Verdean democracy is advancing in three dimensions. A representation and a decision-making process with more equality between the sexes that recognizes the space and plurality of women, the development of civil society, and the civic dimensions of Cape Verdean civil society that can later contribute to the reversal of the tendency toward low electoral participation.

REFERENCES

Afrobarometer. "Atitudes Em Relação À Qualidade Da Democracia Em Cabo Verde": Praia, Cape Verde, 2002–2016.

Atwood, J Brian. "Reflections on the Transition in Eastern and Central Europe." In Garber, Larry and Bjornlund, Eric: *The New Democratic Frontier: A Country by Country Report on Election in Central and Eastern Europe.* Washington: National Democratic Institute for International Affairs, 1992.

Bobbio, Norberto. *O Futuro Da Democracia.* São Paulo: Paz E Terra, 2000.

Bratton, Michael. "Second Elections in Africa." *Journal of Democracy* 9, no. 3: 51–63. Afrobarometer Policy Paper, No 36, 1998.

Bratton, Michael, and Robert Mattes. "Do Africans Still Want Democracy?" Afrobarometer Policy Paper No 36, 2016.

Costa, Suzano. "Mulheres E Participação Política No Cabo Verde Democrático." In Silva, Carmelita E Fortes, Celeste (Org). *As Mulheres Em Cabo Verde: Experiências E Perspectivas*. Praia: Edunicv, Vol. 4, 2011.

Coutinho, Ângela. Mulheres Na «Sombra»: As Cabo-Verdianas E A Luta De Libertação Nacional. In Silva E Fortes (Org). Ob. Cit. Gomes, Crispina. 2011. Mulher E Poder: O Caso De Cabo Verde. Ed: Ibnl, Praia/Cabo Verde, 2011.

Linz, Juan E., and Alfred A. Stepan. *Transição E Consolidação Da Democracia- A Experiência Do Sul Da Europa E Da América Do Sul*. São Paulo: Ed Paz E Terra, 1999.

Matland, Richard. "Institutional Variables Affecting Female Representation in National Legislatures: The Case of Norway." *The Journal of Politics* 55, no. 3: 737–755, 1993.

Monteiro, Euridice. *Mulheres, Democracia E Representação Politica*. Praia: Ed Unicv, 2008.

———. "Racism and Sexism: Between Colonial Discourse and Postcolonial Challenge." In Cape Verde. In Bussotti, Luca and Ngoenha (Org). *Cabo Verde Da Indepência A Hoje A Hoje Estudos Pós-Coloniais*. Italy: Aviani & Aviani, 2011.

———. "Quem Governa? Da Ausencia À Emergência De Mulheres No Campo Político Em Cabo Verde." In Sarmento, Cristina Montalvão E Costa, Suzano (Org). *Entre África E A Europa: Nação, Estado E Democracia Em Cabo Verde*. Coimbra: Almedina, 2013.

———. "Crioulidade, Colonialidade E Género: As Representações De Cabo Verde." *Estudos Feminista* 24, no. 3: 398, 983–996, Florianopolis, 2016.

Osório, Conceição. *Género E Democracia: As Eleições De 2009 Em Moçambique*. Ed: Wlsa, Maputo, 2010.

Pnud/Unicef/Unfpa. *Estudo Sobre A Participação Eleitoral Em Cabo Verde - Relatório Final. Elaborado Por Évora, Roselma & Ramos, Noemi*. Praia, 2013.

Putnam, Robert D. *Comunidade E Democracia – A Experiência Da Itália Moderna*. Rio De Janeiro: Fgv, 1996.

Rule, Wilma. "Why Women Don't Run: The Critical Contextual Factors in Women's Legislative Recruitment." *Western Political Quarterly*, 61–77, 1997.

Silva, Mário. *Código Eleitoral*. Praia: Ed Do Autor, 2007.

Toqueville, Alex De. *A Democracia Na América*. São Paulo: Ed:Martins Fontes, 1999.

Chapter 6

Public Policies and Gender Equality in Cabo Verde from the Study on the Use of Time to the National Care System

Clementina Baptista de Jesus Furtado

In[1] Cabo Verde, the mainstreaming of gender equality is seen as a factor in the development and promotion of social justice. Current policies aim to promote gender equality and empowerment and social justice. The results of the survey on the Use of Time and Unpaid Work (UTUW) showed that 77 percent of the work performed in the country is unpaid and the majority is done by women. These results were fundamental for the design of the National Care Plan (NCP 2017–2021).[2]

This data brought to light the problems of sexual division of labor and the weight of unpaid work for women, especially those less educated, socioeconomically vulnerable residents in rural and peri-urban areas. This situation proved to be urgent for the elaboration and implementation of public policies, aiming at societal changes. The population of the country is young; however, life expectancy has been increasing and, consequently, the number of elderly, and along with them, the need for care. Likewise, there are people with disabilities who depend, for the most part, on special care from their relatives, usually women. Many live in a situation of extreme socioeconomic vulnerability, jeopardizing their human dignity hence the need for a restructuring of efficient public support services for families and the redistribution of care tasks and services (care seen as a public concern and its inclusion in the national, social, political, and governmental agenda, involving different actors from the society).

Based on the results of the study of the UTUW[3] and in these sociodemographic dynamics, the National Care Plan (2017/2021) was prepared. Consequently, two new dual categories emerged: caregivers of the dependents (for children and elderly and people with disabilities) and young people of both sexes benefiting from specific training for the professional exercise of care.

This work aims to reflect on the process that takes place from the elaboration of UTUW Study to the elaboration of the National Care Plan, from one hand and, on the other, to evaluate the challenges and impacts of its implementation, based on semi-structured interviews with the National General Department of Social Inclusion (DGIS) and two young people who benefited from the care of the training project. It is a qualitative study including a brief literature review, guiding documents for the design of the NCP, as well as other documents related to the theme in the study. The analysis is complemented with statistical information analyzed from a gendered perspective.

This study is divided into four parts, in addition to the introduction. They are as follows: Public Policies on Equality and Gender Empowerment: Contextualization; The Study on the UTUW and the Sexual Division of Work; From the Care Crises to the National Care Plan; and the Implementation of the National Care System-Gains and Challenges.

PUBLIC POLICIES ON EQUALITY AND GENDER EMPOWERMENT: CONTEXTUALIZATION

Cabo Verde has been investing in the adoption of efficient public policies, promoting equality and gender empowerment, and emphasizing inclusion and social justice. The efforts are made both through its accession and ratification of international treaties and conventions (CEDAW),[4] the Declaration of the Platform of the Actions of Beijing), and through the adoption of diplomas and national legislative measures promoting gender equality and social inclusion. The commitments assumed in relation to MDG's (Millennium Development Goals) Agenda 2063 and, later, the SDOs (Sustainable Development Objectives) reflect this commitment to the country. At the national level, the legal framework is quite favorable. Equality is embedded in the country's Constitution.[5] In the Government Program (IX Legislature, 2016–2021), transversality is the basic principle, and the Strategic Plan for Sustainable Development (PEDS, 2017/2021),[6] particularly through its Objective 3, *to ensure social inclusion and the reduction of inequalities and social and regional asymmetries* reinforces this vision of the country. There are also other diplomas, namely the Family Code (1997), the Labor Code (2007), among others. It should be noted that the programs of previous governments also had transversality as the basic guiding principle of policies.[7]

The very creation of the Institute for Gender Equality and Equity (ICIEG) in 2006 that came to replace the Institute for Female Condition Institute (ICF, created in 994) is the result of measures taken in the framework of promoting gender equality and social justice. ICIEG is the national structure responsible for the design, coordination, and implementation of public policies. It works in conjunction with several national institutions, both public and within academia, and it gives responses to its objectives and missions. The various plans and diplomas designed and implemented in direct partnership with international organizations based in the country are the result of these commitments. This information is highlighted in the first National Action Plan for the Promotion of Woman (1996–2000), The National Plan for Gender Equality and Equity (PNIEG, 2005–2011), the First and Second National Plans to Combat Gender-Based Violence (I PNVBG, 2008–2011 and II PNVBG, 2014–2016), the special law on GBV (Law 84/VII/11, January 10), Action Program for the Promotion of Gender Equality (PAPIG, 2011–2012), and the National Plan for Gender Equality (PNIG, 2014–2018).[8]

Municipalities also had initiatives, for example, there is the Common Gender Agenda of the Municipalities of Praia and São Miguel (2014), an initiative of the Democratic Women of these municipalities, where they demand a fairer and promoting gender equality. Similarly, there are the Municipal Plans for Gender Equality (PMIG), as is the case of São Salvador do Mundo (PMIGSSM, 2019–2022). Another aspect to mention is the Parity law, approved in November of 2019.

Therefore, all the conditions for inclusive public policies were created. However, after all, what are public policies? Souza (2002) defines public policies as

> a branch of political science capable of guiding governments in their decisions and understanding how and why the governments choose certain actions (p.3). In his turn, Peters (1986) understands that public policy is the sum of government activities, which act directly or through delegation, and which influence the lives of citizens. (4)

And this is what is proposed with the National Care Plan/System (2017–2021) to impact the lives of people and to allow that all have an equal opportunity. According to Tude (n.d.), public policy is the sum of all the activities of the governments, which act directly or through delegation, influence the life of the citizens, and allow that all have the same opportunity. Also, public policies traditionally comprise a set of decisions and actions usually proposed by a state entity in a given area (health, education, transport, land, reform, etc.) in a discretionary manner or by combining efforts with a particular community or sectors of the civil society.

Policymaking takes place from evidence. And the evidence is presented through data. Gender-disaggregated data allows us to identify more vulnerable groups and gender gaps, influencing the design of appropriate policies.

In this particular case, the Study of the Use of Time and Unpaid Work (UTUW) was fundamental for the design of the National Care Plan.

THE STUDY ON THE UTUW AND THE
SEXUAL DIVISION OF WORK

With an extension of 4.033 km², Cabo Verde is located on the West African Coast and has a total population of 491.575 people (INE 2010). The census reports a population of 50.5 percent women (248,260) and 49.5 percent men (243,315). The annual growth rate of the population was 2.4 in 2000, having decreased to 1.2 in 2010. In 2018, it was estimated that 543,492 were residents (data from INE, National Institute of Statistics),[9] among which 273,546 were men and 269,956 were women. Regarding the head of the households, men represented 55 percent and women 45 percent. As for households, women were reported to have a higher rate of poverty at 31 percent compared to 26 percent of men.

In 2012, as part of the IMC's achievements, the study on the UTUW was carried out through a partnership between INE, ICIEG, and UN Women. This project also involved other institutions, namely UNFPA,[10] and the University of Cabo Verde (Uni-CV), through the Center of Investigation and Training for Gender and Family (CIGEF), with the technical collaboration of the University of the Republic of Uruguay. Until then, there was little available information about the unpaid workload, mainly housework and care and its weight on the national economy. The study would fill a large gap in this regard, and the information would be crucial to take action to meet justice and social inclusion. It brought quite pertinent conclusions about the participation of men and women in the national economy, revealing the sexual division of work, as well as the situation about the care and the weight of unpaid work in the national economy. Similarly, it gave greater visibility to the role of women in the national economy and in unpaid work, especially domestic and care labor.

The results showed that around a third of the week time is devoted to unpaid work with significant differences between men and women, that is, 90 percent of the women declared their participation compared to 73 percent of the men. Women reported dedicating around twice as many hours to unpaid work than men (63 and 38, respectively). In short, the use of time is unequal between genders, and there is a clear overload of women's work, which reflects negatively on their participation in other sectors of social life, including self-care. In general, the exercise of their citizenship is compromised. The situation is more delicate for women with less education, young people, those in poverty, heads of single-parent families, and those in urban and rural areas.

The study also found that in domestic work they dedicate more time, that is, 77 percent (49:35) followed by care 33 percent (27:25) provided to children and dependent people (the elderly and people with disabilities). These tasks are practically exclusive to women (87 percent against 66 percent of men), who depend around twice as long as men (59:40 against 36 hours). Particularly in the time dedicated to the care of the household, women contribute 72 percent of the time and men only 28 percent.

It is evident that women are "responsible" for the well-being of the families, ending up, themselves, not enjoying these benefits. This, in a way, is the reflection of a society marked by patriarchy, where domestic and care tasks are reserved for women. These, many times, will have to unfold between the private space and the public space, when working outside the home, which translates into a double or triple journey. As can be seen in the picture below, it is just in the maintenance and management services that the men stand out in terms of performance. All other household tasks are the responsibility of women.

The results also made it possible to verify that children under six years demand the greatest care, mainly due to the absence of daycare. When they existed, that was a privilege of a few. It is in this sector that the main gender gaps are found, and the situation is more critical in children aged zero to three

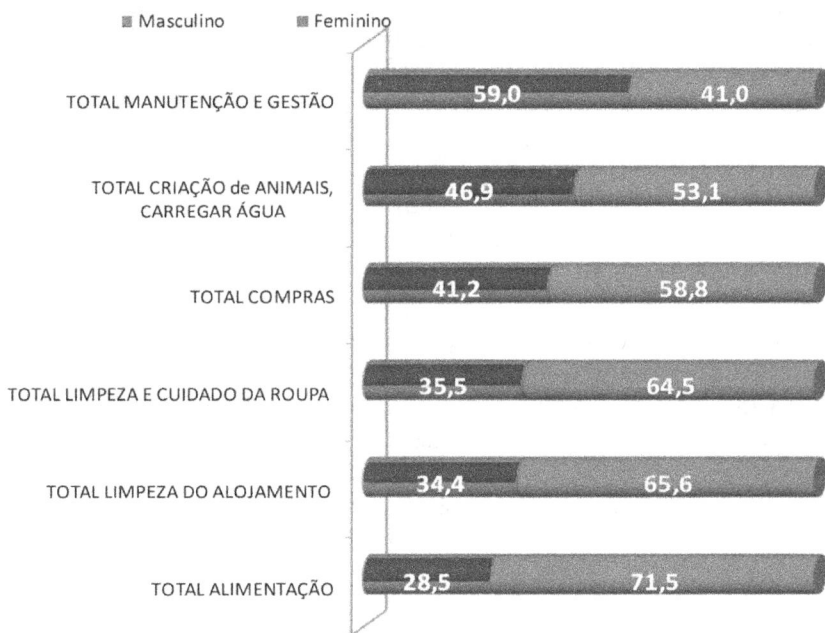

Figure 6.1   Percentage Distribution of the Participation in Housework by Sex
Source: INE, IMC 2012.

years, due to the lack of effective responses to the existent needs. Between zero to two years, the care is not practically verified (Soares 2004). The poorer, the greater the responsibility with housework and care.

It was also found that, despite a tendency toward a decrease in intensity, as age increases, among men, the time devoted to unpaid work decreases continuously; however, in women there are variations. With the exception of the ten to fourteen age group, in all others, the participation of women is higher than that of men. It is in the age groups between fifteen and nineteen and twenty-five to forty-four that there is a greater female participation. In addition, the presence of children decreases the participation of men in unpaid work, while it increases in women.

Based on these results, it was concluded that we were facing a crisis of care due to the lack of provision of these services by the State, leaving everything under the responsibility of women, with the evident division of sexual labor. In this regard, according to Soares (2004),[11]

Women continue to be considered as the only ones responsible for the innumerable tasks of the house, care for children and family, and, ultimately, responsible for the well-being. When the State does not provide the services, they are the women who do them. And, of course, the impact on adjustment policies which aim to reduce and decrease the services provided by the State, is already known. Domestic work naturalizes the division of public and private and establishes a place for each and every one in society. An analysis of the household shows an even distribution of work within the family—women invest more time in unpaid work activities than men. (121)

To better understand this issue of the care crisis (as a universal right), it is first necessary to understand what care consists of. In this case, according to Aguirre and Ferrari (2014),

In specialized literature and current political debates, the concept of care refers to the multiplicity of activities and relationships, whether paid or unpaid, intended to maintain the physical and emotional welfare of people, as well as to the normative, economic, and social frameworks where those activities and relationships are defined and performed (Daly and Lewis 2000, 285). It is conceived as a form of multidimensional support: material, economic, moral, and emotional to dependent individuals, but also to all persons in situations that threaten a loss of autonomy. The concept of care implies not just material aspects (the production of goods and services, as well the time spent in productive activities) but also moral aspects (responsibility, interactions based on what is considered fair and adequate) and affective ones (concern for the other, love, tensions, and conflict). (11)[12]

For her part, the author believes that the care crisis has to do with the relationship between people who require it and people available to offer this type of service. It is a relationship that happens in a proportionally inverse way, that is, it increases the number of people who require care and decreases the number of people, usually women, able to offer these services, a situation linked to the increase of life expectancy and other social and economic and cultural factors. In other words, the crisis affects both those who seek and those who are dedicated to offering this care. In Cabo Verde, the reduction in natural growth rate and the increase in the number of elderly population, along with a considerable number of people with disabilities and the lack of reception facilities and support structures for the needs of this group means that these responsibilities are assumed by the families, women in particular.

This issue is associated with what is called poverty of time (and money), that is, if, on the one hand, there was an almost total absence of care services, on the other, when they existed, they were the privilege of a few families. The poorest women did not have the money to buy these services, and, on the other hand, they had to sell their own time, often at low costs, as a way of guaranteeing the survival of their families. And that implied, even, having no time available to take care of themselves.

In summary, we would say that UTUW Study was an important tool for the production of knowledge concerning inequality between men and women at a national level, social inequality, and sexual division of labor, as well as how women, especially the poorest, live in vulnerable situations. Consequently, it opened a path for the elaboration of a public policy to combat poverty, social exclusion, and to promote gender equality and social justice, aiming at reducing poverty and promoting social justice. It is in this sense that the proposal for the National Care Plan was made, where the co-responsibility of the State and the Civil Society was fundamental. That is, care ceases to be a private responsibility to become collective.

FROM THE CARE CRISES TO THE NATIONAL CARE PLAN

The Care Crises in Cabo Verde is evidenced by the results of the UTUW Survey which include the overload of domestic work and care in the bosom of women associated with a constant increase in average life expectancy, with the consequent increase in the elderly population and the number of dependent people (with disabilities) under the care of the family members; they raise concrete measures for the unfamiliarization of the care policy and redistribution of tasks and co-responsibility.

Thus, in 2016, CIGEF (Uni-CV) in partnership with ICIEG and UN Women, hired a team to carry out a National Consultancy for the Analysis of Social Policies and Proposals for Gender-Sensitive Social Public Policies, with the objective to analyze "the situation of Cabo Verde in terms of social protection and gender mainstreaming in the design and implementation of social policies" (para. 1). These results were complemented with a cost-benefit analysis over a 24-year-old period (2016–2040), in order to highlight the economic viability of the plan. Subsequently, a proposal was made to create the Interministerial Group (GI) for the design of the access to the Income, Education, Care, and Health Program (2016), which would later work on the proposal for the National Health System Care (NCS/National Care Plan 2017–2021).

The results of the analysis showed that the country had some infrastructure and a fragmented set of policies; however, there was no integrated system of care that, until then, was in charge of women who were affected by poverty and did not benefit from the care, contrary to what is said in the Constitution of the Republic which determines, in its article 6, the principles of universality and equality. Thus, many children at risk were left on the streets by mothers, unable to leave them inadequate supports structures, increasing the risks of juvenile delinquency; the majority of elderly and disabled people lived in a situation of vulnerability and lacked care coverage, with the consequence of fragility of families, leading to the disintegration of ties, in addition to mutilating projects and life opportunities for women reduced to the condition of caregivers (Anjos et al. 2016).

Consequently, it was recommended that Cabo Verde needed a Care System, as an instrument to reduce poverty and inequality, where the rights of people with disabilities, gender equality, and economic and social development would be guaranteed. The proposal should integrate principles of integrity, universality, transversality in gender equality, and symmetry of focus on dependents and caregivers, among others. The question of universality and focus is debatable. For, on the one hand, universality was defended, on the other, priorities had to be established. And that meant focusing on specific groups. In this case, the caregivers, who needed to be minimally trained to give a more dignified response to the sector (visibility of/ attendants—decent employment), and dependent people, due to the lack of structures, that would respond to their needs (homes and daycare centers and rehabilitation centers). As Dighiero (2015) says,[13]

> The analyzed experiences show that even when the discursive level aims for universality, particularity imposes itself at the terrain of implementation. The second challenge refers to the tension between the development of fair policies from the point of view of gender that may balance care and incentivize the

incorporation of women into the workforce, with an approach that prioritizes social investment in childhood in its sanitary aspects aimed at the most disadvantaged sectors. This tension emerges, even at its extremes, as a conflict between children's rights and women's rights. (44)

Thus, using our own method of cost-benefit analysis, they concluded that, among others, in socioeconomic terms, the gains would be visible. That is, "for every 1.000 CVE spent on the program (infrastructures + paid salary + other costs) in a 24-year horizon, the economy will have a gain of 3.1000 CVE, that is, the benefits to the economy will be more than three times more than costs in a 24-year period" (Digihiero 2015, para. 1). They concluded that with the possible insertion of women in the formal market, with higher income, they would contribute positively to GDP and at the same time to tax collection.

Subsequently, they considered that it would make perfect sense to create an interministerial group for the design of a Proposal of Gender-sensitive Social and Economic Policies. The Committee would be under the tutelage of the Ministry of Family and Social Inclusion (MFSI) and would be coordinated by DGIS, which would lead the National Care System (SNC).

In parallel, several activities took place, namely the Dialogue on Social Policies. Dialogue on Protection and Social Policies in Cabo Verde (July 19–20, 2016), at the initiative of the involved institutions, with the objective of collecting subsidies for the definition of the protection and social policies agenda in the country; the "Workshops on Gender-Sensitive Social Policies" on July 22 (Praia) and 26 (Mindelo), aimed at Civil Society Organizations, Academies, and Private Sector to promote a space for debate and reflection, from the presentation of concrete proposals for social protection policy, with the view of contributing to the definition of the protection agenda and social policy proposals in Cabo Verde in an integrative and inclusive approach. The final result of these discussions would then give rise to the National Care Plan (2017–2021), considered an indisputable gain in terms of public policies, which took into account the issues of gender and sexual division of labor.

IMPLEMENTATION OF THE NATIONAL CARE SYSTEM-GAINS AND CHALLENGES

As mentioned earlier, the implementation of the NCP is coordinated by DGIS. Some activities were already being performed in parallel with the NCP discussion. In this case, the creation/certification of the professional categories (childhood, caregivers, and dependents) stood out.

Through semi-structured interviews carried out in the first half of July 2019, we sought to identify the main gains and challenges seen in the first months of its implementation. Training actions for caregivers were carried out. In the first session that took place in Praia, ninety young people were selected. Unfortunately, despite efforts to promote parity, only six trainees were male, which still reflects gender stereotypes regarding care services. It is a somewhat paradoxical situation, as the focus is on the empowerment of women who are the most affected; however, males were encouraged to participate, as a way to avoid reinforcing gender imbalances and stereotypes. As our DGIS interviewee said,

> On the one hand, we also have the majority of people looking for these courses, are female. On the other hand, the policy itself has chosen, in some cases . . . for training for women, exclusively. For the first situation, what is still verified is that this is a task that is considered women's. Hence, the low demand on the part of men. For the second situation,[14] we can look for two explanations: it can be soon be criticized for only to be directed at women. However, and secondly, it must be taken into account that the National Care System proposes exactly of the class that is at a disadvantage, which is women. Thus . . . it could minimize the situation of inequality between the two groups . . . and guarantee women's economic autonomy and their participation in the decision-making space.

She reported that they have information that boys (trained mainly in the care of the elderly) obtained jobs faster than girls. Despite it being too early to discuss the impact, she pointed out several gains after the beginning of the implementation of the NCP, namely with the daycare centers and preschools that started to be assumed by the State through the direct participation of the Municipalities (municipalization of care services); the approval of the Decree-law for the implementation of daycare centers, the design of the ludo-pedagogical guidance Guide, and the allocation of funding to NGOs in the care are by the MFIS, prioritizing children aged zero to three years old. Here, the alliance between state, civil society, and companies stand out, highlighting the entrance of the private sector in the activity of capacity building of the caregivers.

Other positive aspects highlighted are free education for people with disabilities (from basic to higher education), the emergence of new organized civil society groups of care and the promotion of care for dependent people, the partnership of new international organizations, and financing health training projects: UNICEF, Portuguese Cooperation, Spanish Cooperation, IWO. The State Budget itself (through the MFIS) provides funding for NGOs. New equipment (daycare centers and care centers) appeared and others were improved (municipal daycare centers are more accessible in terms of cost).

Day spaces started to offer sleeping conditions. Several municipalities (in several islands) took their own initiatives; such is the case of the municipalities of Ribeira Grande (Santo Antão), which already has its care plan for the elderly, Santa Catarina de Santiago, Tarrafal de Santiago, S. Vicente, and São Salvador do Mundo (recently approved its plan for gender equality).

The assumption of daycare centers and preschools by the municipalities is considered one of the great gains achieved, revealing itself an important step toward guaranteeing women's autonomy, their economic independence, with the possibility of having a self-sustained job. According to the DGIS interviewee,

> The advantage that the daycare centers will have is diverse: for example, we now have more children to attend kindergartens and be in their own places while their mothers are in their daily toil in search of family support. Another advantage is that when assumed by the city councils, the prices of kindergartens will be more accessible, as it has been usual practice to charge a minimum monthly amount for each child, unlike the private ones, where the amount is different and less accessible for low-income families.

Therefore, as a result, women have more time to dedicate to other tasks, will have more time available to look for paid jobs, and even will be able to use their training to gain a decent job. Paraphrasing Silveira (2003), it is,

> About the possibility of that women can have some control over their time and be able to dedicate themselves to paid work, but also see the overload of the domestic work reduced; they can also be professionally trained, study or have some leisure time and culture. Largely it depends on the state reviewing its gender approach in a very broad spectrum of policies (73).[15]

She considers that labor integration is practically immediate, especially in kindergartens and in the provision of care services for the elderly, saying that there have been many people contacting DGIS and requesting contacts for this type of service. There is also a project to extend the project to the rural world, so as not to leave care under the responsibility of women, and some municipalities without nursing homes are creating the conditions to do so.

Regarding the challenges, our interviewee indicated the poor adherence of male candidates to the training sessions (they tended to choose the area of care for the elderly), the need to mobilize resources for the design and management of Municipal Plans, the lack of definition for financing mechanisms, the lack of clarity in the financing, and the economic viability of the NCS, as it is yet not clear who covers expenses with people from non-contributory schemes (minimum wage in the order of 130 USD); similarly, a platform that would aggregate all the information in a single database for a better control of the beneficiaries as needed, to avoid duplication and injustice. In addition, daycare costs were still borne by MFIS (it is hoped to resolve this with the creation of municipal daycare centers).

There is also the challenge related to the transformation of existing spaces into care spaces, as there are centers with other designations that, though providing care services, they have other designations (childcare centers, for street children, for example)

The two other interviews were analyzed, one from a young man and another female who trained in the care of independent people. They said it was something new, and it was a great job opportunity to work in something noble and that they always liked. So, there were many expectations in relation to their professional future. At the time of the interview, they were attending the internship. The possibility of a quick insertion in the labor market was a great incentive.

However, they expressed some frustration because they and many others were volunteering, while waiting to get paid employment, somewhat contradicting the initial expectation that it was to enter the labor market as soon as they finish. This did not happen right away. Despite this, they both said they would go on personal projects, which is a good thing, because they could also claim that their services had been sought by people who were essentially of the middle class. This is a positive aspect to be highlighted since one of the great objectives of this plan is that they have their own business ideas, hence, the Startup Challenge to promote business ideas.

One of the winning projects received an approximately 5,000 USD prize to implement their business, dedicated to the provision of Care and Occupational Therapy services. In fact, it already employs other young people who also received training in the area of care. A great asset is, during this period of confinement because of COVID 19, the MFIS has requested its services, having extended the universe of people to receive care.

There is some concern in relation to the families they work with, related to the need to work on their mentality, mainly due to hygiene issues; likewise, they are concerned about people with dependency whose spouses also need a minimum social pension and who are not covered. Just because they have a home, benefits are not often granted causing less accessibility to purchase medication.

In summary, we can say that efforts to promote gender equality and empowerment, inclusion, and social justice have always been seen as fundamental. This is visible, whether through the country's adherence to international conventions and treaties or internal mechanisms in terms of laws, decrees, projects, or programs.

However, despite the efforts made, on the one hand, problems of gender equality persisted, and there was no integrated public policy that responded to the inequalities found. There was a clear need for public/social policies (robust and equitable) to combat poverty and social exclusion and to promote gender equality and social justice, aiming at poverty reduction and inclusion. The UTUW (2012) brought concrete data that exposed the sexual division and unpaid workload among women, especially the most vulnerable socioeconomically. It also made it possible to see that the care of children and dependent people was under the care of women, and it was certain that measures were needed to avoid the risks of a greater gender and inequality at all levels.

The gender analysis of the results of this study showed that the measures should be taken concerning unequal opportunities and the task of care should be of the responsibility of all sectors of society: state, families, and sectors of civil and private society. Thus, the Proposal in the National Care System would come to fill the gaps and provide more dignity to families. This is how the 2017–2021 National Care Plan came about. It is an innovative policy that brings with it several positive aspects, namely defamiliarization and joint responsibility for care, through redefinition of responsibilities.

Some concrete gains have already been noted since the beginning of its implementation; however, there are still challenges that need to be overcome. A positive aspect to highlight—at this moment that we are experiencing changes in the context of COVID 19. More families are benefiting from care services, which, in a way, reduces their vulnerability and exposure to the risks of exclusion.

NOTES

1. This work is the result of a lecture presented in the scope the II International ICIEG Congress, Gender, Feminist and Women's Studies: Reflexivity, resistance and action. Lisbon, July 24, 25, and 26, 2019.

2. It is NCP 2017–2021, however, due to a printing error, we found 2017–2019.

3. Conducted under the Continuous-Multi-Objective Survey I (IMC – 2012), and presented through the Report of the module on the use of time and unpaid work, in Cabo Verde, 2012.

4. International Convention of All Forms of Discrimination Against Women.

5. Approved by the Constitutional Law n° 1/IV/92, of September 25, changed by the Constitutional Laws is now 1/IV/95, of November 13 and 1/V/99, of November 23, Constitutional Law n° 1/VII/2010. Revision. SÉRIE — N° 17 «B. O.» Of the Republic of Cabo Verde — May 3, 2010.

6. Following, the National Strategic Plan for Sustainable Development (PEMDS).

7. The Poverty Alleviation and Growth Strategy (DECRP III, 2012-2016) that precedes the PEDS is also another important instrument to consider

8. Cf. Carvalho 2019 and República de Cabo Verde. Relatório Cabo Verde Beijing+20 (2014).

9. IMC (Inquérito Multi-Objetivo Contínuo) 2018. Indicators for living conditions.

10. ONU-Mulheres e o UNFPA supported this Project.

11. Our translation, from the original in Portuguese.

12. Our translation, from the original in Spanish.

13. Our translation, from the original in Spanish.

14. In the Island of Boa Vista, for example, the twenty-five people beneficiaries in the area of Child Care from zero to three years old were women and girls, exclusively. The training took place between July 8 and September 2019. This is a joint initiative DGIS, ICIEG and the Municipality of Boa Vista, with financial support of the Spanish Cooperation in Cabo Verde.

15. Our translation, from the original in Portuguese.

REFERENCES

Aguirre, Rosario and Ferrari, Fernanda. *La construcción del sistema de cuidados en el Uruguay En busca de consensos para una protección social más igualitaria.* Nações Unidas, Santiago de Chile, 2014. https://repositorio.cepal.org/bitstream/handle/11362/36721/1/S2014269_es.pdf.

Anjos, José Carlos and others, eds. *Consultoria Nacional para a Análise de Políticas Sociais e Propostas de Políticas Públicas Sociais Sensíveis ao Género (Relatório).* Praia, 2016.

Cabo Verde. Lei nº 1/IV/92, of September 25 Constitutional Laws is now 1/IV/95, of November 13 and 1/V/99, of November 23, Constitutional Law nº 1/VII/2010. Revision. SÉRIE — Nº 17 «B. O.» Of the Republic of Cabo Verde — May 3, 2010.

———. Lei nº 131/V/2001, de 22 de Janeiro. *Bases da Protecção Social.* Lei nº 131/V/2001 de 22 de Janeiro.

———. *Plano Estratégico de Desenvolvimento Sustentável (PEDS) 2017/2021.* Cabo Verde.

———. *Relatório Cabo Verde Beijing+20. Sobre A Implementação Da Declaração E Plataforma De Ação De Beijing.* Praia, Junho de 2014.

———. Conselho de Ministros. *Plano Nacional de Cuidados.* 2017/2021. Resolução nº 143/2017.

Carvalho, Carla Santos de. "A Questão de Gênero na Agenda Pública e Política de CaboVerde, África: Papel das ONG Feministas na Luta pelos Direitos das Mulheres." *Outros Tempos* 12(19): 135–152, 2015. ISNN: 1808-8031.

Carvalho, Carla Santos de. *Os donos da terra. As donas da terra. Ou... As terras de ninguém. Questões agrárias e desenvolvimento em Santiago, Cabo Verde.* PhD Thesis, ISEG, Universidade de Lisboa, 2019.

Dighiero, Karina Batthyány. *Las políticas y el cuidado en América Latina. Una mirada a las experiencias regionales.* Naciones Unidas, Santiago de Chile, 2015. https://repositorio.cepal.org/bitstream/handle/11362/37726/S1500041_es.pdf?sequence=1&isAllowed=y.

Instituto Nacional de Estatística. *Recenseamento Geral da População e Habitação 2010. População e Condições de Vida.* Praia, 2010.
———. *Inquérito Multi-Objetivo Contínuo (IMC—2012). Relatório do módulo sobre uso do tempo e trabalho não remunerado, em Cabo Verde.* Praia, 2012.
———. *IMC (Inquérito Multi-Objetivo Contínuo) 2018. Indicadores de Condições de Vida.* Praia, 2018.
Soares, Vera. *Políticas públicas para igualdade: papel do Estado e diretrizes.* Lecture given at the National Seminar of Women's Coordinator Public Policies to tackle gender inequalities in local governments. Table 3 - Guidelines for Equality policies. Organized by the Special Coordination ofa Women, Municipality of São Paulo. in URBIS—International Fair and Congress of Cities. São Paulo, 2004.
Souza, Celina. Políticas Públicas: Conceitos, Tipologias e Sub-Áreas. Work designed Luís Eduardo Magalhães Foundation, in December 2002. http://professor.pucgoias .edu.br/SiteDocente/admin/arquivosUpload/3843/material/001-%20A- percent-20POLITICAS%20PUBLICAS.pdf.
Tude, João Martins. *Conceitos Gerais de Políticas Públicas.* s.l., n.d. http://www2 .videolivraria.com.br/pdfs/24132.pdf.

Chapter 7

Democracy and Social Inclusion

State-Society Relations in Cabo Verde

Aleida Mendes Borges

The patriarchal and authoritarian legacy of colonialism left the postcolonial state in Lusophone Africa with a tradition of apartheid between politics and the people (Monteiro 2015; Sarmento 2013; Chabal 1992). Cabo Verde, a small, insular, resource-poor country, has over the years impressed the world and won international recognition as a state of good governance and democratic example in Africa. However, despite its reputation for "good governance" (Mo Ibrahim 2017), the Cabo Verdean political system is characterized by a "top-down" governance model dominated by a small, predominantly male, political elite which emerged from the independence struggle as the *fidjus de terra*("sons of the land") (Sarmento 2013; Monteiro 2015).

More recently, the inability of state institutions to respond to the needs of the vast majority of citizens has led to an ensuing feeling of "democratic deficit" (Costa 2013) affecting particularly marginalized groups such as women and youth and contributing to high levels of dissatisfaction with the quality of democracy (Afrobarometer 2017) in the country.

This chapter will analyze the ways in which the population in Cabo Verde perceives their social contract with the State and the extent to which the current governance model in Cabo Verde can be said to be fit for purpose. Particular focus will be placed on the perspective of the population/society to examine current levels of engagement with the state.

INTRODUCTION

"For Europe, for ourselves and for humanity, we must turn over a new leaf, we must work out new concepts, and try to set afoot a new man," stated by Fanon (Falola 2018, 1).

As a young Cabo Verdean woman in the Diaspora, it is a remarkable experience to be able to share my insights and research in this wonderful project celebrating the work of Cabo Verdean women all over the world. My research focuses on state-society relations and political participation in Cabo Verde. I am particularly interested in political representation and in the experience of young women and men as they navigate spaces of political marginalization in traditionally patriarchal states.

We are preparing, in Cabo Verde, to enter a period of interesting change and reflection about our values and the direction of our nation. In relation to gender, there has been institutional recognition that something needs to be done to address the gender gap in our society with proposals currently being discussed for the passing of a gender parity law for parliamentary representation (Varela 2018; Comissão para a Cidadania e Igualdade de Género 2018). Furthermore, the government has recently announced that Cabo Verde wishes to become a model in the world for gender parity (Governo de Cabo Verde 2018). These developments represent a continuous momentum building on the consolidation of past achievements such as the passing of a gender-based violence law[1] and becoming in 2008, the first and only gender-balanced government (ministerial positions) in Africa (Monteiro 2015). This project celebrates the fact that we women have entered onto the scene and found our own voices as lawyers, policymakers, governors but also as writers and filmmakers who continue, therefore, transforming our societies and our standing within it (Taoua 2018).

Despite the many achievements attained since independence from Portugal in 1975 and the democratization in the 1990s, it remains important to not lose sight of the significant challenges that still remain. According to the Global Index of Gender Inequality (2016), Cabo Verde is classified in thirty-sixth place out of 144 countries. Considering that, for instance, Mauritius, a country which is often compared with Cabo Verde in terms of good governance and has systematically scored first for good governance in Africa according to the Mo Ibrahim Index (Mo Ibrahim 2017) scored very poorly on the Gender Inequality Index, and is placed 113th/144; there is scope for optimism. However, there are countries that are doing much better, such as Rwanda (fifth), Burundi (twelfth), Namibia (fourteenth), South Africa (fifteenth), and Mozambique (twenty-first) (World Economic Forum 2016).

Furthermore, in relation to economic opportunity and participation, Cabo Verde is placed 104th and 23rd for the political empowerment of women (World Economic Forum 2016). For parliamentary representation, it is placed sixty-second well behind other Lusophone countries in Africa such as Mozambique and Angola which are tenth and eleventh in the world, respectively (Mendes de Barros 2016).

This chapter will not focus exclusively on women and their relationship with the state, which is the outcome of complex historical and sociological processes but will instead seek to analyze more generally how the state in Cabo Verde relates to the population at large. From an analytical standpoint, it will, on the one hand, address the question of the emergence of the post-colonial state in Africa and how its agents, the politico-administrative elite seek to engage with its main legitimizers, the people. On the other hand, it will also examine how society perceives the state and rates its performance in terms of responding to societal needs and operating through a democratic, non-personalized logic, as expected of a country which systematically, in the last decade, scored among the top 5 countries in Africa for good governance according to the Ibrahim Index of African Governance (Mo Ibrahim 2017; Allison 2018). Based on data collected by the Afrobarometer research team, we aim to consider the limitations of the Ibrahim Index, based on a poorly defined, multidimensional concept (Gisselquist 2014), that of governance, which follows a neoliberal, market-based logic and focuses more on what is important to businesses and investors than on the well-being of society and their perception of governance and state performance.

We ultimately argue that the good governance agenda, which theo-retically should be concerned with public service delivery and state-society relation is biased. The emphasis of the neoliberal project is not on the relationship between the state and the people, but rather on the process, the democratic process, focusing on how power is attained, that is through fair elections and on whether there is a contestation of power by the opposing political elite. There is, therefore, little preoccupation with the substantial dimension of democracy related to the efficiency of democratic institutions and the overall quality of the governance. We thus ask, good governance, yes, but for whom? As argued by Khan (2012) "many of the dominant views on governance reform priorities for developing countries implicitly draw on a particular view of the role of the state that is based on a view of markets as largely able on their own to allocate resources . . . that are necessary for sustaining economic growth" (52). This enforces a fixation on the part of states with ensuring the maintenance of the rule of law, stable property rights, corruption control, and stable political institutions through a demo-cratic process that serves the interest of businesses and investors. It is thus important to start by considering the different dimensions of the concept of the state.

FROM THE IDEAL OF THE WEBERIAN STATE TO THE REALITY OF THE POSTCOLONIAL STATE IN AFRICA

From a Weberian perspective, the modern state is the outcome of a process by which the realm of politics is gradually emancipated from society and constituted into increasingly autonomous political institutions (Sellers 2011; Lottholz and Lemay-Hébert 2016). The public and private spheres, theoretically, become functionally distinct. If, on the one hand, as argued by Chabal and Daluz (1999), one of the main challenges with the conceptualization of the state in Africa is that it did not become properly institutionalized as there was never significant emancipation from society. On the other hand, the "informalization of politics" in Africa (Chabal and Daloz 1999) is also the consequence of the imposition of what Bayart (2009) called an "artificial construction" based on colonial foundations as opposed to a development stemming from "organic" growth from the entrails of civil society (Chabal 1986). Consequently, what emerged from the decolonization struggle was a "state without structural roots in society, a sort of 'balloon floating in the air'" (Bayart 2009, 1).

It is worth emphasizing that the institutionalized political structure proposed by Weber alluded to an ideal type of state which has been the exception rather than the rule (Chabal and Daloz 1999) meaning that this Weberian ideal of a state in which the public and private spheres become functionally distinct did not fully materialize in the majority of states, industrialized or otherwise.

Furthermore, the concept of state is linked to the idea of public authority in terms of common organizational, administrative, legal, territorial, and sociocultural attributes (Sellers 2011). This conceptualization is inspired by traditional European state forms, which continue to portray the state as a Weberian bureaucratic apparatus (Kohli 2002), hierarchical in nature. Consistent with this view of the state is an underlying assumption in the literature that there is a sharp analytical distinction, if not always an actual separation, between the state and society (Sellers 2011). State-society relations, thus, emerged as a field of study focusing on the interactions and interdependence between the state and society. However, in recent years, the traditional state-society dichotomy has given way to a more nuanced, more complex conceptualization of relations between state and society, which recognizes that there are different ways of capturing power dynamics in the relationship the society has with the state. There was thus a move away from predominantly state-centered approaches to more bottom-up perspectives on the interaction between state actors and civil society at large. This development in the literature comes from an understanding that the changing nature of the micro-level relations between society and the state will ultimately necessitate a wider rethinking of power dynamics between the center and the periphery. We shall proceed with a discussion about democracy, as one of the main systems to regulate the relationship between state and society.

CONCEPTUALIZING DEMOCRACY

Since its advent, a couple of centuries ago, democracy has been about exclusion. From women and slaves to people with no property and foreigners, democracy has been intrinsically as much about inclusion as it has been about exclusion. State-society relations have been characterized by a gap between the governors and the governed. A relationship that has been conditioned by power relations and confined to a network of interests based on a narrow social stratum usually consisting of bourgeois and aristocratic men (Sartori 1987; Pateman 2000; Young 2010).

Theoretically, orthodox democratic theory (Schumpeter 1942) has been conditioned by an underlining understanding that the "electoral mass" is incapable of political action other than to vote. Schumpeter (1942) proposed a minimalist definition of the democratic method as "an institutional arrangement for arriving at political decisions which realizes the common good by making the people itself decide issues through the election of individuals who are to assemble in order to carry out its will" (250). In *Polyarchy*, Dahl (1971), expanding this definition identified eight key criteria which define democracy: "the right to vote; the right to be elected; the right of political leaders to compete for support and votes; elections that are free and fair; freedom of association; freedom of expression; alternative sources of information; and institutions that depend on votes and other expressions of preference" (3). Like other democratic theorists, Dahl (1971) conceptualized democracy as essentially concerning the existence of institutions and electoral processes. Thus, if it can be shown that citizens can participate equally in free and fair elections, and if elections direct the actions of the government, then that is democracy. The focus is therefore on procedure rather than substance and such an approach has for long legitimized regimes that are democratic in form but lack any substantive democratic dimension.

Collier and Levitsky (1997) emphasized that the most widely employed definitions of democracy focus on the procedures of governance. However, besides the procedural aspects of democracy, it is equally important to ensure that governments are able to adequately respond to demands from citizens. A well-functioning democracy is, therefore, first and foremost one that constitutes a broadly legitimated regime that is able to satisfy citizens and provide quality in terms of result (Morlino 2009).

In the context of postcolonial African nations, the definition of Marshall (1992) is more in line with people's expectations of what democratic systems ought to deliver. Marshall (1992) discussed a social dimension to democratic citizenship, which offers more than civil and political rights and includes social rights, such as social services, providing for those in need, and ensuring the general welfare of citizens. This approach posits that unless the basic social needs of individuals are met, democratic principles of political equality and participation are meaningless (Huber et al. 1997).

The predominantly narrow understanding of the role citizens play in a democratic system emphasizes the construction of democracy which is intended to preserve elite domination and maintain the *status quo* under the false pretence of a common good. It is an approach that does not see democracy as a tool for inclusion but instead further marginalizes the majority of the population which is perceived as incapable of directly participating in decision-making processes.

A GLOBAL CRISIS OF POLITICAL REPRESENTATION?

Despite the many efforts to move away from orthodox democratic theory through more participatory democratic practices, for quite a few decades now we have seen a growth in feelings of democratic deficit and political alienation within the electorate all over the world. Social movements emerged as a reaction and developed on the basis of contesting the political marginalization that many different strata of the population claim they face from the central structures of power.

In more recent years, building on the events of the so-called "Arab Spring," many other movements with different context-specific demands and claims have emerged. Within the African context, these include movements as varied as mass student protests in South Africa, under the banner of "Rhodes Must Fall," demanding free, quality, and decolonized higher education (Ndlovu-Gatsheni 2018), and youth protests in Senegal, under the movement *'Y'en Marre'* (Dieng 2015; Dimé 2017), directly challenging the legitimacy of Abdoulaye Wade's government by successfully pushing their political agenda to ensure that the voice of the marginalized, denied by formal institutions, is heard through rap, graffiti, and street protest. There were also similar youth protests in Cabo Verde and Ethiopia and what these movements have in common, from West to East Africa, is the expression of disillusionment with the inability of the state to respond to what is considered as basic societal needs, leading to the generalized questioning of the legitimacy, logic, and raison d'être of many modern states.

This call for the "rethinking of thinking" (Ndlovu-Gatsheni 2018) in terms of how modern states relate to the overall society might be more emphasized in postcolonial nations as a result of the promises made during the decolonization struggle about the future of the emerging nations. For the most part, these promises did not materialize and the colonial power was replaced by a dominant "local class'" formed by a stratum of people who have learned to manipulate the apparatus of the state in the service of imperialism—the African petit bourgeoisie (Chabal 1981).

In Lusophone Africa, the 1990s epitomized a second chance to embrace democratization and full citizenship. Nonetheless, by the new millennium, questions were already being raised about the postcolonial state, seen as a Western "façade" (Chabal and Daloz 1999) that served to mask personalized political relations with the sole purpose of benefiting the African and European elites. It thus became clear that the fall of authoritarian governments and single-party states did not necessarily produce consolidated democracies (Sarmento 2013; Costa 2013; Francisco and Agostinho 2011). Instead, it resulted in increased competition for power between different political elite fractions (Seibert 1999; Sarmento 2013), continuing thus to serve the needs of that same elite and marginalizing the same people, the poor.

In Europe, the most recent mass protests in France, the *"gilet jaune"* (BBC News 2018), has yet again drawn our attention to the fundamental issue of the perceived inability of the political elite to relate to their electorate. Through what is already being called the Yellow Vest movement (The Spectator 2018), cutting across age, occupation, and geographic region, the main sentiment is the urge to challenge and bring to account a leader who is perceived to have broken his election promise of changing the way politics are done in France and instead has shown that he is arrogantly out-of-touch with the needs of the majority of the population (BBC News 2018).

There is scope, therefore, to talk about a growing global crisis in political representation (Chabal and Green 2016) characterized by the increasing public disenchantment with the political establishment and the consequent erosion of the legitimacy of authority. Already in the 2000s, there were discussions about a "tidal wave" of citizen withdrawal from traditional channels of political participation (Norris 2004), which affected the *polis* all over the world.

THE POLITICAL SYSTEM IN CABO VERDE

After attaining independence in 1975, a single-party state was established in the archipelago until the early 1990s when the country joined the third wave of democratization (Huntington 1993). Subsequently, a multiparty system was put in place, with the necessary constitutional amendments, which opened the way to the development of a democratic system based on free and fair elections (Freedom House 2018).

One of the main criticisms made to postcolonial states in Africa is the lack of rupture with colonial systems despite the official rhetoric of political freedom. Cabral argued that the biggest challenge of newly established states was to destroy the colonial system (Chabal 1981). Instead, political elites in newly founded states, such as Cabo Verde and other African nations, attempted to create a "copy-paste" process of democratization and state-building, which mimicked the institutional frameworks of Western states, oftentimes former colonial powers, without taking notice of the local realities of the societies in questions. In other words, there was a process of mimicking in Africa of Western institutions and States with little effort to reflect on the needs of the territories and populations in question, in a remarkable repro-duction of the post-Berlin Conference colonial project. This in turn led to the development of weak institutions with an "imported character" (Gomes Dos Anjos 2013), which were ill-adapted to meet the new demands of the build-ing of the postcolonial state and alienated the masses by serving the interests of small elites.

The 2000s, in Cabo Verde, coincided with the first decade since the begin-ning of the democratization process, and thus citizen withdrawal from official channels of political participation and expressions of distrust of institutions symbolized a critical crisis of the democratic project. Thinking about the expectations in line with the promises of the rupture which the democra-tization should have symbolized, namely in terms of access to power and decision-making by sections of the population such as women, youth, and poor people from the rural areas, the conclusion in the words of Monteiro (2015) was that there remained "the systematic persistence of the sub-representation [of women] in the structures of power, despite the significant progress attained during the democratic process" (196). The same can be said of the political margination of youth in a continent where the overwhelming majority of the population is under 35 (Mo Ibrahim Foundation 2012). As posited by Mo Ibrahim (Allison 2018) in a discussion about the last decade of governance in the continent:

> The lost opportunity of the past decade is deeply concerning. Africa has a huge challenge ahead. Its large and youthful potential workforce could transform the continent for the better, but this opportunity is close to being squandered. The evidence is clear—young citizens of Africa need hope, prospects, and opportu-nities. Its leaders need to speed up job creation to sustain progress and stave off deterioration. The time to act is now. (para. 3)

The issuing widespread rejection of the system by the masses can be interpreted as a form of protest against the idea of a state which is perceived as both strong and powerless, overdeveloped in size and underdeveloped in functional terms (Chabal and Daloz 1999) for it remains incapable of fulfill-ing its main competences. A state which, therefore, fails to achieve the very objectives which define its raison d'être. It also symbolizes a challenge to a political and administrative elite that stands accused of using the State to advance its own personal interests.

THE GOOD GOVERNANCE
PARADIGM IN CABO VERDE

Weakness in governance has received significant attention in Africa and has been identified as a hindering factor to the development of the continent. Therefore, significant emphasis has been put on reporting the levels of the so-called "good governance" as an indicator that the state and its institutions are performing adequately and delivering on their basic responsibilities. However, more recently, the debate has also considered the "good governance" agenda in Africa and questioned who the main beneficiaries of this agenda are.

Governance is itself a contested concept (Gisselquist 2014), generally used to refer to how state and society interact. It is often used to capture very varying social phenomena. In the context of Africa, the Ibrahim Index for African Governance (IIAG) has four main categories (Safety & Rule of Law; Participation and Human Rights; Sustainable Economic Opportunity; and Human Development) with more than ninety indicators. It claims to consider governance from the perspective of the citizen and to have an intentionally broad definition to capture all of the political, social, and economic goods and services that any citizen has the right to expect from his or her state and that any state has the responsibility to deliver to its citizens. It posits that its "definition of governance does not focus on de jure measurements, but rather aims to capture attainments or results, reflecting the actual status of governance performance in a given context—be it national, regional or continental" (Mo Ibrahim Foundation 2012, 1).

As with other governance indexes, the IIAG has limitations in terms of following the fundamentals of social science methodology, which entails particular attention given to concept formation, content validity, reliability, replicability, and robustness (Gisselquist 2014). Furthermore, it is not clear whether its components, in terms of indicators and sub-indicators, form a coherent whole, and as their definition is not based on a theoretical framework, their utility is not theoretically obvious. However, the IIAG remains a useful indicator of general trends of governance in Africa and a very useful tool to compare different performances over time in the continent.

In Cabo Verde, despite the relatively good reputation for "good governance" and quality of democracy (Baker 2006; Mo Ibrahim 2017), there remain very low levels of civic participation outside the election period (Sarmento 2013; Varela and Lima 2014). This is a result of the negotiated nature of the independence movement which claimed to fight against imperialism and colonial dominance but brought back authoritarianism, totalitarianism, and neutralized dissent during the single-party period (Sarmento 2013). This negotiated transition did not lead to the emergence of democrats; instead, it gave rise to the development of an authoritarian political habitus within the small politico-administrative elite.

After the democratization in the 1990s, there was renewed hope for democracy in Cabo Verde. The newly formed opposition had a discourse of change and progress which the country needed after more than fifteen years of the rule of what was then seen as an economically and politically failing party. However, the negotiated nature of the democratization process between political elites, as if it was family conflict, resulted in little change for the people. The institutional routine, the political privileges as well as the decision-making processes were retained leaving once again, the people marginalized by the process (Costa 2013; Sarmento 2013; Varela and Lima 2014). In this context of elitist rivalry, there persists a substantial deficit of democracy in Cabo Verde (Costa 2013).

As a country of limited economic viability, it was quickly understood by the political elite that it was important to keep a certain level of a governmental function. Cabo Verde became what is often referred to as a "donor darling" and through the strict deadlines to submit reports, funding applications, and strategic plans, produced by the small political and administrative elite, there was subsequently a process of "de-subjectification" (Gomes Dos Anjos 2013), in which the local knowledge, perspective, and experience were emptied of the documents produced by the government. In this context, Cabo Verde was upgraded to middle-income country status in 2008, despite large pockets of the population still living in abject poverty with no roads or access to electricity. This disconnect, which could also be seen as a rejection of reality, stems from the fact that the vast majority of politicians and civil servants are educated in Western institutions and there is a sort of globalization, convergence, and Westernization of the language used in governmental documents and strategic plans, which systematically ignores the local context and the needs of the majority of the population.

Thus, there is a general feeling of frustration that the country's reputation for "good governance," political stability, and sound economic policy, often presented to international organizations, does not correspond to the reality felt by the majority of the population. In the next section, we will focus on the manifestations of the disconnect which exists between those who govern and those who are governed in Cabo Verde.

LESSONS FROM THE LATEST ROUND (7)
OF THE AFROBAROMETER SURVEY

In line with national and global trends, despite the significant levels of disenchantment and discontent with the way democracy is being performed in Cabo Verde, most citizens continue to accept the legitimacy of elections by participating through voting. However, a key challenge of modern democratic theory is that individual citizens have increasingly less and less of a role to play in decision-making processes relative to representative collective actors who occupy the scenery of political life.

The Afrobarometer survey provides an interesting insight into democracy and state-society relations from the perspective of citizens. The sampling of the 2017 (Afrobarometer 2017) survey in Cabo Verde consists of youth (eighteen to thirty-five) majority of 53 percent in urban areas and 49 percent in urban areas, as well as a gender balance of 55 percent male and 48 percent female. Considering that youth make up around 70 percent of the total population (INE 2017), it is important that their views were reflected in the study.

When asked about the direction of the country, the majority of people in Cabo Verde, (54 percent in urban areas; 64 percent in rural areas) agreed that they felt that the country is going in the wrong direction. There were slightly different perceptions between men and women with 55 percent male and 61 percent female. It might also be the case that perceptions on governance and democracy are gendered in Cabo Verde as men take the lead in positions of leadership and decision-making. In total, this means that only 38 percent of the people interviewed think that the country is going in the right direction. Furthermore, with almost no difference in gender and urban vs rural, the overwhelming majority of Cabo Verdeans thinks that the situation in the country is neither good nor bad (38 percent) or fairly bad (34 percent), with only 13 percent thinking that it is very bad and 12 percent thinking that it is very good. This middle ground in terms of the situation of the country might be reflective of the fact that in the last elections in 2016, the opposition party, the *Movimento para Democracia* (MpD), managed to win against the incumbent *Partido para Independência de Cabo Verde* (PAICV), which had been in power for fifteen years. It is reasonable to conclude that the nation is in the process of observing the performance of the newly elected party in relation to their election manifesto.

Considering that Cabo Verde was ranked first in Africa for Participation and Human Rights in 2016 (IIAG) and second in 2017, it is rather striking that 81 percent of the people interviewed stated that they are not a member of a voluntary organization or community group. In addition, 52 percent said that they have never attended a community meeting but would if they had a chance. When asked if they have ever, as citizens, got together with others to raise an issue, 52 percent said that they have not but that they would if they had the chance. As the IIAG bases its scores also on data from the Afrobarometer, the analysis takes us to the consideration of concepts and what is understood by participation and disappointingly, the factor considered is not whether there is de facto participation in its various forms, but rather whether there is the freedom to participate, to assemble publicly, focusing, once again, on the process, rather than on experience or substance.

As argued by Costa (2013), the potential for mobilization and civic participation within the Cabo Verdean society in bottom-up initiatives which could potentially better respond to their needs is largely limited by the absence of spaces and opportunities which foster non-conventional political participation in the archipelago. If, on the one hand, it could be argued that such spaces are not given, but claimed and appropriated as spaces of political contestation (Cornwall and Shankland 2013). On the other hand, there is also an argument to be made that the negotiated nature of all political transitions in Cabo Verde fostered what Costa (2013) termed the *sociedade servil*, a society which is mostly at service, with little emancipation from the state.

Furthermore, the insular nature of the Cabo Verdean state renders any prospect of creating a social movement, insular and heavily influenced by local dynamics. The socio-economic conditions of the country also render the potential of getting together to create a movement tenuous as communication technology remains very expensive in the country. A factor that is even mentioned by politicians as making political elections more costly (Borges 2018) and which is mitigated by the fact that elections are state-funded in Cabo Verde. Therefore, the society in the country has evolved over time to become quite dependent on the state and has shown little initiative in terms of challenging the state. An interesting exception to this was the MAC 114 youth-led movement, which in 2016, just a few weeks after the general elections, managed to gather momentum for a multi-island simultaneous protest to demand that the president veto a law approved by parliament to increase the salaries of MPs and other public servants. This proved quite successful and showed to young people the realm of possibilities which can be open by organized civil society action. Only time will tell us more about the legacy of this movement.

When asked more specific questions relating to their relationship with the state and its agencies, 79 percent answered that they had never, in the past year, contacted a local government councilor about some important problem or to give them their views. Likewise, 88 percent admitted that they had never contacted a member of the National Assembly (within the past year), 89 percent said that they have never contacted an official or a government agency and 81 percent said that they never contacted a political party official. These results are in line with conclusions drawn by the main critics of the Cabo Verdean political system as they highlight that there is a significant distance between the governors and those being governed and the communication between the two forces, government and society, only happens during the election period (Varela and Lima 2014; Costa 2013). As argued by Monteiro (2015), there are residues of a colonial relationship between the political domain and the community in Cabo Verde which renders the latter an area of both reception and submission of what is decided, demanded, and imposed by the center.

It does not therefore come as a surprise that the majority of those interviewed admitted being either not very satisfied (48 percent) or not at all satisfied (28 percent) with the way democracy works in Cabo Verde. On a more alarming note, 71 percent agreed with the statement: "For someone like me it doesn't matter what kind of government we have, with only 15 percent agreeing that democracy is preferable to any other kind of government" (Mo Ibrahim 2017). Lastly, despite the former prime minister and main political actors defending that Cabo Verde is an example of a consolidated democracy (Africa 21 Online 2015), 44 percent of the population agrees that Cabo Verde is indeed a democracy but with major problems with only 13 percent agreeing that it is a full democracy. In relation to the differing perspectives between the government and society, it is worth noting that "one's schemes of perception, expectations, aspirations and the scope of one's imagination are determined by one's position in the social structures, the world and the opportunities it offers look different for the dominated and for the dominant" (Mihai 2016, 9).

The crisis of legitimacy or crisis of democracy in Cabo Verde is, thus, highly associated with the limited capacity for action by the government, which is not able to keep up with the rising demands of its citizens. As Foucault (1978) rightly posited, the main challenge with the concept of government is knowing "how to be governed, by whom, to what extent, with which aims and through which methods" (385). This is also known as the art of governmentality, a set of organized practices (mentalities, rationalities, and techniques) through which subjects are governed; the "how" of governing, the art of government (1978). In other words, the maintenance of the often-fragile link between those who govern and those who are governed.

Another interesting dimension of the Cabo Verdean political system which can be observed from the Afrobarometer survey is the expression of dissatisfaction with the government. When asked if they would join others in their community to request action from the government, 71 percent said that they would if they had a chance but had never done so (within the past year) and 70 percent admitted that they never contacted a government official to ask for help or make a complaint but would if they had a chance. In terms of what could be considered a more radical form of contestation, the refusal to pay a tax or fee to the government as a way of protest, only 24 percent said they would if they had a chance, with 68 percent saying that they would never do this. This illustrates that despite their disillusionment with the system, the majority still believe in the value of institutions and in the credibility of the system.

As posited by Claus Offe (2009), political disaffection is oftentimes

> associated to the idea of a group of phenomena that have to do with negative attitudes and behavioral patterns of people towards political life in general, political institutions (above all parties and party elites) and the practice of citizenship (such as a minimum, voting). It relates to the primarily emotional and passionate (rather than cognitive) condition of absence of a "sense of belonging," not "feeling-at-home" in the political community, marginalization, perceived lack of representation, institutionally mediated lack of capacity to make one's voice heard, deprivation of political resources, lack of horizontal and vertical trust, as well as a profound aversion to the political order. (12)

Such feelings or sentiments do not have to necessarily translate into political action or rejection of the system. However, active citizenship (Wong 2008) requires engagement with political institutions which "make citizens" in a sense that they engender in them, a perception of duties, opportunities, and meanings (Offe 2009). The citizen is constituted and positioned as an agent in politics by the institutions in and through which politics takes place. Therefore, a fundamental paradigm shift, arguably already underway, is needed in order to position the citizens in Cabo Verde, at the very center of politics and the political. As argued by Ndlovu-Gatsheni (2018), it requires a "moving the center" away from the dominant social stratum, usually composed of a male bourgeois minority. It requires the continuation of the project initiated during the liberation struggle of freeing the subject of oppression and marginalization by creating spaces, public spaces, of decision-making and participation, at an equal level to all citizens.

CONCLUSION

Through an analysis of the idea of the State and its interaction with society, this chapter has sought to understand whether the interaction between citizens, political elites, organizations (parties), and institutions (government/ parliament/ local authority) should not be a central aspect of both the consolidation of democracy and the measurement of the quality of governance in a given country. It argued that the "good governance" agenda, based on neoliberal assumptions, has posed an excessive focus on whether the procedure is democratic, that is, regular, uncontested elections within a system of respect for the rule of law. Although these are equally important considerations, these seem to be serving the interests of business and foreign investors rather than being a democratic system that is at the service of the people.

The fundamental paradox which this chapter has tried to emphasize is how a country can be internationally recognized for its good governance when the majority of the population is unsatisfied with its governance system and modus operandi. In light of the data collected by the Afrobarometer research team, the question that remains is whether it is possible to dissociate the quality of governance in Cabo Verde with that of its democracy? In other words, are we able to read the perceptions of the population in relation to the state in a way that is compatible with its reputation as a democratic example in Africa? (Baker 2006)

It was also argued that a key challenge for the Cabo Verdean society is the fact that there was no complete rupture through the decolonization process, which as Fanon (2001) argued, is fundamental, in order for the colonial subject to find itself in a new system. There was no paradigm shift in Cabo Verde due to the negotiated nature of all political transitions which occurred in the country. Societal transformation requires, unequivocally, a *prise de conscience* by all members of the community that could provoke a shift in the categories of the political common sense (Mihai 2016).

NOTE

1. Lei 84/Vll/2011 (Lei VBG).

REFERENCES

Africa 21 Online. "PM de Cabo Verde considera democracia cabo-verdiana consolidada." http://africa21online.com/artigo.php?a=8721&e=Pol%C3%ADtica, 2015.

Afrobarometer. *Atitudes em Relação à Qualidade da Democracia em Cabo Verde.* Praia: Cabo Verde, 2017.

Allison, Simon. "Mo Ibrahim: Africa's Decade of 'Lost Opportunity.'" *The M&G Online.* https://mg.co.za/article/2018-10-30-mo-ibrahim-africas-decade-of-lost-opportunity/, 2018.

Baker, Bruce. "Cape Verde: The Most Democratic Nation in Africa?" *The Journal of Modern African Studies* 44(4): 493–511, 2006.

Bayart, Jean-François. *The State in Africa: The Politics of the Belly* (2nd ed.). Cambridge; Malden, MA: Polity, 2009.

BBC News. "Why the 'Yellow Vests' Won't Stop Protests." *sec. Europe.* https://www.bbc.com/news/world-europe-46480867, 2018.

Aleida Mendes Borges

Borges, Aleida. *Does Money Matter? Women's Political Representation in Cabo Verde*. Bergen, Norway, 2018.

Chabal, Patrick. "The Social and Political Thought of Amilcar Cabral: A Reassessment." *The Journal of Modern African Studies* 19(1): 31–56, 1981.

Chabal, Patrick, ed. "Political Domination in Africa: Reflections on the Limits of Power." *African Studies Series 50*. Cambridge [Cambridgeshire]; New York: Cambridge University Press, 1986.

Chabal, Patrick, and Jean-Pascal Daloz. "Africa Works: Disorder as Political Instrument." *African Issues*. [London]; Bloomington: International African Institute in Association with James Currey, Oxford: Indiana University Press, 1999.

Chabal, Patrick, and Toby Green, eds. *Guinea-Bissau: Micro-State to "Narco-State*. First Published. London: Hurst & Company, 2016.

Collier, David, and Steven Levitsky. "Democracy with Adjectives: Conceptual Innovation in Comparative Research." *World Politics* 49: 430–451, 1997.

Comissão para a Cidadania e Igualdade de Género. "Reunião entre a CIG e Cabo Verde sobre a Lei da Paridade." Presidência do Conselho de Ministros. Comissão para a Cidadania e Igualdade de Género. September 17, 2018. https://www.cig.gov.pt/2018/09/reuniao-cig-cabo-verde-lei-da-paridade/, 2018.

Cornwall, Andrea, and Alex Shankland. "Cultures of Politics, Spaces of Power: Contextualizing Brazilian Experiences of Participation." *Journal of Political Power* 6(2): 309–333. https://doi.org/10.1080/2158379X.2013.811859. 2013.

Costa, Suzano. *Sociedade Civil, Estado e Qualidade Da Democracia Em Cabo Verde: Entre a Letargia Cívica e a Omnipresença Do Leviathã*. Entre África e a Europa: Nação, Estado e Democracia Em Cabo Verde, Coimbra, Almedina, 273–329, 2013.

Dahl, Robert Alan. *Polyarchy: Participation and Opposition*. 26. Print. New Haven: Yale University Press, 1971.

Dieng, Moda. "La Contribution Des Jeunes à l'alternance Politique Au Sénégal : Le Rôle de Bul Faale et de Y'en a Marre." *African Sociological Review/Revue Africaine de Sociologie* 19(2): 75–95, 2015.

Dimé, Mamadou. "De Bul Faale à Y'en a Marre : Continuités et Dissonances Dans Les Dynamiques de Contestation Sociopolitique et d'affirmation Citoyenne Chez Les Jeunes Au Sénégal." *Africa Development* 42(2): 83–105, 2017.

Falola, Toyin. "Foreword: Optimism for Afro-Futurism." In *Epistemic Freedom in Africa: Deprovincialization and Decolonization*, edited by Sabelo J. Ndlovu-Gatsheni. Rethinking Development. New York: Routledge, Taylor & Francis Group, 2018.

Fanon, Frantz, Constance Farrington, and Jean-Paul Sartre. *The Wretched of the Earth*. Repr. Penguin Classics. London: Penguin Books, 2011.

Foucault, Michel. "La gouvernementalité." In *1976–1988*, edited by Daniel Defert and François Ewald, Vol. II. Dits et écrits. 1954–1988, Michel Foucault. Ed. établie sous la dir. de Daniel Defert ...; 2. Quarto Gallimard, 1978.

Francisco, Albertino, and Nujoma Agostinho. *Exorcising Devils from the Throne: São Tomé and Príncipe in the Chaos of Democratization*. New York: Algora Pub, 2011.

Freedom House. "Cape Verde." *Country Report 2018*. https://freedomhouse.org/report/freedom-world/2018/cape-verde, 2018.

Gisselquist, Rachel M. "Developing and Evaluating Governance Indexes: 10 Questions." *Policy Studies* 35(5): 513–531. https://doi.org/10.1080/01442872.2014 .946484, 2014.

Gomes Dos Anjos, José Carlos. "De Políticos-literários a Político-técnicos: a Perda da Imaginação Política e o Mimetismo Estatal Pós-Colonial em Cabo Verde." In *Entre África e Europa: nação, estado e democracia em Cabo Verde*, edited by Cristina Montalvão Sarmento, 117–139. Coimbra: Almedina, 2013.

Governo de Cabo Verde. "Igualdade de Género: Governo quer posicionar Cabo Verde como uma nação exemplo no mundo." Offical Government Portal. Governo de Cabo Verde. November 26, 2018. http://www.governo.cv/index.php/rss/10024 -igualdade-de-genero-governo-quer-posicionar-cabo-verde-como-uma-nacao -exemplo-no-mundo, 2018.

Huber, Evelyne, Dietrich Rueschemeyer, and John D. Stephens. 1997. "The Paradoxes of Contemporary Democracy: Formal, Participatory, and Social Dimensions." *Comparative Politics* 29(3): 323–342. https://doi.org/10.2307/422124, 1997.

Huntington, Samuel P. *The Third Wave: Democratization in the Late Twentieth Century*. The Julian J. Rothbaum Distinguished Lecture Series 4. Norman: University of Oklahoma Press, 1993.

INE. "Mulheres e Homens em Cabo Verde - Factos e Números 2017." http://ine.cv/ publicacoes/mulheres-homens-cabo-verde-factos-numeros-2017/, 2017.

Khan, Mushtaq H. 2012. "Governance, Institutions, and the State." In *Good Growth and Governance in Africa: Rethinking Development Strategies*, edited by Akbar Noman, Kwesi Botchwey, Howard Stein, and Joseph E. Stiglitz. The Initiative for Policy Dialogue Series. Oxford: Oxford University Press, 2012.

Kohli, Ravi. "Immigration Controls, the Family and the Welfare State." *Child & Family Social Work* 7(1): 69–70. https://doi.org/10.1046/j.1365-2206.2002._229e .x, 2002.

Lottholz, Philipp, and Nicolas Lemay-Hébert. "Re-Reading Weber, Re-Conceptualizing State-Building: From Neo-Weberian to Post-Weberian Approaches to State, Legitimacy and State-Building." *Cambridge Review of International Affairs* 29(4): 1467–1485. https://doi.org/10.1080/09557571.2016.1230588, 2016.

Marshall, Thomas H. *Citizenship and Social Class*. Edited by Tom Bottomore. Pluto Perspectives. London: Pluto Press, 1992.

Mendes de Barros, Clara. "Análise de Género e Plano de Ação de Género (GAP 2016-2020) no âmbito da cooperação." *European Union*. https://www.icieg.cv/ images/phocadownload/Gender-Action-Plan-CV-2016-2020-PORT.pdf, 2016.

Mihai, Mihaela. "Theorizing Change: Between Reflective Judgment and the Inertia of Political Habitus." *European Journal of Political Theory* 15(1): 22–42. https:// doi.org/10.1177/1474885114537634, 2016.

Mo Ibrahim. "Good Governance in Africa." *Addis Ababa*. http://iiag.online, 2017.

Mo Ibrahim Foundation. "African Youth: Fulfilling the Potential." *2012 Ibrahim Forum Facts & Figures*. Dakar, Senegal: Mo Ibrahim Foundation, 2012.

Monteiro, Eurídice Furtado. "Entre Os Senhores Das Ilhas e as Descontentes: Identidade, Classe e Género Na Estruturação Do Campo Político Em Cabo Verde." Colecção Sociedade, Vol. 6. Praia: Edições Uni-CV, 2015.

Morlino, Leonardo. *Qualities of Democracy: How to Analyze Them.* Florence: Istituto Italiano di Scienze Umane. http://indicatorsinfo.pbworks.com/f/Morlino+Qualities +of+Democracy.pdf, 2009.

Ndlovu-Gatsheni, Sabelo J. *Epistemic Freedom in Africa: Deprovincialization and Decolonization. Rethinking Development.* New York: Routledge, Taylor & Francis Group, 2018.

Norris, Pippa. "Young People & Political Activism." Harvard University, John F. Kennedy School of Government. (32p). https://www.hks.harvard.edu/fs/pnorris/ Acrobat/COE%20Young%20People%20and%20Political%20Activism.pdf, 2004.

Offe, Claus. "Political Disaffection as an Outcome of Institutional Practices? Some Post-Tocquevillean Speculations." In *Bedrohungen Der Demokratie*, edited by André Brodocz, Marcus Llanque, and Gary S. Schaal, 42–60. Wiesbaden: VS Verlag für Sozialwissenschaften. https://doi.org/10.1007/978-3-531-91156-4_3, 2009.

Pateman, Carole. *Participation and Democratic Theory.* Reprinted. Cambridge: Cambridge University Press, 2000.

Sarmento, Cristina Montalvão, ed. *Entre África e Europa: Nação, Estado e Democracia Em Cabo Verde.* Coimbra: Almedina, 2013.

Sartori, Giovanni. *The Theory of Democracy Revisited.* Chatham, NJ: Chatham House Publishers, 1987.

Schumpeter, Joseph A. *Capitalism, Socialism, and Democracy.* 1st ed. New York: Harper Perennial Modern Thought, 1942.

Seibert, Gerhard. *Comrades, Clients, and Cousins: Colonialism, Socialism, and Democratization in São Tomé and Príncipe.* CNWS Publications, Vol. 73. Leiden, The Netherlands: Research School of Asian, African, and Amerindian Studies, Leiden University, 1999.

Sellers, Jefferey. "State-Society Relations Beyond the Weberian State." In *The SAGE Handbook of Governance*, edited by Mark Bevir. London: SAGE Publications Ltd. https://doi.org/10.4135/9781446200964, 2011.

Taoua, Phyllis. *African Freedom: How Africa Responded to Independence.* New York: Cambridge University Press, 2018.

The Spectator. "How the Gilets Jaunes Movement Could Spread Across Europe." *Coffee House (blog).* https://blogs.spectator.co.uk/2018/12/how-the-gilets-jaunes -movement-could-spread-across-europe/, 2018.

Varela, Aquilino, and Redy Wilson Lima. "Esferas (Ocultas) de Participação Política Dos Jovens Na Cidade Da Praia, Cabo Verde: Do Político Ao Parapolítico." *Revista Debates* 8(2), 2014.

Varela, José Maria. "Lei da Paridade é uma conquista da sociedade cabo-verdiana que merece ser reconhecida - Presidente do Parlamento." *Inforpress.* http://www .inforpress.publ.cv/lei-da-paridade-e-uma-conquista-da-sociedade-cabo-verdiana -que-merece-ser-reconhecida-presidente-do-parlamento/, 2018.

Wong, Lloyd L. "Transnationalism, Active Citizenship, and Belonging in Canada." *International Journal* 63(1): 79–100, 2008.

World Economic Forum. "Global Gender Gap Index." *Data-Based Index.* Geneva, Switzerland: World Economic Forum. http://wef.ch/1YKx0JW, 2016.

Part IV

POESIAS ("POETRY")

Chapter 8

Let

Shauna Barbosa

Let[1]

my father be a pregnant palm.
Or Cesaria Évora's voice
on Christmas with *Sodade* on her lips.
Let him be Amilcar Cabral's fist in the air.
And the pardon for all the stints
the sun fixed on his baby girl.

Let him be an instrument
in a jazz song: trombone, bass and snare.
The ship carrying his brothers and sisters.
If rain falls on the land he can't live on,
let him be a wildflower there.

Be a dancer, be a volcano with good intentions.
Be thousands of drums shipped to Cape Verde.
The cell phones, the shirts, & the shoes inside.

Let the sky be my father on his knees.
Let the sun be my father.
When the blues are the sun,
let me be the words he holds tight.

I wrote *Cape Verdean Blues* in service to those whose first language was silence. The original title for "Let" was "Quick Prayer." I cannot remember why I changed it. "Quick Prayer" was heavily lineated, impulsed toward urgent prayer. If I had to answer why I changed the title, I'd say, I wanted permission. For myself, and for you. Allowance. I wanted and still want freedom. I wanted and still want to hear stories that were conceived in the pit of the belly. Bellies. Of yours. Of mine. Of every immigrant. Of every Cape Verdean. Of every Cape Verdean woman. Of my father whose mother is the story that is genetically mine. "Let" is a world of music and material. Morna and mourning people and objects given to the sea. This poem, as an editor described, "combines the natural world (beach, sun, sky) with the dynamics of family." The original title of *Cape Verdean Blues* was *The Genetics of Leaving*. Culture can't leave when we give it voice. When we run back and forth, mic traveling, raised hand to raised hand, like a television host in service to her audience, letting different voices reach high volume. Every prayer without my name hums my father's. Every prayer not about you is about you.

NOTE

1. "Let" from *Cape Verdean Blues* by Shauna Barbosa, © 2018. Reprinted by permission of the University of Pittsburgh Press.

Chapter 9

A Kriola's Work through Poetry
Iva Brito

My work takes a critical look at the intersectionality of cultural, social, and political issues. Like the waters surrounding the islands, one theme that runs throughout my work is social justice and activism. At its peaks, it reflects the rugged terrain of inequalities of our societies past and present and the need for critical ideology regarding the issues. In its tranquil valleys, it provides opportunities to empower and unite. Always in line with the power of faith, it seeks to create agents of change that are continuously transforming with the tropical winds of expressive thought and evolving toward love.

As a Kriola, the Cabo Verdean experience is embedded in my soul. It is in my smile, laughter, sorrow, stories, lived experiences, and connection with my ancestors. I am constantly inspired by Cabo Verde's vibrancy, history, beauty, and unique culture. As a visual and performing artist and poet, I create opportunities that incorporate the arts in different modalities inclusive of writing, painting, sound, and movement. I utilize my strengths in these areas to create connections with the Cape Verdean experience that allow individuals to explore and create connections with themselves, our diverse community, and the rich history we share. These experiences allow one to connect to our heritage and tap into the power of our ancestors' stories. This is exemplified in my poems "Kriola" and "Nos Terra" from my book *Essence, Tones, Whispers and Shouts.*

Kriola

She stands grounded in her roots
She carries the world on her back
Wrapped around in African wraps
Winds in her hips

143

Fire exudes from her fingertips
Sunshine in her smile
And the mystery of moon in her eyes
Regardless of hair texture or length
Skin tone, orientation,
Living in third world
Or developed nation
Her heart overflows for ten little gems
She calls home

The poem Kriola is representative of the strength and beauty of a Cabo Verdean women/Kriola. Beauty not only in aesthetics but from the warmth and strength of her soul. She is grounded in the strength of her heritage and African roots. She is a Poderoza. She has the strength of Mother Nature and is the source of life and light in our world. Irrespective of the differences in the appearance of Kriolas, we all carry the love for our home and Cabo Verde in our hearts.

Nos Terra (Our Land)

My ancestors whisper to me their stories
My lips spoke their names
Boa Vista, Santiago, San Antao, Maio e Fogo
Es des ilhas, Moda na des dedos de mo (these ten islands like my ten finger tips)
Sal, Santa Luzia, San Nicolau, Sao Vicente and Brava
Each with its own essence
All within me
From the lava rocks of Fogo
To the white sands of Maio
From San Vincent's coladera
To Santiago's batuko
I sway to their rhythm
I caress myself in San Nicolau's sunset
I slide across Boa Vista's sand dunes
I elevate to San Antao's peaks
I bloom in Brava's gardens
At a distance, I see my silent sister Santa Luzia
Watching over me
Finally, I land to open arms at Cabral's door in Sal
As I transcend in this vast sea of history
Engraved in me
Selfishly I want to keep you hidden

Fearful of Exposure's sin
I want you hidden as my secret hiding place
Where childhood memory lies
In bright blue skies of fading faces
My roots are painted in vibrant hues of reds, yellows and greens
A grandmother's kiss on the forehead
Makes time stand still
Sun light rays darken skin tones
And enlighten souls
As your beauty transcends time and distance
Like a farewell of childhood
Into womanhood's truth
All that I ask
Is for you to wear this gift
This conta de ojo around your soul[1]
Molded by ancestor's sweat and tears[2]
Engraved with morabeza smiles of yesterday
Remembrances of our ancestors' whispers
Nos terra, Nos terra, Cabo Verde (Our land, our land, Cabo Verde)
Ca bo esquese de bo conta de ojo (Don't forget your conta de ojo)

The poem, Nos Terra is about the unique beautiful essence of the Cabo Verde Islands. It also shares the longing and love Cabo Verdeans have for their homeland. Cabo Verde Islands is a sacred space, in our hearts, that we want to protect. In recent years, there have been many changes within the islands. The poem also speaks to the concerns and negative impacts of tourism and Western ideology such as disregard of our sacred land and the environment, inadequate wages and conditions for workers, an increase in crime, and overall negative disruption to our cultural landscape. It is a reminder to hear our ancestral song of hope, in faith, it will shape our future for the better.

NOTES

1. Conta de ojo is a black bead with white dots, each unique in their own way. As the African legend goes the "conta" will protect you from evil.
2. Morabeza is a word that characterizes being Cabo Verdean, that is, welcoming spirit, friendly, hospitable, relaxed joyous.

Chapter 10

Poderoza

Rosilda DePina James, Aminah
Fernandes Pilgrim, and Stephanie Andrade

She stands firmly on all continents
The matriarch and the midwife
An African footprint says
The original woman
Resilient and versatile
Standing on the shoulders of the ancestors' power and perseverance
The keeper of the culture that strengthens and nurtures the Diaspora
The spark and the fire of an unbreakable spirit
Of she and we and her
Beauty and passion that was birthed in the tears of immigration
Silence and grace
Peace and hope
Yesterday, Today, Forever
The Cabo Verdean woman
Uma Deklarasau
El é Poderoza
Nau pamodi Se Beleza
Nau pamodi Se Forsa
Pamodi é El ki ta desidi Se Kaminhu
El ka kes kuzas otu algen fazé
El ka kes circumstansias di vida
Nen di nos komunidadi
El é kel ki El ta defini
Remembering the past, she chooses to be herself,
    a divine mirror of God's perfection
Reflecting on family, she chooses a crown for her
    inner glow not external superficiality

Aware of her community, she carries her throne into a bright
    future united by the blood of sisterhood, holding her sisters,
    brothers, sons, daughters, mothers, fathers, All
She feeds the family, the village and the nation in hope of a brighter tomorrow
Adopted by a foreign land
A solid mountain fighting for equality
She is the still and powerful water cleansing, flowing, restoring
The infinite sky offering opportunities
Ten dots in the ocean, a reminder of growth
The pull and push of the wind
The provider of wings
Original
Free
Primeru y Ultimo
Un Alma ki ka ten midida
Poderoza

Part V

IDENTIDADI ("IDENTITY")

Chapter 11

Where Blackness and Cape Verdeanness Intersect

Reflections on a Monoracial and Multiethnic Reality in the United States

Callie Watkins Liu

Frequently[1] Cape Verdean scholarship focuses on the Cape Verdeans in the Cape Verde islands, or immigrant experiences and Diaspora communities. Immigrant-related research might address questions of integration, identity, or challenges such as deportation. The broader research looks at the transnational relationships across the diaspora as they relate back to Cape Verde (Lima-Neves 2015; Resende-Santos 2015; Rosa 2015; Silva 2015). There is very little work in the research based in the United States that moves past the initial immigration questions to look at life "post-integration." This leaves out the experiences of families like mine, where I am the fourth generation in the United States yet maintain a Cape Verdean and American identity.

Scholarship about race and Cape Verdeans in the United States tends to stop at the point where Cape Verdeans and Cape Verdean Americans must confront the United States' racial categories and learn how to understand these initial foreign categories (Lima-Neves 2015; Pilgrim 2015; Halter 1993). What does it mean for those of us for whom these racial categories are not new, but rather are integral to our own upbringing and sense of self? Building on work that demonstrates the significance of embodied and lived experience (Bakare-Yusef 2008; Collins 2000), I use my own ethno-racial experience in the United States as a touchpoint of reflection and exploration. This examination reveals ways in which race and ethnicity intersect in an integrated fashion in the United States and what that can mean for identity within this context.

SOCIAL CONSTRUCTION OF IDENTITY

To understand my ethno-racial journey in the United States, it is important to understand the social construction of identity itself. Though identity is frequently thought of as a fixed element of a person, identity is constantly in construction as the result of both internal and external factors. Miller and Garran (2017) describe this identity construction as the story we tell ourselves and others about who we are; and like stories, this can change over time, or in different contexts, with some aspects being more malleable than others

Internal factors that might shape an identity story could be personal experiences, preferences, personalities, or traits. External factors that might affect a person's identity could include the community one grows up in, how one is perceived and treated by other people, family relationships, and other interpersonal ties. For example, on an internal level, while my lineage has remained unchanged throughout my life, the way I relate to and understand that lineage has transformed as the result of different life experiences. And although I've always understood myself as Black, when I've traveled to other countries with different understandings of race, such as Brazil, other people might understand me as "mulatta," rather than Black or Negra, and engage with me differently as a result.

This identity formation process occurs within a broader context of social disparities, privilege, and oppression. A person's position within the power hierarchy influences one's perception of self and others and the relationship between self and others. Those in a privileged position may automatically understand themselves superior relative to a person in a marginalized or oppressed position, and the inverse may happen for those in the marginalized positions. Any individual may hold both privileged and oppressed—or targeted—identities simultaneously (Collins 2000), such as a wealthy Black woman who might be privileged in terms of class yet targeted with respect to race and gender. This article focuses primarily on race and ethnicity, but it is important to remember that these structures interact with other social hierarchies in society as well.

An individual may be more aware of their identity with respect to their targeted categories, which may be charged with a heavily negative significance or stigmatization in society—such as being Black, an immigrant, queer, or poor—and less aware of their privileged identities which are usually normalized and valued in society, such as being White, a citizen, heterosexual, or wealthy. This means that targeted people must learn how to reject negative stories about themselves for the stigmatized aspects of their identity and need to learn how to recognize the unearned benefits and power related to the privileged aspects of their identity (Miller and Garran 2017). For example, in her book *Why Are All the Black Kids Sitting Together in the Cafeteria?*, Beverly

Tatum examined how adolescents navigate their own understandings of self and others based on their racial positions within the United States, the factors that shape the processes, and the consequences for their sense of self. She identified how racism and discrimination may make Black children hyper-aware of their racial identity, while White ones would not become aware of it until later in life (Tatum 2017). My own identity formation took place in a highly racialized context of the United States with Black American and Cape Verdean ancestry. My social position within this context resulted in my being hyper-aware of my race, ethnicity, and Cape Verdean immigrant background and my integrated sense of self actively engaged with all these components.

THE FALSE DICHOTOMY OF RACE OR ETHNICITY: WORKING TO SEE EACH AND BOTH

Born to a Black American Father and Cape Verdean American mother, I was raised and always identified as Black (or Black American)[2] and Cape Verdean, yet at different moments in my life people have asked me if I consider myself "Black or Cape Verdean?" This question confused me tremendously, as though the person had just asked whether I was left-handed OR did I have two feet. Two coexisting parts of myself are unnecessarily and suddenly put into opposition with each other. Over time, I've come to believe that much of this confusion comes from how the distinct yet interrelated social constructions of race and ethnicity are often conflated into one construct.

Ethnicity is commonly understood in the United States as culture and heritage related to ancestry and place of origin (Treitler 2013). Though it may correlate with phenotypic traits (such as skin color, body type, hair texture), ethnicity is not defined by phenotype. Such an identity comes from a combination of heritage and internal assertion of belonging to that group. For example, my Cape Verdean ethnic identity comes from my ancestors being Cape Verdean combined with my own internal association with this ethnic membership. It is internally and not relatively defined. Ethnicities are not mutually exclusive. The association with one ethnic heritage does not automatically negate the validity of another heritage within the same person. Furthermore, this identity is in no way affected by the presence of someone else's ethnicity. I am no more or less Cape Verdean if I stand next to a person who is ethnically Greek, Nicaraguan, or Nigerian. My relationship to this identity only varies depending on my relationship to the Cape Verdean culture and community.

Ethnicity is not necessarily hierarchical or polar, while race is inherently so. Race in the United States is an externally constructed (through policy, norms, practices, and culture), polarized power relation based on phenotype into which everyone is placed (Quinones-Rosado 2016). White only exists because there is "Black." The sole definition of White is to not be Black and to have more access to power, privilege, and resources relative to Black or non-White populations (Harris 1993). The United States is a white supremacist society, where White, heterosexual, Christian, wealthy, cis-gendered men are supposed to be at the top, and everyone else is supposed to be varying degrees below that. Though the United States, like every society, is based on intersecting power structures, race is a dominant social structure and one generally does better the closer one is to White and the further one is from Black.

Even though the white supremacist racial hierarchy is socially constructed, it still carries very real implications for people's lives. Although the first Africans to arrive in the United States had many different ethnicities, generations of living this racialized existence together has generated a Black American ethnic culture, contingent upon, yet distinct from, the initial African ethnicities (Lewis 1995). For example, as Vilna Treitler (2013) describes in her book:

> If I asked you to identify a group of people and told you that they are presumed to be dark in skin tone, were largely concentrated in the Southern United States prior to 1970; believe their people descend from persons who traveled from the African continent involuntarily even if, more often than not, they cannot pinpoint the national origin of their ancestor with any certainty; identify in great numbers with the Baptist faith; founded the music tradition known as "jazz" and are known for "soul music" and "soul food"; and that other Americans tend not to intermarry with them, your mind would conjure up the ethnic group "African Americans." (21)

This reality that Treitler describes is unique to the United States and to this racialized group. Even though ethnicity is usually rendered invisible when talking about Black Americans, the Black American reality is that of a specific ethnic group constructed within the United States. Thus, my own identity is the integration of two U.S.-based ethnicities, Cape Verdean American and Black American.

While there are no externally imposed laws or policies regarding ethnic identification, there have been very rigid (yet frequently contradictory) ones with respect to race (Ngai 2014). The specific requirements of what made someone "Black" in the United States would vary state by state, but the "one-drop" rule where a single drop of Black ancestry made a person Black is a prevalent ideology. Regardless of how light or dark your own skin may be, if you have parents or any ancestors considered Black, you are Black. In contrast, Whiteness is lost once there is any non-White mixing because White is defined by "purity." This means that even though there are numerous

phenotypic varieties in the United States, and a long history of "miscegena-
tion," those nuances are ignored because they are erased from the national
narrative.

There have been some fluctuations in terms of how groups are racialized,
but the overall system stays intact. For example, historically, the Irish and
Italian immigrants were considered "ethnic Whites" and "non-White," but
now they are considered White. Similarly, Arab Americans, who had been
racially considered White, are recently becoming racialized into a distinct
"non-White" category (Shryock 2008; Mahdawi 2017). Though non-Black
groups in between may shift closer to one end of the racial spectrum or the
other, Black and White are always in structural hierarchical opposition to
each other with White always being on top and groups considered Black
is never re-racialized into the White category (Treitler 2013). In contrast to
the U.S. system, Cape Verdean national identity assumes mixed populations
(racially and ethnically) and phenotypic diversity. The rigid racial system in
the United States is often an unwelcome and invasive experience for immigrants who come from places like Cape Verde, where the social hierarchy is
not based on such stringent racial categorizations (Halter 1993).

As a part of the "Americanization" assimilation process, immigrants are
expected to rid themselves of ethnic identity and embrace a solely racial
Americanized one (Vega and Ortiz 2018). This assimilation narrative comes
from the idea that the United States is a "melting pot" where everyone's differences are merged into one monolithic "American" identity. This ideology
resulted in generations of immigrants being pushed or shamed into rejecting their unique ethnic characteristics, such as language, food, or cultural
traits, and conforming to White, middle-class social norms in pursuit of the
"American Dream." Scholars have shown that assimilation is not the only
way that immigrant populations get incorporated into U.S. society (Portes
and Zhou 2008).

While both White and Black Americans are identified primarily by racial
markers to the exclusion of race, this happens through distinct processes.
For White Americans that process was more voluntary, where they may suppress their own ethnic identifiers and relationships to appear Americanized/
White and gain access to the benefits and privileges associated with that. For
Black Americans, this has been a violently imposed process, from explicit
attempts to strip enslaved Africans of their ethnic identity, violently break
family lineages which disrupted the transference of ethnic identity and
cultural knowledge, and finally the erasure and denial of ethnic roots in the
present. Black Americans have worked to reconnect with ethnic roots by
constructing the "African American" identity label (Bennett 1967), which
shifts the categorization from a racialized to a more ethnic conception. Yet,
the racialized position still prevails and those who are considered Black

American are not generally conceptualized in terms of ethnicity (Treitler 2013)

Ethnicity is distinct from race, but ethnicity is used to racialize, or racially categorize, groups in the United States and place them in the social hierarchy. Groups are categorized as White or non-White, then they may be Black or perhaps a racialized "other." Racialization occurs based on phenotype, lineage, and even place of origin. Regional racialization occurs when whole geographies along with anyone from that geography carries that racialization (Paschel 2016). For example, Latin American countries are racialized as "non-White" or "Brown" and even though a person may be racially White within Latin America, once they are in the United States, they are placed in the non-White category of "Latino." Cape Verdean population and families have vast phenotypic variety that challenge U.S.-based racial assumptions, like many other communities in the United States and globally (e.g., Latin America, The Caribbean, or Creole communities in the United States); however, given that Cape Verde is considered part of Africa (which then defines you as Black) and almost everyone of Cape Verdean descent has (or is assumed to have) at least "one-drop" of Black blood, Cape Verdeans in the United States would always be considered Black and not White. Making Cape Verdean and Black racially synonymous, while ethnic particularities remain.

This structural reality of racialization may decide a person's racial designation, yet individuals may or may not internalize that designation. Within my own family, even though Cape Verdeans would generally be considered Black, the degree to which individuals might embrace that (if at all) would vary. For example, my light-skinned Cape Verdean grandmother was angry that my mother had come home from college with a dark-skinned Black American boyfriend, and even when I was coming to understand race as a child, this same grandmother loved when I said she was White because of her skin tone, while my politically racialized mother who strongly identified as Black cried when I said she looked White. As Black immigrants from the same immigrant community, each person navigates these dimensions differently.

Everyone in the United States has a race and an ethnicity, though one may be more salient than the other for a variety of reasons. Race is an identity that is largely externally constructed and defined. If everyone else in society perceives you as part of that racial category, then that is part of your racialization regardless of how you see yourself. Ethnicity is largely an internal construction process, primarily determined by individual assertion as opposed to external imposition. To ask the question are you "Black or Cape Verdean" is to take a racial framework (polarized and hierarchal) and apply it to an ethnic question (multiple and not inherently hierarchical). To assert Cape Verdeanness is to primarily assert ethnic identity, even though that ethnicity has been racialized as Black. To assert Black Americanness is to primarily assert a racial identity, even though it also carries cultural and ethnic attributes. Even if the weights may shift more one way or the other, racial and ethnic identity are both present and do not have to exist in opposition to each other.

Phenotypically, I have brown skin with characteristics such as hair texture and nose shape that clearly mark me as a Black person in the United States. I have Black American ancestry from my Black American father. I am both perceived and understand myself as a Black person, in addition to the ways in which Cape Verdeans are automatically racialized as Black in the United States. Given my Cape Verdean American mother, personal engagement with my Cape Verdean heritage, and phenotypic diversity within Cape Verdean populations, I am also accepted and understood as Cape Verdean or Cape Verdean American. Because of my racial and ethnic embeddedness, I relate to, but am not limited by, either of the social structures. Instead, I draw on both to expand how I relate to myself and others.

POWER STRUCTURES, REVOLUTIONS, AND IDENTITY CONSTRUCTION

White supremacy (particularly, though not exclusively U.S.-based), colonial legacies in the United States and Cape Verde, and the subsequent movements to resist those power systems are vital external forces in the construction of my own identity as Black American and Cape Verdean American. Colonialism and white supremacy are foundational power structures for Cape Verde and the United States. Both the United States and Cape Verde were the products of colonialism; however, the United States was subject to settler colonialism in which the colonial power not only extracts resources from the colonial territory but also settles on the land itself. In the United States, settlers gained independence from England in 1776; however, colonizers who had settled here stayed in power, and white supremacy remained intact. Thus, the white supremacist system in the United States is embedded within a settler colonialist legacy (Glenn 2015). When Cape Verde gained independence in 1975, after about 500 years of Portuguese colonial rule, the colonial power left the territory. Even though the Portuguese may have still held economic or informal power in many ways, the government and country were formally in the hands of the Cape Verdean people.

In both cases, the subjugated populations are forced to fit into the norms, values, systems, and structures put into place to benefit the dominating population. Colonialism embedded a sense of valuing European and specifically Portuguese/White traits and devaluing African/Black ones. White supremacy instituted a similar value system around Whiteness (Harris 1993; Lima-Neves 2015). The contours of these power dynamics become evident in the myriad ways that people negotiate identity and survival in the face of these inequalities. Subjugated populations may seek out proximity to Whiteness or the colonial power (European and White in this case) to gain access to power and resources for themselves and their communities, or they might embrace Africanness and Blackness in resistance to the white supremacy and imperialism.

Within the United States, everyone navigates the white supremacy systems in their own way and Whiteness has come with a plethora of resources and advantages. Cape Verdeans, like every community, have their own internalized supremacy before coming to the United States, which then interacts with the internalized supremacy system in the United States. Immigrants in the United States frequently try to get as close to Whiteness as possible, or at the very least try to resist being perceived as Black. This has been true with Latinx communities, West Indian Communities, Asian, African, and even indigenous communities that have made efforts to be distinguished from Black American populations (Nagai 2016; Waters 1999). While Black people who phenotypically appeared White have used this proximity to Whiteness to gain access to resources and opportunity at various points in history (Harris 1993). People use whatever tools they have to find space for their sense of self and for survival within this system. In the Cape Verdean case, Aminah Pilgrim (2015) notes that

> Cape Verdeans frequently manipulated their conditions according to the use of identity politics—often through the choice of language spoken, political or religious affiliations, etc.—and thus, their "blackness" or status as African-Americans is/was never fixed. This was the case for those from Cape Verde and arguably for many other immigrants from the African Diaspora in the US racial context, in spite of the fact that they faced institutionalized racism that sought to categorize and define them otherwise.

> The descendants of African slaves in the United States—according to the "one drop rule" all those of any traceable African descent or the traditionally defined "African-Americans"— always sought alternatives to one definition of blackness and collectively resisted that definition, and its attendant stereotypes, in transforming their collective "name" . . . "Neo-African-Americans," or "African-non-Americans," . . . maintain their cultural identities and resist over-determinant blackness by similarly naming themselves—holding on to the names associated with their countries of origin. (112)

Even though there is ample literature documenting Black immigrant resistance to being labeled Black as described here, some important literature has also documented how some ethnic groups specifically identify with Blackness and Black American culture. For example, in Ana Aparicio's (2007) work with Dominican Youth in New York, she found that many second-generation youths attributed their parent's resistance to Black people, to not actually knowing any real Black people and ignorance about their own African ancestry. In this sense, immigrant populations are rejecting stereotypes but have very little knowledge about actual people.

Usually, immigrants only learn about Black populations in the United States through stereotypes. It is important, however, not to reduce Blackness to merely being undesirable within the White supremacist system but to also recognize the unique values of Blackness. Not only is it vital to acknowledge the social assets we have developed (Yosso 2005) it is essential that cultural products such as hip hop (Rosa 2018) or resistance struggles not to be discussed in a way that ignores their Black American foundation (Lewis 1995).

The U.S. supremacy system has created a false dichotomy of race and ethnicity (through policy, norms, and national narratives), where the presence of one frequently implies the denial or erasure of the other. This dichotomization and erasure can generate distance and hostility within and between Black and Cape Verdean (or Black immigrant) communities. Asserting ethnic identity may be interpreted (or may in fact be) as denying Blackness, and immigrant communities may shun Blackness in a range of implicit and explicit ways. Though I have experienced my identity in an integrated way, this has required that I push back on erasure or antagonism within my own communities. On my Cape Verdean side, I was frequently simply swept into the Kriola identity[3] and the Black Americanness would mostly be ignored. While on the Black side, a person might respond "Naw girl, you just black," in response to me naming my Cape Verdean identity.

I would suggest that Black immigrants are not simply rejecting Blackness but that this might be a place where race and ethnicity are being conflated in this resistance. There may be both an ethnic resistance—to refuse the loss of ethnic connection in the face of an assumed assimilationist immigration trajectory in the United States and/or a racial resistance—the refusal to be categorized or see oneself in terms of stereotypes and perceived Blackness.

Black resistance to ethnic naming may be more nuanced as well. Given the myriad of ways that our Black existence is constantly being invalidated, threatened, and undermined, along with the persistent denial of Black ethnicity, and polarized racial structure, it's not surprising that affirming ethnicity can be experienced as racial invalidation. By decoupling race and ethnicity and interrogating these resistances further, I believe we would discover a more multifaceted understanding of these experiences. Historically, global liberation movements have played an important role in bridging racial and ethnic resentment fostered by the dominant power systems.

The 1950s through the 1970s was a time of asserting positive identities in the African Diaspora. Cape Verde was entrenched in the struggle for independence while Black Americans in the United States were asserting their own Black racial identity and fighting for their own independence. As Cape Verdeans were going from Portuguese to Black Portuguese to Cape Verdean (Pilgrim 2015), Black Americans were going from colored to negro to African American and Black (Bennett 1967). Each striving to construct an identity and sense of self separate from the colonizer or oppressor. The cultural revolutions of the mid-twentieth century brought many Black immigrants into a new racialized consciousness and connection to Black America. Pilgrim (2015) further notes,

> Arguably, many Cape Verdean American men and women (if not most) of Salah's generation experienced a so-called "Negro" phase; this phenomenon has continued until now where it is evident that some newer and younger Cape Verdean arrivals in the US embrace commercial, African-American hip hop identity. (117)

Salah may have felt aligned with the Black Power movement, yet it does not appear that he personally accepted a Black identity but rather held a strong affinity. While other Cape Verdeans of Salah's generation and current Cape Verdean immigrants may have a "Negro phase," my Black identity is not optional. Being Black American and Cape Verdean American especially living outside of the Cape Verdean enclave, my Blackness is never a choice. To deny my Blackness would not just be to reject what I interpret as a foreign community but would mean negating an integral part of myself and the rich social legacy that accompanies it.

I was born to parents who were each affirmatively defining themselves as Cape Verdean and Black in a community of Black and Pan African consciousness. My Blackness was always a beautiful thing that carries meaning, integrity, pride, and substance. My Blackness and the Blackness of others brought joy and fullness and significance to me. I was understood as Black and was proud to understand myself as Black. I was simultaneously imbued with a deep connection to my Cape Verdeanness, being intimately familiar with our immigration history and connecting directly with some of our ethnic traits, such as language. For me to be situated and to identify the way I do is to be firmly embedded within the anti-oppressive nexus of these power structures which means being connected to my targeted identities, while pushing against the social structures that subjugate people based on them.

EXTENDING TO THE DIASPORA IDENTITY

In her article, "Free men name themselves: U.S. Cape Verdeans & Black Identity Politics in the Era of Revolutions, 1955–75," Aminah Pilgrim discusses racialized identity processes for Cape Verdean Americans and situates the discussion firmly within critical race and diaspora (specifically afro-diaspora) studies and within the historical context of cultural identity revolutions. She describes the Cape Verdean diaspora as

> being made up of "overlapping diasporas" (a term coined by Earl Lewis), having multiple points of origin and settlement, and consistently moving communities, with multiple identities and subjectivities that themselves shift according to time and place. (Pilgrim 2015, 109)

Diasporas are constantly in flux, remaining connected yet always changing. I think of it as river channels where water flows and collects and moves into other water basins while remaining part of the initial water system. From a Diaspora perspective, it's easy to see how the two sides of my family are part of the same legacy. I am the product of African Diaspora trajectories (Cape Verdean and Black American) re-merging in the United States.

Diaspora is an explicitly integral component of Cape Verdean identity and nationality. Uninhabited prior to discovery, the Cape Verde islands were colonized by the Portuguese, and Cape Verdeans as a people are the product of the violent integration of African and European peoples through the trans-Atlantic slave trade and colonialism. Kidnapped Africans were first taken to Cape Verde to be conditioned and "broken in" for slavery. Some remained on the islands to become the foundation for our Cape Verdean society, some were shipped off to a wide range of destinations in the transatlantic slave trade—creating the foundation for our Afro-Diaspora. In addition to this role, Cape Verde has also served as a vital throughway for migrant, wandering, or fleeing populations across the globe at different points in history and regular cycles of drought and famine have made emigration a vital component of survival. As a result, we have been a country characterized by massive emigration and Diaspora communities. We have a very strong diaspora community and identity that allows for the integration of other nationalities and ethnicities while retaining a Cape Verdean identity (Halter 1993; Resende-Santos 2015).

Black Americans are part of the global Black Diaspora while also having a U.S. domestic diaspora trajectory (Gregory 2005). From families being broken up and sold to people fleeing enslavement and the great migration North post-reconstruction, Black migration within the United States has continued to be an important part of our reality. On my Black American side, I can trace my lineage back to around reconstruction, when an ancestor that had been enslaved in Texas escaped to Virginia and went back to free their mother. I know that the great migration North resulted in my family settling in a steel mill town in Pennsylvania. I know that civil rights and black power moved even more of my family into colleges and professions across the country, including to the college town where my parents met.

On my Cape Verdean side, ongoing challenges in the islands combined with economic opportunity in the United States pushed my great-grandparents to migrate to Cape Verdean immigrant enclaves in New England in the 1900s. The opportunities that attracted my Cape Verdean ancestors were the result of industry and labor shifts post-slavery. These same forces led to my Black American side pursuing new life and opportunities up North. I am the third generation to be born in the United States, but generally the first generation to have parents who married outside of the Cape Verdean community and the first to live outside the enclave. Like my Black American side, civil rights and Black power moved many of my family members into higher education, and for many, into a newfound racial consciousness as well.

Not only are the sides of my family united racially, but they are also connected through interwoven Diaspora streams that merge in my identity. Throughout the long history of the trans-Atlantic slave trade and enslavement in the United States, it is very likely that ancestors on my Black American father's side overlapped with ancestors on my Cape Verdean American mother's side. Perhaps my first Black American ancestor came to the United States through Cape Verde, perhaps there were Cape Verdeans working on the slave ship, or perhaps a British ship traded with a Portuguese one on the way to the U.S. colonies. Then global pressures continued to push my Cape Verdean ancestors toward migration, as U.S. structures and norms continued to feed into forced and chosen internal migration. And finally, liberation movements of the 1950s and 1970s facilitated each of my parents accessing new opportunities and attending college at the same time and place, where they met and then made a family.

UNDERSTANDING THE MONORACIAL MULTIETHNIC REALITY

As with all identities, mine was constructed through a confluence of internal and external forces that shape how I am understood, how I understand myself and my experiences. This was shaped in the U.S. social context in which both sides of my family have distinct ethnic legacies, yet both are legacies of being racially Black in the United States. Thus, I understand myself as being monoracially Black and multiethnically Black American and Cape Verdean American.

I grew up with Blackness and Cape Verdeanness existing as one. My Cape Verdeanness is an extension of my Blackness, and my Blackness is never removed by my Cape Verdeanness. These parts of my identity have come together in an enriching fashion that allows me to draw from the long traditions of resistance, survival, and resilience that both strains have provided to me and make it possible for me to exist, thrive, and resist within the United States. To understand this reality, it was essential to explicitly address race and ethnicity as well as their interactions and integrate that into an analysis of attitudes and experiences; pay attention to broader historical and structural context; examine what identity means for those who are post-the initial immigrant integration; and expand to a Diaspora identity that unites the interwoven Cape Verdean and Black American trajectories.

Cape Verdeans have been coming to the United States for a long time; it is one of the oldest CV diaspora communities in the world, and each generation must contend with the racial reality of the United States (Halter 1993; Andrade-Watkins 2006). To deepen our understanding of individual and collective identity formation and experiences, it is vital that we use frameworks that match this U.S. reality and we must continue to examine other post-integration positionalities. Work like this can shed light on experiences within the United States and across the Diaspora while providing more insight into local and global social structures.

NOTES

1. This chapter was originally published as Liu, Callie Watkins. (2019). Where Blackness and Cape Verdeanness Intersect: Reflections on a Monoracial and Multiethnic Reality in the United States. *Journal of Cape Verdean Studies*, 4(1), 43–62. Available at: https://vc.bridgew.edu/jcvs/vol4/iss1/4 and is reprinted with permission.

2. I specify Black American here because while the racial category of Black is not exclusive to the United States, the U.S. experience of being Black is a particular one.

3. "Kriola" meaning a Cape Verdean woman

REFERENCES

Andrade-Watkins, Claire. *Some Kind of Funny Porto Rican: A Cape Verdean American Story*. [USA]: SPIA Media Productions, 2006.

Aparicio, Ana. "Contesting Race and Power Through the Diaspora: Second-Generation Dominican Youth in the New Gotham." Special issue on youth and globalization, *City and Society* 19, no. 2: 179–201, 2007.

Bakare-Yusuf, Bibi. "Rethinking Diasporicity: Embodiment, Emotion, and the Displaced Origin." *Africana and Black Diaspora* 1, 2008. doi: 10.1080/17528630802224056.

Bennett, Lerone. "What's in a Name? Negro vs. Afro-American vs. Black." *Ebony Magazine*, (November): 46–48, 50–52, 54. http://www.virginia.edu/woodson/courses/aas102%20(spring%2001)/articles/names/bennett.htm, 1967.

Collins, Patricia Hill. *Black Feminist Thought Knowledge, Consciousness, and the Politics of Empowerment*. New York: Routledge, 2000.

Glenn, Evelyn N. "Settler Colonialism as Structure: A Framework for Comparative Studies of U.S. Race and Gender Formation." *Sociology of Race and Ethnicity* 1, no. 1: 54–74, 2015.

Gregory, James M. *The Southern Diaspora: How the Great Migrations of Black and White Southerners Transformed America*. Chapel Hill: University of North Carolina Press, 2005.

Halter, Marilyn. *Between Race and Ethnicity: Cape Verdean American Immigrants, 1860–1965*. Urbana and Chicago: University of Illinois Press, 1993.

Harris, Cheryl. "Whiteness as Property." *Harvard Law Review* 106, no. 8: 1707–1791, 1993.

Lewis, Earl. "To Turn as on a Pivot: Writing African-Americans into a History of Overlapping Diasporas." *American Historical Review* 100: 765–787, 1995.

Lima-Neves, Terza Alice Silva. "D'NOS MANERA: Gender, Collective Identity and Leadership in the Cape Verdean Community in the United States." *Journal of Cape Verdean Studies* 1, no. 1: 57–82, 2015.

Mahdawi, Arwa. "I'm a Bit Brown. But in America I'm White. Not for Much Longer." *The Guardian* (March). https://www.theguardian.com/commentisfree/2017/mar/21/us-census-whiteness-race-colour-middle-east-north-africa-america, 2017.

Miller, Joshua, and Ann Marie Garran. *Racism in the United States: Implications for the Helping Professions*. New York: Spring Publishing Company, 2017.

Nagai, Tyrone. "Multiracial Americans Throughout the History of the US." In *Race Policy and Multiracial Americans*, edited by K. O. Korgen, 13–28. Chicago, IL: Policy Press, 2016.

Paschel, Tianna S. *Becoming Black Political Subjects: Movements and Ethno-Racial Rights in Colombia and Brazil*. Princeton, NJ: Princeton University Press, 2016.

Pilgrim, Aminah. "Free Men Name Themselves": U.S. Cape Verdeans & Black Identity Politics in the Era of Revolutions, 1955–75." *Journal of Cape Verdean Studies* 1, no. 1: 101–120, 2015.

Portes, Alejandro, and Min Zhou. "The New Second Generation: Segmented Assimilation and Its Variants." In *Social Stratification: Class, Race, and Gender in Sociological Perspective*, edited by D. B. Grusky, 658–669. Boulder, CO: Westview Press, 2008.

Quinones-Rosado, Raul. "Latinos and Multiracial America." In *Race Policy and Multiracial Americans*, edited by K. O. Korgen, 51–66. Chicago, IL: Policy Press, 2016.

Resende-Santos, João. 2015. "Cape Verde and Its Diaspora: Economic Transnationalism and Homeland Development." *Journal of Cape Verdean Studies* 2, no. 1: 69–107, 2015.

Rosa, Leila. "'This Country Does Not Have My Back!': Youth Experiences with a Parent Threatened by Deportation." *Journal of Cape Verdean Studies* 2, no. 1: 35–68, 2015.

Rosa, Ricardo D. "Cape Verdean Counter Cultural Hip-Hop(s) & the Mobilization of the Culture of Radical Memory: Public Pedagogy for Liberation or Continued Colonial Enslavement." *Journal of Cape Verdean Studies* 3, no. 1: 92–113, 2018.

Shryock, Andrew. "The Moral Analogies of Race: Arab American Identity, Color Politics, and the Limits of Racialized Citizenship." In *Race and Arab Americans Before and After 9/11: From Invisible Subjects to Visible Subjects*, edited by A. Jamal Editor and N. Naber, 81–113. Syracuse, New York: Syracuse University Press, 2008.

Silva, Clara. "Immigrants from Cabo Verde in Italy: History and Paths of Socio-Educative Integration." *Journal of Cape Verdean Studies* 2, no. 1: 25–34, 2015.

Tatum, Beverly. *Why Are All the Black Kids Sitting Together in the Cafeteria? And Other Conversations About Race.* New York, NY: Basic Books, 2017.

Treitler, Vilna. *The Ethnic Project: Transforming Racial Fiction into Ethnic Factions.* Stanford, CA: Stanford University Press, 2013.

Vega, Irene I., and Vilma Ortiz. "Mexican Americans and Immigration Attitudes: A Cohort Analysis of Assimilation and Group Consciousness." *Social Problems* 65: 137–153, 2018.

Waters, Mary C. "West Indian Immigrant Dreams and American Realities." In *Black Identities: West Indian Immigrant Dreams and American Realities*, 5–8, 336–338. Cambridge, MA: Harvard University Press, 1999.

Yosso, Tara. "Whose Culture Has Capital? A Critical Race Theory Discussion of Community Cultural Wealth." *Race Ethnicity and Education* 8, no. 1: 69–91, 2005.

Chapter 12

The Experience of One in the Many

LGBTQI+ History of Cape Verde

Idalina Pina

BACK IN MY DAY

I stood at the top of the hill with my friends, Bruna, Bruno, and Katia, gazing at the scene before us. We sometimes encountered the older students on our way home as they made their way to school. Us second graders did not dare try to talk to them, so we looked and pondered from afar. Such was the way in my primary school in the little village of As-Hortas in São Filipe, Fogo. This day they had gathered at the bottom of the hill, hollering and screaming about some new gossip. It seemed they had conjured this one themselves, crowning their fourth-grade intellects for figuring out this mystery.

"He's gay," they whisper-yelled, again and again.

I wasn't sure who he was, nor what gay really was, but it seemed to excite them. I had only heard that word once or twice in the Brazilian telenovelas my family watched in the evenings. The scene was usually chaotic and sad, a moment of heartbreak and anguish. I never understood it, but there wasn't much my eight-year-old self could at the time. My family, as usual, stayed quiet during these moments, watching the telenovela as fiercely as any other moment.

My friends and I stood for another moment or two, but eventually, we all got bored of this spectacle and made our way home. The older students continued with their circus for as far as we could hear, and again and again, I could hear that word. I wasn't enticed to ask any family members; I somehow knew better than to bring up this topic. So, for the time being, I forgot about that encounter.

This moment didn't particularly stick with me, not until I figured out the meaning of this word. Gay. It wasn't uttered in my household and, as far as I knew, none of the other ones in my small village. It didn't take long, however, for me to notice what was there before. It started when I was in the third grade, a couple of years after my encounter with the older students. My family sat outside our home, looking toward the sunset and Brava, another island, as a conversation about the neighbors struck. I usually ignored these long drawls, but the topic intrigued me. Here it was again—that word. As it got thrown around, again and again, my eight-year-old self dared to do the unthinkable and asked a question. As I expected, my inquiry was ignored, and I was left to add from the pieces of the conversation. Here's what I conjured: being gay is a sin. There wasn't much that wasn't those days, so I added this qualification to my already long list of things that could bring me to hell, and I moved on without understanding much beyond that point.

What is left unsaid is often seen. That particular truth lives through our shared ancestral trauma, in the ways we bury our hurt and shame our happiness. Such is the case with gender norms on my island, at least at the time of my childhood. All my experiences with the fluidity of sexuality on the island had been as such. Most of the time, my people danced around the subject, choosing to ignore its sway, but, of course, sexuality has a way of finding itself in our daily lives. Most, if not all, homes in my village and probably the islands at large were two-parent households. Most mothers stayed at home while fathers worked. Although the distribution of work is so much more nuanced than this view, it is that which the people held at that time. Such was the way for my mother, my grandmother, and so forth. I didn't question it much, but I did not have the capacity to doubt what I did not understand, but when that time came, I did nothing but that.

PANSEXUAL, CAPE VERDEAN, AND EXHAUSTED

In 2008, most of my family moved from Fogo to Massachusetts in search of better opportunities. We settled in Boston with the rest of the predominantly Cape Verdean community. In some ways, it was still the islands—my first encounter with the diaspora. In my attempt to acclimate, I, for the most part, assimilated into the American culture. Although I was an immigrant child, I learned to hide this part of my life pretty well early on. Such was my coping mechanism and that of many other people. This way of living soon became a part of me, another characteristic of my already intersectional identity. By sixteen, I had achieved much more than myself and my family imagined possible. I was attending a boarding school in the suburbs of Boston on full financial aid—the first of my family to do so. That, however, was all I allowed my family to know about me, at that time. At home, I was the same person I was on the islands, but at school a completely different woman, one who had grown up in the twenty-first century with liberal ideals and a nonconforming identity. In my first year at this boarding school, I became somewhat of a little Black Marxist, as tends to happen to some Black students in predominantly white institutions. I joined all the social justice clubs, from the Young Democrats group to the school's Gay-Straight Alliance. I became an active member of these societies, fighting for the rights of people to become equal members in institutions like mine. What I didn't realize at the time was that not only was I fighting for the humanity of underprivileged people, but I was creating a safe space for myself, as well.

It was summer 2015. I was a budding teenager, recently turned sixteen with illusions of maturity and adulthood. One afternoon, on the 26th of June, as I sat on my grandmother's porch babysitting my younger cousins at my Boston home, I decided to update myself on the day's news. Obergefell v. Hodges was everywhere. The Supreme Court decision legalized same-sex marriage throughout the United States. I was ecstatic; I started playing music and dancing with my little cousins, celebrating this milestone for the LGBTQI+ community. It was at this moment that I truly questioned my involvement in queer spaces and communities. No longer could I hide that part of myself. It was a second, but I finally realized I was gay. I liked girls in the same ways I liked boys, but not only did I like girls and boys, I loved people. I knew of the term pansexual but hadn't met many people who identified as such at this time. For so long, I suppressed this part of myself in order to cope with my family and my community. I internalized the sinful teachings of the church, so much so I couldn't discover parts of myself. In that first year of boarding school, I had grown more distant from the traditional teachings of the church, even to the point of considering myself an atheist for a period of time. I kept this newfound freedom to myself and found other ways of expressing my identity without the knowledge of my family. Boarding school provided the space for me to grow into the person I wanted, not the person my family envisioned. This new discovery would just be another part of myself I kept hidden.

I first came out to my friends as pansexual. I was always surrounded by their love and never doubted their acceptance. As time progressed, I learned to heal that part of myself that hid for safety. I became more outspoken about my character, my personhood. In the summer of 2018, I finally came out to my mother. It wasn't the moment I envisioned, but it was much better than the one I had feared. Just like our community has learned to do in the past decades, my mother came to accept me. As time progresses, I hope I can find the courage to present my full self to my family. But therapy and life have taught me that not all parts of the self have to be open at all times. It may be a remnant of my old coping mechanisms, but I like to see it from a different perspective, one of a person who is pansexual, Cape Verdean, and living an exhausting life in the United States.

HISTORY OF LGBTQI+ PRESENCE
AND RIGHTS IN CABO VERDE

Myths about African sexuality have clouded its beautiful history for far too long. Prior to colonization, there existed a variety of gender identities and sexualities that neither excluded non-gender-conforming individuals nor exulted particular gender norms (Alimi 2015). Throughout the West Coast, different chiefdoms and kingdoms functioned with the presence of other genders and sexualities and even flourished under the rule of people identifying as such. With the introduction of colonial traditions such as Christianity, these before accepted behaviors and identities were marginalized and persecuted. Most of West African history is oral, a tradition which proves difficult to uphold in a Western academic system; however, as the paradigms of education shift, the value and significance of oral traditions are being recognized. Such is the case with the histories of LGBTQI+ peoples in the continent. As more of it is being unearthed, the acknowledgment of the spectrum of African people is being heard and appreciated.

Cape Verde's history, however, is a particular one to the continent. In 1456, Portuguese mariners landed on this uninhabited island, later settling and colonizing it. As was practiced during these voyages, the Portuguese claimed these lands to belong to God, but secondly, and, most importantly, to be a part of the Portuguese empire. As the Transatlantic slave trade accelerated, Cape Verde became an important bridge between Europe, Africa, and the Americas. Other European empires became jealous of the particular location of the islands, often leading to invasions. All of this chaos ultimately led to the creation of a new culture, a new people who weren't so much so—a mixture of old traditions and newer ones, a synchronizing of cultures, and an amalgamation of peoples, mostly from the West Coast of Africa and southern Europe. This occurrence wasn't particular to Cape Verde, of course, but the circumstances on the island make it an isolated and unique one. Moreover, because the islands were colonized until the late twentieth century, the influence and power of the Portuguese empire were very strong and continues to be so. For centuries, Portugal and other European nations were directly involved in manufacturing Christian, capital societies like theirs throughout their colonies. Such perpetuation of norms looked like two-gender households, ones in which the male figure provided the income and the female figure took care of household matters. In fact, in 1886, at the creation of a penal code, the Portuguese empire criminalized all "unnatural acts" (Vibrant 2015). Hence, same-sex couples were forbidden by law. This ruling was not particular to Cape Verde. Throughout the continent, countries adopted similar punitive laws against same-sex couples and nongender conforming individuals. Centuries of percussion led to the eradication of the idea of African sexuality, but it could not erase the many queer people on the lands.

When Cabo Verde gained its independence in 1975, it maintained a close relationship with its former colonizer; however, Cabo Verde paved its path in history from the moments it could. In 1992, when Cabo Verde wrote its articles of the constitution, freedom of expression was emphasized as one of the country's main values. In 2004, the parliament progressed this right toward more citizens and provisioned the former penal code to decriminalize same-gender relations (Epprecht 2012). With this decree, Cape Verde became the second African nation to legalize same-gender relationships. In 2008, not only did Cape Verde sign a United Nations document stating that human rights were not limited based on sexual preference, but the nation also instated a ban on discrimination based on sexual orientation (Itaborahy 2013). This was a huge milestone for an African nation that not too long ago gained its independence. Although discrimination and prejudice are still a very real problem, the situation for LGBTQI+ individuals has improved on the islands.

In 2011, the Cape Verdean Gay Association (AGC) was created by a group of transgender activists in Mindelo, the queer capital of Cape Verde. It is on this beautiful island that one finds Tchinda Andrade, the country's first transgender activist and matriarch of the association. Tchinda's story is one of beauty, grace, hardship, and struggle. Like any other Cape Verdean experience, life on a mostly barren rock can prove difficult to maneuver; however, the life of an LGBTQI+ person in a mostly Catholic community is never an easy one. In 1998, in an act of bravery, Tchinda announced at a local newspaper that she was transgender (Page 2016). The small community of people in São Vicente was, for the most part, welcoming of Tchinda. Although she still encounters resistance from some, she lives a vibrant life and has even cultivated a safe, welcoming community for others like herself. Indeed, the transgender people of the islands are known as Tchindas. This queer-identifying group ultimately created the Association of Gay Cape Verdeans. The group states that its mission is to provide visibility to the country's queer individuals (Associacaogaycaboverdiana 2013).

In 2013, it did just that by organizing the first Pride Week in the country and the second in the continent (May 17, 2014). From the 24th to the 29th of June, AGC, with the support of other organizations, hosted parades, live music, food, and all things festival related. Carnival is a celebration of good fortune, good weather, and all of the sinful things of life before handing them off to God in a forty-day period as we repent and lent. Although most Cape Verdean customs and traditions are rooted in colonial practices, there are those which are entrenched in our African ancestry and roots—such is carnival. On their way to a cultural fair in Portugal in the 1960s, the Mandinka people of West Africa stopped and performed for Cape Verdeans on their route. These performances ultimately lead to the creation of carnival on the islands, the primary one occurring in Mindelo, São Vicente.

In 2015, with the support of the United Nations' Free and Equal campaign, Helen Tavares speared headed the opening of the Cabo Verdean Gay Association (AGC) in Santiago, a different island (UN Women 2020). As an LBGT Cape Verdean, Tavares yearned for a peaceful life for her and her family—such pursuits proved daunting in the nation's biggest island. However, it was a fight she was willing to pursue. Three years later in 2018, Praia, the nation's capital, hosted its first Pride Week, which included a parade, conversations at the nation's oldest university about LGBTQI+ issues, a gallery exhibition of some of the country's LGBTIQ+ peoples, and more activities (UN Women 2020). The now more permanent associations on the islands attempted to introduce further anti-Homophobic legislations into the parliament; although not successful in pushing for gay marriage, these legislations provided a voice for the islands' LGBTQI+ community.

As these groups push for more inclusion, life for Cape Verdean LGBTQI+ citizens continues to improve. It's vital that organizations such as these continue to exist and flourish in places like our islands home. Only when visible can society once again learn to hear our stories and our truths. As the struggle for this equality continues, hope springs from different wells.

CONCLUDING THOUGHTS

I have been living away from my island for eleven years now. I am now a part of the Cape Verdean diaspora, one which spans many countries and boundaries. At times, it feels lonely on the other side. I yearn for home more days than exist in a year. But home was a difficult place, and I can't imagine my radical, intersectional life on a small island; however, that doesn't mean I can't miss our hospitality, our feijao e arroz com peixe, and all my cousins. I wish for what could have been, what was, and the sun beaming on my face from dawn to dusk.

But I must face reality, and that for me is that I am a student struggling with Bipolar disorder and PTSD, a pansexual woman, and Black in America. My family immigrated to the United States for better opportunities, and, for the most part, that is what our experience in the United States has been. Although our islands are progressing in legislation for the LGBTQI+ community, it is nowhere close to where it should be, nor is the acceptance of the overall Cape Verdean community. Even a decade later, the situation on my island looks about the same; two-parent Christian households with a complex labor divide. However, I am hopeful for the future. Not too long ago most of my family members couldn't utter the word gay, but now they understand that sexuality does not take away one's humanity. It's a small gesture from our families and peers, but it's how prejudice can be fought.

In this ever-changing global, capitalist world, Cape Verdeans are finding themselves in even more intersectional identities and paradigms. Throughout our diaspora, more and more of our brethren are speaking out about their integrity without fear. From the people living their lives in full color on the island to those of us living abroad in our own little worlds, it's important to understand and give visibility to all parts of our community. We're a struggling community, one which needs support from all members of society, not only help but also acceptance and love. Cape Verde struggles to provide for its community of people, it's hard to believe its LGBTQI+ citizens will be receiving adequate assistance any time soon. In the meantime, as a community, the LGBTQI+ Cape Verdeans are becoming more aware of each other, and we are supporting ourselves when we can. In this digital age, Facebook groups, and Instagram pages, such as @CaboQueer, provide safe spaces for our queer-identifying people. It's a space for us to know that, yes, other queer Cape Verdeans do exist. And yes, some day, too, we shall flourish like an arco-íris.

REFERENCES

Alimi, Bisi. "If You Say Being Gay Is Not African, You Don't Know Your History." *CNN*. https://www.theguardian.com/commentisfree/2015/sep/09/being-gay-african-history-homosexuality-christianity, 2015.

Associacaogaycaboverdiana. "Associacaogaycaboverdiana.blogspot.com/(blog)." http://associacaogaycaboverdiana.blogspot.com/2013/06/quem-somos-nos.html, 2013.

Epprecht, Marc. "Sexual Minorities, Human Rights and Public Health Strategies in Africa." *African Affairs* 111(443): 223–243. doi: 10.1093/afraf/ads019, 2012.

Itaborahy, L. P., and Jingshu, Zhu. "State-Sponsored Homophobia: A World Survey of Laws: Criminalisation, Protection and Recognition of Same-Sex Love." (PDF). old.ilga.org. ILGA. Archived from the original (PDF), 2013.

May17. "Cape Verde Gets Ready for First Ever Pride Week." *May17.org*. https://may17.org/cape-verde-gets-ready-for-first-ever-pride-week/, 2014.

Page, Thomas. "Meet Cape Verde's Transgender Hero." CNN. *Cable News Network*. https://www.cnn.com/2016/07/07/africa/tchinda-andrade-transgender-cape-verde-film/index.html, 2016.

UN Women. "From Where I Stand: 'Being LGBT Means Fighting Against Prejudice and Violence Every Day.'" https://www.unwomen.org/en/news/stories/2018/11/from-where-i-stand-helen-tavares, 2020.

Vibrant, Virtual Braz. *Anthr. 12* no. 1 Brasília Jan. http://dx.doi.org/10.1590/1809-43412015v12n1p037, 2015.

Part VI

TRANSFORMING CULTURE
INTO PRACTICE

Chapter 13

Family History and Genealogy

The Benefits for the Listener, the Storyteller, and the Community

Anna Lima

A few years ago, I was asked by another Cape Verdean my name and who my family was. Without thinking twice, I said I'm "Nanie de Ramizi de Rosinha de Nha Maria Rosinha de Cham de Souza, Brava." In that one sentence, I was able to give five generations of my family history including the place they came from. Those few words explained exactly who I was. It was the essence of my identity (The Creola Genealogist 2015).

Although I was born in America, my identity was firmly established within my Cape Verdean culture and the four generations of extended family I lived with. I not only lived with my grandparents, I had the honor of knowing my great grandmother, Maria Coelho Rodrigues for the first thirty years of my life.

I was that persistent child that would grill my great grandmother about her childhood, her parents, grandparents, and great grandparents. I wanted to know about where they were from, what they looked like, and how they lived. I wanted to know my family history and not just my genealogy. I instinctively knew that learning about who they were gave me a greater understanding of who I was.

My identity was shaped by this knowledge of my ancestors that has been passed down to me by my great grandmother and my family. Our culture and traditions, shaped by the ancestors, are the foundation of how we perceive the world, how we present ourselves to the world, and how our ethics and morality are articulated.

I began my genealogical research in earnest after the death of my great grandmother in 2003.

I can still hear her voice though it's been 15 years since she took her last breath. Her words continue to guide me through my trials, her praises ring in my ears. Her gentle reminders of who I am and where I come from steady my foothold in this world. She was my compass, my foundation. My great-grandmother, Bibi, was the heart and soul of our family. She was the Family Griot. As much as I miss her voice, her glare if you dared to do something she didn't approve of, the melodic humming as she held me in her arms to help me fall asleep, I realize that she is with me everyday of my life. Her song, her Griot Song, continues. . . (The Creola Genealogist 2018, para. 1)

There weren't as many resources available back then as there are today. I could only rely on the memory of family members to explore my family history. Once my great grandmother passed away, I felt an urgency to remember everything she taught me. I was afraid I would forget.

I had the opportunity to visit Cabo Verde for the first time in 2009. I will never forget the moment I first stepped onto the land of my ancestors. I felt I was home for the first time in my life. It is not an exaggeration to say that it was the first time that I felt that I belonged. I also realized that I had felt an intense Sodade for this place. . . . A place that I had never been to before.

While in Cabo Verde, I was able to attain information and baptism records for my parents, grandparents, great grandparents, and even great grandparents. I belonged to this place, these people, this community. My connection and my pride to my family, culture, and ancestry had never been as strong.

This was my reason for doing genealogy. Knowing where I came from and, more importantly, from whom I came from made me feel stronger. Understanding how my family lived gave me purpose to want to be a better version of myself. I wanted to honor them. I wanted other Cape Verdeans of the Diaspora to experience the same.

In the years since, I have published some of my research on my blog called The Creola Genealogist as well as a Facebook page by the same name. By 2015, we had a small group of amateur Cape Verdean genealogists on Facebook and so I created a private group called Cape Verde DNA, Inc which has grown to over 5,000 members all over the world. In August 2018, we held the first Cape Verdean Genealogy conference in Boston, Massachusetts. But this question has always remained. Why is researching our family histories and genealogy important?

This is a question I have asked myself many times. What is the purpose of spending countless hours finding elusive ancestors in semi-legible records? Does it solve the drug problem plaguing our communities? Does it end hunger? Does it improve health statistics, increase literacy rates, end violence? Maybe.

To better answer this, a deeper look into what genealogy is, as well as, the history of genealogy needs to be explored.

WHAT IS GENEALOGY?

The tradition of the recording of lineages is as old as civilization, itself. Emperors and kings from ancient civilizations of Sumer (Mesopotamia) to medieval England have used genealogy to validate any claims to the throne. Some have used it to trace their ancestry to Greek, Roman, and Egyptian gods just as Islamic rulers today trace their descent to the Prophet Mohammed.

Genealogy was told and recorded through oral stories that were passed on from one generation to the next. This tradition can be found across continents and cultures from West African Griots, Japanese Kataribe, Celtic Shanachy, and Germanic Scop. These specialized clans carried and preserved the memory of their leaders through not only the names of the ancestors but also with stories of their accomplishments. With the advent of writing systems, the lineages of rulers and leaders relied less on oral stories. As civilizations grew, genealogy became the primary tool for inheritance and land ownership of the nobility and as such, most people had no need to record their genealogies (Hadis 2002).

Most people point to Alex Haley's (1976) *Roots* as the catalyst for today's rising popularity of genealogy. There is not only an interest in genealogy, which serves as a basic outline with facts such as date of birth, marriage, and death dates but family history that puts those facts into a narrative of self, culture, and community.

THE LISTENER, THE STORYTELLER, AND THE COMMUNITY

Hadis (2002) describes specific benefits of family history and genealogy for the listener, the storyteller, and the greater community.

The Listener

For the listener, genealogy is the initial source of identity. The act of listening and learning from one's family history bestows the benefit of identity, guidance, and enrichment upon the audience (Hadis 2002).

Identity

Studies show that researching one's family history gives a better understanding of self which influences choices that are based on knowledge of their ancestors. This knowledge often leads to a greater desire to improve oneself. An increased sense of identity manifests in a greater sense of self-confidence, increased self-understanding, and greater resolve to improve personally. In what has been dubbed "the Ancestor Effect," researchers describe improved test scores among students who were primed to think about their ancestors before answering test questions. Thinking about their ancestors, and therefore, their own identities in a positive way affected each student's performance accordingly (Fischer et al. 2011). While other studies have shown improved performance utilizing various aspects of identity besides ancestry, it is worth noting that exploring one family history can be a valuable tool that can be used in the classroom to help close achievement gaps.

Guidance

Genealogy can be said to provide a blueprint for life by illuminating the wisdom and folly of our ancestors. As stated by Rosenbluth (1997), "Family stories that come down through the generations are often ones of overcoming obstacles, and of courage and survival, and those can be inspiring in our own lives" (101). Even negative and disastrous stories can offer coping strategies that help us to see more possibilities. Our family histories help us see possibilities; they give us what we need to envision a transformed future (Haas-Dyson and Genishi 1994). Family histories are the main building blocks in one's moral compass.

Enrichment

"A well-loved past enriches the world around us" (Lowenthal 1985, 95).

Being able to link one's experiences to that of history gives a greater understanding of the subject matter. Family histories can help put historical facts in an understandable context when it is related to the actual experiences of our ancestors (Ellis and Bruckman 1999).

The Storyteller

For the storyteller, family history and genealogy has the benefit of coherence, generativity, and resulting human connections (Hadis 2002).

Coherence and Continuity

Family history and genealogy enhance one's identity and therefore, perception of self by allowing one to connect their past with their present. There is therapeutic value to look back at life in order to come to terms with experiences and integrating various aspects of a lifetime. Genealogy can be used in counseling whereby a clinician can create a genome to look for traits, etc. that follow an intergenerational framework (Duba et al. 2009). Genealogy can be used as a counseling tool (Humes 1994). This can lead to "Looking back to childhood and young adulthood allows us to integrate those images of our former selves with who we are now" (Rosenbluth 1997, 101).

Generativity

Psychologists refer to generativity as the healthy impulse to "foster, nurture, encourage and guide those that will succeed" us that "involves the creation or elaboration of a product of the self and the selfless and caring surrendering or handing down of this product to others" (McAdams et al. 1986). This process encourages a sense of immortality, whether it is focused on one's own descendants or allowed to encompass a family group, tribal collective, or even a whole country or people (Hadis 2002). For the teller, family history and genealogy gives us hope that our stories, our product, will not only outlive us but will continue to help and inspire generations to come.

Human Connections

"There is no doubt that reminiscing and telling personal stories have therapeutic value" (Rosenbluth 1997). This is evident in my own practice as a Speech and Language Pathologist, where a majority of my patients are elders suffering from varying degrees of dementia. One of my goals is to maintain my patient's current cognitive status, and this most often entails keeping them "connected" with their families. I educate family members on strategies that aim to maintain a person functioning in their own environment for as long as they can.

Dementia is a hideous process that culminates in the slow unlearning of everything one has learned and experienced in their lifetime. It doesn't only rob a person of their memories. Perhaps the most disturbing and scariest part for anyone diagnosed with dementia is the fear of "losing themselves." The most heartbreaking point for family members is when their loved one ceases to be the person they have always known. Strohminger and Nichols (2015) conducted a study in 2015, which surveyed 248 families and caretakers dementia patients. They found that family members noticed that a change in morals was more significant than memory loss, personality change, loss of intelligence, or inability to do daily tasks. Morals shape our lives and our conduct in various environments. One's set of morals affects behavior and social decisions, and shared values are the basis for personal identity and the ability to belong to unique groups. The moral compass seemed to be the last piece of identity to disappear. When patients finally do lose their morality, their families are no longer able to recognize them as the same person (Strohminger and Nichols 2015). When working with my patients and their families, I have found that working on family trees has shown positive outcomes in prolonging a patient's "identity" and overall function by maintaining a connection with their family and external world. Giving someone with dementia the opportunity to tell their "story" is key in maintaining their sense of self and identity.

Community

We all benefit from the sense of community and intimacy that is naturally fostered by a common past. There is often a divide between us and our ancestors consisting of time and familiarity. Learning about who our ancestors were can be an exercise in self-discovery with positive ramifications that can influence self-identity, confidence, and outlook. Human geographer, Catherine Nash (2002), describes genealogy as "a practice through which ideas of personal, familial, collective, ethnic, and sometimes national senses of culture, location, and identity are shaped, imagined, articulated, and enacted. It is said that the pursuit of family history fulfills a psychological need to the extent that it becomes a way of orienting the internal as well as the external worlds" (28). John Triseliotis (1987), who has studied fostered and adopted children, is convinced that "at least in Western Cultures, [people] have a deep emotional and social need and curiosity to know about their families of origin and ancestors" (273). He argues that narrative about the self contributes to a sense of continuity and uniqueness which is vital "to help us complete ourselves or complete the pattern of our lives" and is, therefore, a "necessary ingredient to the building of self and personality" (Triseliotis 1987, 273). I believe our community can benefit by utilizing the skills, privileges, and resources available through family history and genealogy to ask questions about what specific experiences mean to us now and overtime (Madison 2005). Perhaps we can examine historical injustices within particular experiences and disrupt these injustices by bringing to light the marginalized voices that are often silenced in the telling of stories.

Connecting to Our Roots

With the invention of ancestry.com and DNA testing, genealogy has become very popular all over the world. For most, a few simple clicks are all that is needed to trace one's family back to Charlemagne. For those of us of the Cape Verdean diaspora, it's not as easy. Whether first generation or fifth generation, we identify with our Cape Verdean identity but often lack the genealogical information that allows us to trace our ancestry past our most recent immigrant ancestor. As previously stated, genealogy provides the facts while family history provides the narrative. For some of us, the narrative is lacking the facts to make a coherent story of who and what we are. Most of us can identify with growing up with someone who was identified as a cousin without ever knowing exactly how we are related. It can almost seem that our ancestors never had an interest in our genealogies and passing that information down. But this was not actually the case. Hadis (2002) stated, "Flattering though it would be to think otherwise, our recent interest in family history and genealogy is not because of a heightened perception of the past on our behalf, but in the social changes that have brought about the disappearance of those institutions and structures that were in charge of continuity and the transmission of knowledge down through generations. Far from being the first to show an intense curiosity about our own pasts, we are among the first to suffer from its absence" (23).Smith-Barusch and Steen (1996) described the family structure in preindustrial times to include often four generations of a family living within one household. Extended family members lived nearby, and children were almost always ensured contact with family elders. Children would simply absorb information about their families and pass it on to their own children. Families often remained in the same regions and interacted with the same groups their ancestors did for generations before. Industrialization brought about significant changes in the family household structure whereby only the nucleus or immediate family lived in the same house. With extended families scattered and dispersed, the many legacies that one generation passed to the next all but disappeared (Hadis 2007). Cape Verdeans have a long history of migration that has impacted our family and community structures and therefore passing on of family histories and genealogy. Our history of slavery has to also be taken into account where, due to its hideous nature, those of us who are descendants of enslaved Africans cannot connect to all our African family histories and genealogies. In this light, it should not be surprising that we are now showing such a strong interest in connecting with our roots. Unlike that of our ancestors, our grasp of the past is as fragile as it is faint (Hadis 2007).Why is family history and genealogy important when there are so many other problems in our community? Knowing our family history and genealogy has the benefit of giving us a sense of continuity, identity, guidance, and community. Where there is a breakdown in any of these, problems can and will arise.

REFERENCES

Duba, J. D., M. A. Graham, M. Britzman, and N. Minatrea. "Introducing the "Basic Needs Genogram" in Reality Therapy-Based Marriage and Family Counseling." *International of Journal of Reality Therapy*, 28(2), 15–19, 2009.

Ellis Jason B., and Amy Bruckman. "Children and Elders Sharing Stories: Lessons from Two On-Line History Projects." *Computer Support for Collaborative Learning*, 1999.

Fischer, Peter, Anne Sauer, Claudia Vogrincic, and Silke Weisweiler. "The Ancestor Effect: Thinking About Our Genetic Origin Enhances Intellectual Performance." *European Journal of Social Psychology*, *41*, 11–16. doi: 10.1002/ejsp.778, 2011.

Haas-Dyson, Anne, and Celia Genishi. *Introduction to The Need for Story*. Urbana, IL: National Council of Teachers of English, 1994.

Hadis, Martin. *From Generation to Generation: Family Stories, Computers and Genealogy* (Unpublished master's thesis). Massachusetts Institute of Technology, Cambridge, MA, 2002.

Haley, Alex. *Roots*. Garden City, New York: Doubleday, 1976.

Humes, Charles W. "Genealogy: A Counseling Tool." *The School Counselor, 41*(3), 296–299, 1994.

Lowenthal, David. *The Past is a Foreign Country*. Cambridge: Cambridge University Press, 1985.

Madison, D.S. *Critical Ethnography: Method, Ethics, and Performance*. Thousand Oaks, CA: SAGE Publications, 2005.

McAdams, Dan P., Karin Ruetzel, and Jeanne Foley. "Complexity and Generativity at Mid-Life: Relations Among Social Motives, Ego Development and Adults' Plans for the Future." *Journal of Personality and Social Psychology*, *50*(4), 800–807, 1986.

Nash, Catherine. "Genealogical Identities." *Environment and Planning D: Society and Space*, *20*, 27–52, 2002.

Rosenbluth, Vera. *Keeping Family Stories Alive*. Washington: Hartley & Marks, Pub. Point Roberts, 1997.

Smith-Barusch, Amanda, and Peter Steen. "Keepers of Community in a Changing World." *Generations: The Journal of the Western Gerontological Society*, *20*(1), 1996.

Strohminger, N., and S. Nichols. "Neurodegeneration and Identity." *Psychological Science*, *26*(9), 1469–1479, 2015.

The Creola Genealogist. *My Real Name Is...* (Blog post). https://thecreolagenealogist .com/2015/05/18/my-real-name-is/, 2015.

The Creola Genealogist. *The Griot's Song* (Blog post). https://thecreolagenealogist .com/2018/09/06/the-griots-song, 2018.

Triseliotis, John. "Identity and Genealogy." *The Scottish Genealogist* 272–276, 1987.

Chapter 14

Occupational Ancestry

Ayana Pilgrim-Brown

What's your occupational ancestry? You might be thinking "what is occupational ancestry?" This is your professional DNA. Ever wonder what your great-grandparents might have done for a living? Have you ever wondered if your passion was ever felt by anyone else in your family? Well, recently I had a confluence of things happen that led me to this concept of occupational ancestry.

First, on a chilly winter evening, my girls and I ventured out for movie night. My husband was out of town for a work conference, so we decided to have some fun together and catch the latest Disney film called *Coco*. The premise of this film is the story of a young boy who was desperately in love with music and secretly taught himself to play the guitar. He had daily fantasies of being a musician that the people would love, except he had one problem . . . If you are reading this you may very well have this same problem. His parents and his family were vehemently opposed to what he was most passionate about pursuing. They did not support his desire to pursue music. A powerful scene shows his grandmother destroying his guitar and forbidding him to play it ever again only for him to be magically taken away to the land of the dead where he stumbles upon the awareness that his ancestors too were in fact passionate and very talented musicians.

This got me thinking; so often our ancestors—those who came before us in our lineage—often possessed similar gifts, talents, and occupations than we do. So, I started to remember different interviews that I had seen over the years. I once watched the media and homemaking mogul, Martha Stewart, being interviewed and sharing that her mother was a seamstress and her mother before her a designer. It was all built into the strands of her occupational DNA. Then I happened to be watching an interview with famous

Christian pastor, Bishop T. D. Jakes. When asked how he got to be such an industrious entrepreneur and businessperson, he stated his family's involvement in entrepreneurship. He went on to say that his ancestors were Ibo, and they were known for their businesses and industriousness. Then he spoke of his father being a small business owner. He went on to note that he's a teacher with a dramatic flair because his mother was a schoolteacher, and she was very dramatic. All of these stories were reflected in his own, multiple business ventures, his charisma as a storyteller, and his heartbeat as a spiritual educator.

So, I started to think of myself and my recent DNA test. My results revealed that my ancestors were from a variety of places across Africa and Europe. I began to wonder what my ancestors did for work. First, I thought of my maternal grandmother and how I had heard stories of her and my grandfather having a farm that fed the whole neighborhood. Her mother before her was a midwife and healer, and her father a business store owner. Hmmm . . . that got me thinking . . .Then I thought of my father's side. My great-grandmother founded a church and served as a gift of encouragement in her community in Barbados and Cambridge, Massachuttes. Could all of these talents and gifts be intricately woven together like DNA strands and be a part of my *occupational ancestry?*

I started to ponder the idea, and then it came to me. I am spiritual, carry the gift of encouragement, and I minister to people daily. This is a strand of occupational ancestry from my paternal great-grandmother who founded a church and was known for her spiritual gifts of prophecy. I am a healer, as I am constantly serving as the ambassador for wellness wherever I go. In fact, I even got certified as a Holistic Health Counselor years ago out of a desire to help professionals not only pursue the work that they love but to do so with well-being. I take joy in teaching people information that can revolutionize their health and their work life. This is a strand of my maternal great-grandmother's DNA. She was a healer and midwife, helping to bring forth life and cultivate it (as she adopted many in the community who were in need). I am an entrepreneur and innovator at heart. This is my maternal great-grandfather's strand. He was a store owner, responsible for helping the community to thrive and his family to do so with economic empowerment. These examples illuminate why the concept of occupational ancestry makes sense.

We are each made up of unique genetic codes that dictate our features, the way we walk, the way we talk, and the way we curl our lips when we are mad. It is revolutionary to know that we are also woven together by strands of occupational ancestry that make us gravitate toward the arts, make us feel compelled to speak or to write or to heal or to create. How empowering is it to have that knowledge? I'd say very empowering.

MY OCCUPATIONAL ANCESTRY STORY

To further illustrate my hypothesis, allow me to tell you a bit of my story. In the past, I have worked as a professor and career coach at a business school. While working at a local urban university, I had witnessed far too many students of color who would feel like they didn't belong, who were not being encouraged despite their difficult circumstances, and who were in many instances beginning to confront the ugly spirit of racism for the first time in their professional lives. I knew that if I were to make even more of an impact, I would need to ground myself in the spirit of *nos ku nos*. One story that really stuck with me was that of Isabella.

Isabella was from Angola. I had the pleasure of meeting her as she sat in one of my workshops on professional development. As we sat in our Philadelphia campus, I asked if anyone was from another country, as I always did. She raised her hand and said "Angola," I made it a point to chat with her after the session and use what little Portuguese I knew to establish a connection with her and to let her know that I was here to support her while she was on her higher education journey. Once we spoke she had a smile as bright as the sun, comforted by the knowledge that I saw her; there was a shared cultural experience as a Luso-African woman, and I validated that she mattered.

She subsequently took to me and came to yet another one of my workshops, and a coaching session or two. Then one day I engaged in small talk with her in the hallway. It was my custom to always stop and check-in with my students of color to make sure they were okay. She shared that she was tired, her parents were back home, and she was raising her thirteen- and seven-year-old sisters in a pretty rough section of our city. I encouraged her that she was strong and smart and that she would do all the things that she sets out to do. I told her that I was there for her if she needed anything. From there we walked to my office, and I registered her for our major career event that was coming up that week. She worked hard to prepare. Her resume was in good shape, and she commuted to campus several times to meet the criteria to attend. Then the day of the event came. The campus was filled with excitement and nervousness. Some of my colleagues sat apathetic and uninterested in helping, and that made me work even more diligently at my post, welcoming and coaching students along the way. There is a lesson in that—when you are serving in purpose, don't let others apathy impact your energy.

Now back to the story, for me, a turning point in my assignment. I saw Isabella from afar speaking with our assistant dean by the front door. The dean was notorious for not allowing students to attend the career fair if they were not in a literal matching suit. As she would remind them "matching top and bottom must be the same color." Isabella, like many working black students, could not afford a matching suit. She was standing there with a beautiful professional black dress with a navy cardigan, with a simple necklace, and her natural hair thick and pulled back in an elegant bun. She looked great. I watched in horror as the dean turned her away for not having a "matching suit!"

I ran and parted my way through the busy crowd to chase her down and offer a blazer that I had in my office. By the time I made it outside she was gone. I could only imagine that she scurried down the steps of the subway station in defeat after having gotten her sisters off to school, commuted on public transportation to get to campus, prepared herself to get a much-needed job at the fair—only to be turned away for something so arbitrary.

Everything in my body wanted to scream, to confront the dean, to do something, anything! So, I went back to my post determined. I then commenced to helping diverse students connect to the work they desperately needed. It was what my colleague from another department would refer to as "the underground network" in full effect. I was resolved in my own form of personal resistance. I refused to allow her actions to deter me from my purpose. In fact, my own rationale had already shifted because little did she know—I had just accepted a dream job offer that would expand my assignment to leading diversity attraction efforts for a large global organization in the bathroom an hour before!

This whole encounter and experience reminded me of a famous Amilcar Cabral quote as mentioned by Lopes (2010), "I am a simple African doing my duty in my country in the context of our time" (15). As I lay in my bed wide awake and still upset from what happened I thought to myself, this is what that quote means. I too am a simple African—doing my duty, in my country—in the context of my time. I am African, despite the fact that I was born in the United States. I am still African—it is my birthright, it's where my ancestors are from, it's where my forefathers and mothers dreamed of me. I am doing my personal duty—which is uplifting diverse students and professionals to advance their careers with purpose and well-being.

LESSONS LEARNED

In order for us individually to advance professionally, we must align our work with our gifts, many of which have been passed down to us. We must align our work with our purpose and our call to serve. I would argue that we are all called to serve some specific set of people and a particular issue or issues. As Cabral implied, as Africans, we have a duty. What is your duty? What is the context of your time? How can you impact change in the lives of those around you?

As Cabo Verdean women, we have such power. Just as Cabral and other freedom fighters of his time, their stories and our stories start in simplicity.

They came from humble beginnings but their commitment to their duty is what sets them apart. When we commit to our duty, our purpose, our calling that is when we tap into our greatest power. How can you determine your duty? Cabral has given us the formula.

THINK IN SIMPLE TERMS

Don't over complicate things. In too many instances, we take on too much as women. We are daughters, sisters, mothers, workers, caretakers, and so much more. We say "yes" over and over again to our own detriment. Being "simple" in my estimation is being humble, not fixating our attention on material accumulation or accolades but rather focusing our attention inward to attune to our duty, so that our motivations will be pure and those motivations will serve as our career compass, guiding us on our professional journeys and keeping us on the right path.

BE CLEAR ON YOUR DUTY

No one has the right to mandate your duty. So often parents impart their dreams and professional aspirations onto their children. Then in our adulthood, lovers and partners will assert their opinions on our work choices. Who gives them the right to determine your duty? No one! You alone have the right to determine your duty. Others can lend their ideas, but they shouldn't be the final decision maker in what you will pursue. Perhaps your duty is taking care of your family. Perhaps your duty is in the community or at a business. How can you determine your duty? Start with some introspection, evoke prayer to your creator for guidance, and ask yourself the following questions. Remember to be open to how the knowledge of your ancestors can provide you with some clues to your own path. Ask yourself questions such:

- What lights you up? What thing when you do it makes you feel good on the inside?
- How can you be of service? What gifts do you have that improve something or someone?
- Who do you have a heart to serve? (When you are around this group of people you feel deep emotion and connection)
- What issues do you feel most interested in?

UNDERSTAND THE CONTEXT OF YOUR TIME

"Timing is everything" as the famous quote says. This is entirely true when it comes to your career. We must be astute at paying attention to the rhythm of things as it relates to our *work* during the different seasons of our life. As women, our cycle in life often shifts where we serve and when we serve. Our careers often don't follow a linear progression. Our careers often take twists and turns to allow for balance between family and the rest of our lives. Also, I would argue that our society conditions us to think in a very neat black-and-white box of careers. It confines our dreams to the hallway of 9-5 and often does not include entrepreneurship or social impact work. God dreamed something bigger for you. Don't be confined by narrow thinking. Remain open and receptive.

INTERVIEW OTHERS TO INFORM YOUR AWARENESS

Understanding your occupational ancestry will help you to get clear on your gifts, talents, strengths, and career pathways. You will gain insight into why you gravitate toward certain tasks or lines of work. You can also relieve yourself of the pressure of thinking that no one else you know has done this thing before and so who are you to do it. We can ask questions, do research, and it can be freeing to know from whence you came.

There is always liberty when we know ourselves better and a part of our knowing each other better starts with learning where we came from. What did our family members do? What were they known for? Knowledge is power, as they say, so start asking.

If you were not raised by your natural family, even doing a DNA ancestry test and assessing the history of the respective groups of people you come from could lend you some insight.

EXERCISES TO HELP YOU UNDERSTAND
YOUR OCCUPATIONAL ANCESTRY

Interview your parent(s) and/or loved ones by asking the following questions:

1) What did you love to do as a child that your parents/guardians stopped you from doing?
2) What did your parents do for work?
3) What were your parents and grandparents gifted at? What did they offer those around them?

4) What were your siblings good at, passionate about? What did they do for work?

SELF-REFLECTION

1) What was I good at as a child? What have I lost along the way?
2) What did I naturally gravitate toward when I was younger?
3) What attributes do I have that remind you of others in the family?

Tap into your childlike creativity and draw a picture here of your occupational DNA, including words that speak to your inherited gifts.

CONCLUSION

What do the strands of your occupational ancestry look like? Woven together, what has God and the ancestors revealed to you about your duty at this time? Once you are clear, don't forget to share the lessons that you have learned with those around you. Visualize your success and encourage your children and their gifts. It's not too late. Affirm what they are good at, encourage their innate interests, and talk with them about their ancestors before them. The more of us that follow Cabral's model of simplicity, purpose, and timing, the better things will be for the collective. Nos Ku Nos.

REFERENCE

Lopes, Carlos. *Africa's Contemporary Challenges: The Legacy of Amilcar Cabral.* Milton Park: Taylor & Francis, 2013.

Chapter 15

Cooking as Ritual

Elizabette Andrade

OVERVIEW

I am grateful to the founders, organizers, and supporters of the Poderoza Conference for the opportunity and the receptive platform they created to empower women to share their stories of growth, resiliency, and healing. The Poderoza experience allowed me the space to use my native tongue (Kriolu) to tell food stories I never had a chance to tell a wider audience. It reconnected me to the deep oral traditions that make up our ancestral DNA and rekindled stories about cooking and well-being that would hopefully inspire others to reclaim the power of cooking for self-care and well-being. This essay is an outgrowth of, and reflections on my Poderoza experience. I have included snapshots of my presentation on the power of cooking and how it can positively impact our emotional and mental health, practices and rituals that are our birthright, and the hidden beauty of our oral tradition (storytelling) through cooking. Thus, this chapter is less about a prescribed way to eat, and more about a prescribed way to cook, the way our foremothers cooked, the way that connected us deeper to nature, each other, and ourselves.

My life-long relationship with food and cooking is rooted in my cultural upbringing as a descendent of Cabo Verdean immigrants, very much shaped by the generations of women who came before me. Women, who were all functionally illiterate, in the modern sense of the word, who possessed a greater literacy that schooling did not provide, and used the language and ritual of cooking to share energy, stories, emotions, memories, recipes, nourishment, and love. Through observation, story, and recipe telling in the oral tradition of the Cabo Verdean culture, I learned about the art and spirit of cooking.

They knew and emphasized the "how" experience of cooking and the importance of the hands who cooked the food, over the "what" of cooking, how to lean into cooking as a healing, meditation practice, how to transform food into the most powerful form of vibrational medicine. Cooking and being a *"cuzhera"* is my ancestral gift and yours. Memories, stories, and recipes are the buried treasures of our collective matrilineal connection, and cooking is a way to put ritual back into our lives and use it as a "roadmap to spiritual experience"(Bradford 1993, 102). Cooking is spirit work.

The cook, or "cuzhera" in the traditional Cape Verdean household, under most circumstances, was a role fulfilled by the mother or female. The *mundje de caza* or *"cuzhera"* was more than just a cook and keeper of space and recipes. She was the caregiver, the keeper of order, and the CEO of domestic life. More significantly, she was the keeper of ritual. Cooking in the Cape Verdean culture belongs to the domain of the heart and spirit. As a present moment activity, cooking quieted the mind and welcomed a yoking between the self and the food. The *cuzhera* intuitively knew there was no veil of separation, as cooking dissolved the blurred lines. To these trailblazing, wise women, cooking was an act of trust and courage, which done mindfully and intentionally, became a form of energetic intimacy that bridges the connection between the inner and outer worlds.

The generations of women before me were not literate in the functional, systematic sense, we today, qualify as literacy. Because they were unindoctrinated, they possessed an unadulterated awareness of their inner world, the natural world, and the interwoven worlds that created the backbone of community. Literacy, for the older generations of Cape Verdean women, was an innate intelligence that encompassed a whole sense of being. Through the hands, as extensions of the heart, the one who cooks sends their vibrational imprint and emotional energy. An example of this awareness can be found in their relationship with food and why eating food prepared by an unfamiliar cook, was unacceptable. They would often say, "E ka tudo arge se cume, qui bu ta come" ("It's not everyone's food that one should eat"). One can infer that the hands that prepare the food have the power to heal or harm. The responsibility of cooking was too sacred to be taken lightly, marginalized, or sacrificed.

Women have always intuitively known that food is more than fuel and nutrients. As the basis for human experience and health, cooking practices, along with an unspoken philosophy were passed down through the generations. Women knew there were more subtle forces at play and that their intention behind the food was life-giving. They knew that food was a transmitter of emotional and psychic energy and through the process, they could tap into the capacity to heal themselves and facilitate healing in others. Cooking was and is a form of conjuring, a form of magic that ancient alchemists would often refer to when transmuting one element or form into another.

My ancestral foremothers were homemakers and caregivers, working with the natural rhythms and cycles of nature, starting their dinner preparation in the morning hours, alongside breakfast, or shortly thereafter, maintaining the overall order of the kitchen space and nourishment of the family. The family meal was at the foci of care, a priority because growing up they knew night would come and "noite" was moonlight, stories, and rest.

Living well into their nineties and hundreds, *nha Donas*, with the exception of genetics, cooked daily, got proper rest and did not experience the stressors of the industrial, career-driven world. These wise women lived closer to nature, closer to the home, and the heart. They prepared nourishing meals without the latest high-tech equipment, latest nutritional facts, pre-packaged and pre-cooked ingredients. Cooking was a nonlinear and intuitive daily practice. Cooking was a heart-soul-spirit matter. It's what cradles tradition, helps define culture, roots families, and aligns communities.

"Sabola Ku Adju" ("Onions and Garlic")

She wanted to read, to experience life through words, to create new mental constructs of other realities, she wanted the freedom to express her thoughts with written words that captured those strong emotions, but instead her stories were captured in the meal of the day. The cuzinha was her canvas. She used her "cudjerao" ("large spoon") like Sashet's wand, scribing her energetic imprint and soul with each circular motion, as she came full circle to herself. With each stroke, she channeled and imbibed the healing energy of the ancestors far and wide. She felt the process so deeply, Ancient Goddess Bastet, ruler of home and hearth could feel them. She was a magician in the cuzinha. She used her intuitive knowing and wisdom, passed down through the oral recipe telling . . . to *pica* ("chop") *rafuga* ("saute"), *strela* ("scramble"), *giza* ("stew"), *bate* ("beat"), *ferbe* ("boil"), through bounty or famine ("Fome de mil-novsento-tritenove" /1939). She was my first teacher.

Seer and doer, the *cuznhera* was/is attentive to the intricacies of preparing a meal, details that may be overlooked by others. She incubated, processed, stored, and expanded upon them. She internalized the process and manifested, through will, desire and resourcefulness, a well-cared for meal.

If you've ever seen garlic and onions sweat and soften to the point of translucency, and experienced their sharp pungent aroma change to the taste of caramelized sweetness, you know of the power of *sabola ku adju* to transform any dish. A simple cook, my mother would say as long as you had onions and garlic, you had a meal. Onions and garlic were the foundations of most traditional dishes.

The title of *cuznhera* was a badge that had to be earned. *Cuznhera*, as the one who not only cooks but cooks well, demonstrates their aptitude and receives praise and responsibility as a reward for a meal well prepared. As a kind of informal rite of passage, at the age of 12, my mother thought it was a good time to send me to my aunt's house to cook for her family. She beamed with pride as she told my aunt that I would be preparing dinner for their family of eight. I was sent to perform what seemed to be a simple task of cooking rice and beans. I learned that my own energy and fear of failure led to just that. I learned that each *cuzinha* has its own energy and order, each stove its own temperament, each *caldera* its own signature.

These were my first lessons in perceived failure, in scaling up and why recipes, oral or otherwise, are not always successful, even if followed with precision.

> In order to be good at it, you must understand the foods with which you're experimenting: you need to know what temperatures they can withstand, how they react with other foods, how much of them is needed to produce a particular result. This kind of knowledge is difficult and time consuming to obtain. It's also extremely rewarding and useful, for it allows you to create wonderful foods, and it enables you to be flexible in the face of a nearly empty refrigerator (Curtin and Heldke 1992, 219).

This is the kind of knowledge, that has been passed down from generation to generation through oral tradition, from grandmothers to mothers, aunts to daughters. I learned that I still had much to learn about more than cooking.

"Monh Bunh" (Good Hands)

It would be five years after my "rite of passage" that I would arrive in Cabo Verde for the first time and stay in the small two-bedroom house my mother; one out of twelve children, grew up in, that still had no running water and electricity. My adventure began when it was time to prepare dinner before sundown. She gathered the lenha and brought it to the kitchen. Modern conveniences, like an electric stove, a microwave and toaster oven were put to shame. Their partnership was magnetic, as she struck the matchbook, a force seemed to draw the fire closer to greet the lenha to do the fire dance. From the way she guided her breath, to the rhythmic fanning of her hands, and what could be compared to smudging or energy clearing with sage, to the placing of the pots, she was in tune. She was at one with elements and her own voice. At that moment she was the fire, air, earth, water and the sound of her own voice. She baptized my ears with "te arge qui tenh hom bunh," there are those who have good hands ("upon the food"), which reinforces the idea of feeding the soul or soul food.

Women used their innate sensibilities to feel for desired texture, directly from the *panela*, "poorba" (taste) for the balance of salt and spice and to know if the gosto (flavor) was just right and their noses to announce the readiness of baked bread or couscous (a traditional cornbread eaten for breakfast with milk or coffee). They cooked by vibration and felt their way through the process "And when I cook, I never measure or weigh anything. I cook by vibration. I can tell by the look and smell of it. Most of the ingredients in this book are approximate. Some of the recipes that people gave me list the amounts, but for my part, I just do it by vibration" (Smart-Grosvenor 1970, xvii). With intention, their generational wisdom, and staple ingredients, there was not much else to juxtapose the process.

Our ancestors understood the use of the senses to navigate and find the balance between the inner workings of their own psyches and the outer world of homemaking and caregiving. Women who knew the power in their volcanic ash calderas, the power in their hands, how to activate their palm chakras to make magia ("magic"). Women who knew without explanation that in each palm of their hands, lies a vortex of energy, available to *"pila mindju"* ("grind corn with mortar and pestle"). They knew/know that their hands were creative instruments, the right being positively charged, sending directing energy and the left, negatively charged receiver. "Bodily knowledge" "acquired through embodied experience" is one way to describe it. A concept Curtin and Heldke (1992) expands on as a relationship of interconnectedness: "To know food—to know how to cook food well—does not require an abstracted, measurement-conscious knowledge, but rather a knowledge in the eyes and in the hands" (219). To know cooking was to trust and pay concentrated attention to nourishment and have faith in the unknown and unseen.

TRADITIONAL PRACTICES AND COOKING RITUALS

Chances are if you were born in a Cabo Verdean household or visited one, an offering of food and drink is custom upon arrival. In the Cabo Verdean culture, the hearth of the home has traditionally been the domain of women along with guiding the codes of conduct and behaviors associated with hospitality and temperance. It is not out of character for a Cabo Verdean mother to train up their children to understand that it is considered impolite to refuse a food offering, while at the same time, impress that greed, and overindulgence brings disdain and even shame (in extreme cases) to the family name. Hospitality and temperance are at the crux of family life and ritual, and as Some' (1999) defines, "is by its nature, a communal activity and act of creation" (35).

Traditionally, food is at the center of most Cabo Verdean practices, such as the rituals associated with birth, like "Noite Seite," the seven days of safeguarding the new life, and "Misa Seite," the seven days following the transition of a loved one. Culturally, when a person passes on, death is the marking of a yearly ritual. On the same day of each year, that person is honored and remembered. The newborn child was/is safeguarded and protected from negative spirits or energies for seven days and seven nights, during which time, women gathered and prepared food for the mother, such as "papa" (porridge) made with fresh butter, to assist and expedite the healing of the womb. There is a ceremony, there is collective memory, and always food. One of the most traditional foods prepared for rituals was *sopa* ("soup"). Broths ("caldo") whether made plant-based ("caldo verde"), with fish ("caldo piexi"), eggs ("caldo ovo"), meat, or foul. It should not come as a surprise that soups and broths are one of the most nourishing foods we can consume, given their ability to retain nutrients and use water as a way to carry emotions that come from the heart-brain, a more instinctual and non-cognitive way of perceiving reality.

The residual of famine, during the late 1930s and early 1940s, made food a serious matter. Food was not to be wasted or overindulged in. Food was to be respected and honored, yet it was also expected to be prepared well, satiating, and pleasing to the senses. *Gosto* ("flavor") was more about the energetic quality of the one preparing the meal than about the actual ingredients. The process was of higher regard than the product or end result. It's how the "cuznhera" transformed those ingredients that mattered most. The cuznhera was able to completely spiritualize the food so that those who ate it would feel the effects, nourishing food that would "faze arge prubetu" or have an overall positive effect on the eater.

Our foremothers knew that a meal prepared by a cook who there is an emotional connection to or affinity for produced a different response than a meal prepared by a stranger. They knew that emotions, or the "energy in motion," were being transferred. Cabo Verde's cultural cooking practices are heart-centered. Buhner (2004) stated, "When a person projects a heart-coherent field with caring, loving and attention, living organisms respond to the information in the field by becoming more responsive, open, affectionate, animated, and closely connected" (109). Cultures, as far back as Ancient Kemet knew that the heart was/is the highest organ of perception with the largest electromagnetic field in the body. It was the heart that was weighed against the feather of Ma'at. *Nha Donas* knew that true healing could not take place if the heart is out of balance, regardless of what they ate, how well they slept, or how much they moved their bodies.

In traditional African cultures, offerings to the ancestral realm were primarily food stuff, most of which were traditional to each culture or tribe. Traditional foods ground us in culture and fill more than our bellies. Every culture has and needs foodways. Foodways is the cultural, traditional, and historical context in which food is prepared and eaten, it is part of our cellular memory and reflects our ancestral practices. Honoring traditional diets is critical to our cultural connection, yet adaptation is not a new phenomenon and may be necessary, living at the intersection of two cultures.

Given its remote location, Cabo Verde's cuisine is known as one of the world's first fusion cuisines, with life stock coming from Europe; sugar, tropical fruits, and nuts from Africa and Asia; and America's beans, pumpkin, corn, and manioca ("cassava"). Today, more Cape Verdeans are living abroad than there are in the islands, which means our diets have and will continue to evolve. We have also moved further away from traditional agricultural practices that only deepened our connection with our food before cooking it. We are also experiencing more food and health-related illnesses and death. As we incorporate more non-traditional foods and are lured by the age of processed and mechanized, Western food and systems, cooking may be the one activity that can help ensure our health is not holistically neglected. Our ancestors stand behind us, as we reclaim our birthright.

Without foodways, we are disconnected from our ancestors and the collective wisdom that shapes who we are as not only Krioulas but as the powerful women we came from and were born to be. It is an honor, as women, no matter how many generations removed, to keep the cooking practices alive for generations to come.

When we (women and men) retrace the footprints of our ancestors, why and how they cooked, we "see the pot as your own head, and see the water as your lifeblood" (Kosho 2005, 110), that we are not separate, but a part of the process. When we are ready to restore our faith, redirect our attention, and reclaim cooking as a spiritual and ritual practice, then we are on the wider path to better health, harmony, longevity, and well-being.

REFERENCES

Bradford, Michael. *The Healing Energy of Your Hands*. California: Crossing Press, 1993.

Buhner, Steven. *The Secret Teaching of Plants*. Rochester: Bear & Co, 2004.

Curtin, Deanna, and Lisa Heldke. *Cooking, Eating, Thinking: Transformative Philosophies on Food*. Bloomington: Indiana University Press, 1992.

Kosho, Dogen. *How to Cook Your Life: From the Zen Kitchen to Enlightenment*. Boulder: Shambhala Publications, 2005.

Oldways Preservation and Exchange Trust. *Oldways Cultural Food Traditions: The African Heritage Diet*. Oldways Preservation and Exchange Trust, 2019. https://oldwayspt.org/programs/african-heritage-health.

Smart-Grosvenor, Vertamae. *Vibrational Cooking: The Travel Notes of a Geechee Girl*. New York: Doubleday & Co, 1970.

Some', Patrice M. *The Healing Wisdom of Africa: Finding Life Purpose Through Nature, Ritual, and Community*. New York: Penguin Putnam, 1995.

Part VII

PODEROZA REFLECTIONS

Chapter 16

Poderozas

Lifting as We Climb

Jess Évora

Poderoza. A word that means so much to me, to so many Cabo Verdean womxn (Kuns 2019), and the greater Cabo Verdean community. Womxn stems from the word "woman," which is rooted in patriarchy. I choose to use the term "womxn," as it is an intersectional term that aims to be inclusive of transgender womxn and womxn of all personal identities. Furthermore, Poderoza is a Cabo Verdean Kriolu word that translates to "empowered womxn." When I think of a Poderoza, I think of a strong woman who gives back to her community and who empowers other womxn as she moves along her own journey of personal growth.

When I think of a Poderoza, I think of my mother, Maria Teresa Évora, who worked so hard to earn her bachelor's degree while working two jobs and raising three children. To this day, my mother describes this as one of the most difficult times in her life. At times, the thought of giving up would slip into her mind after feeding me and my sisters (Jenni and Karina), doing our hair, putting us to bed after a long day of work, and still having hours of homework to tackle (homework written in English—her third language, which she was still learning).

Yet my mother was too driven to give up. She knew she was not simply doing this for herself but also her daughters, her husband, Jorge Tavares Évora, and her parents, Epifania and Candido. It would take her many years, but my mother would eventually become the first one in her family to earn a college degree.

Maria Teresa Évora walked the stage at the University of Rhode Island in May 2004. I was sixteen years old at the time. To this day, her graduation has been the proudest moment in my life. My mother's journey is my biggest motivator in life. It reminds me that I'm not only pursuing my dreams for myself but also my mother, my family, for all Cabo Verdeans.

A year after my mother graduated from college, my parents took my sisters and me to Cabo Verde for the first time. I was seventeen years old and extremely shy. I felt uncomfortable speaking Kriolu because I was not fluent. This discomfort made me nervous to go to Cabo Verde. This discomfort sat unyielding in my chest during that entire month-long trip. I remember, I simply resorted to speaking as little as possible. Although this is not a strategy I would recommend, it did allow me to observe more, to really take in the entire experience.

I remember realizing how far my mother had come, from the mountains of Gonçalinho-Ribeira Grande in Santo Antão, Cabo Verde—a country where there were no universities—to becoming the first in her family to go to college. That first trip allowed me to experience the land where my parents were born, the land that influenced so much of my childhood. It was life changing. I felt whole for the first time. I found a piece of my identity I didn't realize was missing.

After that trip, I left Cabo Verde even more proud to be Cabo Verdean, and even more grateful for every strong Cabo Verdean womxn in my life. My mother's story is just one of the countless stories showcasing the resilience of Cabo Verdean womxn. When I think of a Poderoza, I think of Michelle Rosa of Pawtucket, Rhode Island, who dedicates her time to giving back to her community by raising money for college scholarships for seniors at her former high school. I think of Mónica Coelho, a community advocate against domestic violence, and owner of English for All, an English language learning center in Praia, Cabo Verde.

Lory Brito, currently the only marine biologist in Cabo Verde who specializes in aquaculture, also represents Poderozas well. Lory is passionate about advocating for environmental responsibility within the Cabo Verdean community. I also think of Gina Sanchez Gibau, currently serving as associate vice chancellor of faculty diversity and inclusion at the University of Indiana in the United States. Through her dedicated work, Dr. Gibau demonstrates dynamic leadership as a Poderoza who advocates for womxn and leaders from underrepresented backgrounds.

I think often of the countless Cabo Verdean mothers, aunts, sisters, cousins, *vovós* (grandmothers) who made the difficult journey from Cabo Verde to a foreign country in the hopes of providing a better life for their family.

These Poderozas are all so beautifully unique. The common denominator here is that they all continue to engage in heavy lifting to make a positive impact in our community. They all lift as they climb. They unite and help others along the way as they move through their own individual journeys. In Kriolu, we like to say, *Junto, nos é mas forte* (together, we are stronger). This is a sentiment I hear often from the Poderozas in my life. And it is a belief I hold dear to my heart.

RAISING OUR VOICES TOGETHER

It was in 2017 that I first heard of Poderoza: International Conference on Cabo Verdean Women. The Poderoza conference was founded in 2016 and takes place every two years in Providence, Rhode Island. I had just moved back to Rhode Island after leaving for college eleven years prior. Leaving Rhode Island was not only a culture shock, but it was a reality check for me as a Cabo Verdean American from Rhode Island. I have often joked that a Cabo Verdean that steps foot outside of Rhode Island or eastern Massachusetts automatically turned into a unicorn. It's one thing to joke about this, but it's another thing to live it. The lack of visibility is a reality for many Cabo Verdeans living outside of Cabo Verde. We are often living unseen in plain sight.

Editors Luis Batalha and Jørgen Carling described the challenge of Cabo Verdean visibility in their 2008 book *Transnational Archipelago: Perspectives on Cape Verdean Migration and Diaspora*:

> While the emigrants have been central to Cape Verdean nation-building, they have nonetheless been an elusive minority in most of the places they have settled. Cape Verde is a remote country that most people in other parts of the world have never heard of. Cape Verdean immigrants have been mistaken for Surinamese in the Netherlands, Somalis in Sweden and Puerto Ricans and Dominicans in the U.S. (13)

After feeling invisible for so many years living in communities that had never heard of Cabo Verde, I made it a priority to attend the March 2018 Poderoza Conference. I didn't realize just how validating it would feel to be acknowledged as a Cabo Verdean womxn in such a public way. The event left me in awe of the incredible Poderozas in our community. I was re-energized and even more motivated to get involved in the CV community. I felt truly seen for the first time in a long time. I felt empowered.

I also left the conference grateful for the knowledge I had gained. This was actually the first time I had learned of the word *Poderoza*. I grew up with strong, empowered Cabo Verdean womxn in my life. Now, to be able to attach a meaningful name to these powerful individuals was a true gift.

As I continue to think of Poderozas in my life, I think of Professors Dr. Aminah Pilgrim of University of Massachusetts–Boston, and Dr. Terza Lima-Neves of Johnson C. Smith University, co-founders of the Poderoza Conference. They work hard to ensure that every Poderoza can have a voice and be celebrated both during the Poderoza Conference, as well as year-round.

Today, as a member of the Poderoza Conference planning committee, I am constantly filled with gratitude to have the responsibility to contribute to the empowerment of Poderozas. My role as the director of Content entails celebrating the accomplishments of Poderoza on a weekly basis. Essentially, my role is to lift as I climb.

A HISTORY OF UNITY FOR SURVIVAL

It was not until thirteen years later in 2018, at the age of 30, that I would return to Cabo Verde for my second visit. This time I returned on my own. Although my Kriolu wasn't any better, I was no longer that shy teenager. I am most certainly still uncomfortable with my Kriolu, but I've learned to lean into that discomfort as motivation to continue to improve.

This second trip allowed me to experience Cabo Verde through adult eyes. I better understood the impact of our history, our resilient people, and our rich culture. I better understood the important role that Cabo Verdean womxn played in both the development and survival of our culture in Cabo Verde and abroad.

The history of Cabo Verde's mass immigration has primed Cabo Verdean womxn to practice unity and support. In the 1980s, a whopping 90 percent of all Cabo Verdeans who migrated to Italy were womxn looking to secure employment to provide for families left behind in Cabo Verde (Silva 2015).

In the United States, although the first waves of mass migration were comprised of majority men, once Cabo Verdean womxn did arrive, they began depending on each other immediately, serving as heads of the households while remaining engaged in the CV community (Lima-Neves 2015). Depending on their community of sisters is a survival strategy that Cabo Verdean womxn continue to use today.

THE POWER OF LIFTING AS WE CLIMB

Psychologist Shawn Anchor's life work is focused on the pursuit of happiness and full potential. He explains in his 2018 book, *Big Potential*, that extensive research indicates that the secret to reaching big potential is to support and uplift those around us (Anchor 2018). In other words, we must lift as we climb.

In Michelle Obama's 2018 memoir *Becoming*, she writes, "There's power in allowing yourself to be known and heard, in owning your unique story, in using your authentic voice. And there's grace in being willing to know and hear others. This to me is how we become" (Obama 2018, 101).

This, in a sense, is the essence of lifting as we climb. This is also one of the main goals of the Poderoza Conference. The conference is about celebrating our story and our voices, which, as Michelle Obama writes in *Becoming*, is extremely important for both our personal *and* collective success.

This concept of lifting as we climb is the reason I created RanjaCV.org. *Ranja* means "to prepare" in Cabo Verdean Kriolu. Ranja CV is a nonprofit organization that aims to prepare, unite, and empower Cabo Verdeans to do great work in our community. One of the major focus areas of Ranja CV is our initiative to share stories of Cabo Verdeans across the world who are doing great things for our community. Our goal is to better connect with one another so that we can lift as we climb and make a collective impact in the Cabo Verdean community. This initiative has allowed us to celebrate incredible Cabo Verdean womxn—Poderozas!

We've published interviews with womxn like Samira Gomes, of Sweden, who are empowering women of color in the tech industry. We've highlighted the story of Marisa Solange, who is creating a bridge between Cabo Verdean and in her current home in Rotterdam, Netherlands, by empowering Cabo Verdean designers. We have also had the pleasure of sharing the story of Andrea Cleary, of Virginia, the United States, who discovered the power of mental wellness during her successful battle with Leukemia and is now sharing her lessons learned along the way.

Ranja CV is just one of the countless organizations aiming to empower and unite Poderozas, as well as the general Cabo Verdean population. We now have new organizations like Kriolas Professional Association and Kriolas Wellness Retreat, in addition to the longer-standing community organizations like Criolas Contra Cancer and Poderoza Conference. I am excited for the great impact we will make as we work together to tackle the complex challenges of the Cabo Verdean communities across the diaspora. I am especially inspired by the possibilities.

As I continue to witness the increase in unity among Poderozas across the world, I am often reminded of an African proverb that so beautifully defines the power of unity: "If you want to go fast, go alone. If you want to go far, go together" (Goldberg 2016, para. 1). Mary Church Terrell (1898), a black feminist pioneer and suffragist (and the co-founder of the National Association for Colored Women in 1896) seems to have agreed with this sentiment as well:

> And so, lifting as we climb, onward and upward we go, struggling and striving, and hoping that the buds and blossoms of our desires will burst into glorious fruition 'ere long. With courage, born of success achieved in the past, with a keen sense of the responsibility which we shall continue to assume, we look forward to a future large with promise and hope. Seeking no favors because of our color, nor patronage because of our needs, we knock at the bar of justice, asking an equal chance. (para. 24)

I'm rooting for all Poderozas. May we all continue to lift as we climb.

REFERENCES

Anchor, Shawn. *Big Potential: How Transforming the Pursuit of Success Raises Our Achievement, Happiness, and Well-being.* First Edition. New York: Currency, 2018.

Batalha, Luís, and Jørgen Carling, eds. *Transnational Archipelago: Perspectives on Cape Verdean Migration and Diaspora.* Amsterdam: Amsterdam University Press. doi: 10.2307/j.ctt46msd4, 2008.

Goldberg, Joel. "It Takes a Village to Determine the Origins of an African Proverb." *National Public Radio.* https://www.npr.org/sections/goatsandsoda/2016/07/30 /487925796/it-takes-a-village-to-determine-the-origins-of-an-african-proverb, 2016.

Kuns, Ash D. "WOMXN: An Evolution of Identity." *Summit to Salish Sea: Inquiries and Essays* 4, no. 16: 2–3. https://cedar.wwu.edu/s2ss/, 2019.

Lima-Neves, Terza S. "D'NOS MANERA: Gender, Collective Identity and Leadership in the Cape Verdean Community in the United States." *Journal of Cape Verdean Studies* 1, no. 1: 57–82. http://vc.bridgew.edu/jcvs/vol1/iss1/6, 2015.

Obama, Michelle. *Becoming.* New York: Crown, 2018.

Silva, Clara. "Immigrants from Cabo Verde in Italy: History and Paths of Socio-Educative Integration." *Journal of Cape Verdean Studies* 2, no. 1: 25–34. https:// vc.bridgew.edu/jcvs/vol2/iss1/4, 2015.

Terrell, Mary Church. "The Progress of Colored Women." *Gifts of Speech.* http://gos .sbc.edu/t/terrellmary.html, 1898.

Chapter 17

Poderoza Magic

Thoughts from the Audience

Stephanie Miranda Andrade

So much of our worthiness is tied to how much we can endure as women. This brand of "resilience" is cultural, is societal, is so very, very familiar to young girls who grow into women groomed for men who reject our humanity as part of their own conditioning. We learn to show grace, to swallow our pain whole, to live through violence, to give of ourselves, to remain soft, to remain silent—our mother's first tongue.

And much like women the world over, we learn to create magic where none exists. The Poderoza conference, in particular, was affirming, was moving, was timely, was indeed magic. A radical reimagination of how we tell our stories, it was an ode to our grandmothers who made our villages strong and our mothers who dare cross entire oceans so that we may have the audacity to see ourselves fully and outside the male gaze.

The gathering was dedicated to scholarship, to ownership, to visibility, to healing, to creating community. A safe space to take up space. An opportunity to learn, to reconsider our limiting beliefs, and permission to celebrate ourselves and women to look like us. To unpack and to grieve, to share, to feel valued and seen and heard.

Chapter 18

Sabura

Reflections and Intentions

Ivette Centeio Monteiro

When I first walked into a SABURA classroom, I immediately felt the spirit of the organization. SABURA stands for *S*tudent *A*mbassadors *B*onded *U*nder *R*ecreation and *A*chievement. At the time, I was a stay-at-home mom raising two boys, wondering if I would ever get back into a classroom. I had recently completed my graduate degree in elementary education. I wanted to become a teacher because of all the great teachers that impacted my life. When I reflect on my educational experience, I think about the personal impact that these educators had on me. I do not remember the lessons that were taught, the assignments that were given, or the tests I took. I remember the relationships that shaped me to become the educator I am today.

On my journey to becoming a teacher, I was exposed to the many challenges facing education today, as well as the many injustices. As a substitute teacher in Boston, I learned how many classrooms lacked adequate supplies for students. This made it difficult for students to thrive in the classroom. Interning at a private independent school made me realize how different education can be for those who can afford a quality education which caused me to ask the question, "Is a quality education only for those who can afford it?" During my student teaching experience, I realized the importance of having a teacher of color who resembled and validated students' experiences in the classroom and the effects of a lack thereof. I witnessed white teachers set low expectations for students of color and witnessed students secretly ask me for help when teachers failed to accommodate English language learners with comprehension. However, volunteering at SABURA exposed me to the joys of education again, where work became family.

I began teaching at SABURA in 2015. I volunteered by facilitating culturally and linguistically tailored arts and crafts activities. I worked with some students on creating family trees, and in the process, discovered my own family members. Who could've imagined meeting my cousin during a teaching lesson?! Only at SABURA! It was invigorating working on culturally inspired lessons, while speaking Kriolu, and connecting with students and their families. I then began building upon the "Back to Our Roots" curriculum and introduced students to the Cape Verdean folktale of "Nho Lobo." It was when the students created their own finger puppets of "Nho Lobo" and "Xinbinhu" while speaking Kriolu that I realized this is how I always imagined teaching.

When I reflect on what makes SABURA unique, I think about the two women who founded the organization. Dr. Aminah Fernandes-Pilgrim, a college professor of Africana and Transdisciplinary Cultural Community Studies, and Anita "Leny" Monteiro, the director of SABURA, created this grassroots organization to engage, teach, and empower students and their families. They created a board of directors that consists entirely of parents and grandparents within the community. These stakeholders, who are directly invested in the community, have provided their time, energy, and passion to continue to make the program run each and every year. For a program that began serving 50 students to now serve over 150 students in and around the Brockton area directly speaks to the power of influence these women have. They work tirelessly to meet the demands of the community in which they serve.

Anita "Leny" Monteiro began her SABURA journey while working at the Cabo Verdean Association in Brockton. She began working as a Youth Coordinator, developing programming and establishing a solid after-school and summer program that students and families trusted and truly enjoyed and benefited from. She later became the director at the Cabo Verdean Association and also served as a board member. It was there that she met Dr. Aminah Pilgrim, who was also a board member. When the two left the association, they then decided to build upon what they started at the Cabo Verdean Association and create SABURA, due to the demands of the families they left behind. The families felt the programming was no longer the same without the two women who started it. These families now serve as board members of SABURA. The evolution of SABURA is significant because it demonstrates how keenly aware they are of the needs of the community and how they actively work to serve those needs.

The mission of the organization, as stated on their website is "to educate, engage and empower youth and families through carefully designed, culturally and linguistically tailored programming that is affordable, safe and affirming" (SABURA 2018, para. 1). Although many schools and programs across the country are recognizing the diversity among their student body, it is known that our education system "is steeped in norms, traditions, and a lens that too often does not reflect and may not be supportive of this diversity" (Massachusetts

Department of Education n.d.). Many parents of Brockton today are keenly aware of the struggle for a quality education that is sometimes not afforded to them. Education can be viewed as a privilege instead of a basic human right. As one parent stated, "You have to ask, they won't offer [help]" (SABURA 2018, para. 1). As immigrant families struggle to navigate the American education system, programs like SABURA exists to help bridge that gap.

SABURA is the Cabo Verdean Kriolu word for fun. "It's the joy you feel at seeing a loved one or experiencing your passion. We chose this name to rebrand the experiences of education & recreation for Brockton children and parents" (SABURA 2018, para. 1). Today SABURA is more than a summer camp. SABURA has expanded to include an after-school program servicing recently arrived immigrant children, as well as providing ESL classes for families. SABURA is effectively bridging the gap by establishing strong partnerships with other organizations in the community, including Brockton Public Schools, Coordinated Family and Community Engagement, Coordinated Parent Leadership Action Network, and Harbor One to name a few.

The founders of the organization understand the complexities of education and the importance of rebranding and reshaping the experiences that Cabo Verdean children, Caribbean children, and African children in the Brockton area have collectively shared. Matias (2013) describes it as the constant struggle against the whitening of education and stated that culturally responsive educators "consciously or subconsciously were responding to a pre-existing loveless condition of the largely White teaching force providing instruction to students of color" (71). That is exactly what Aminah and Leny did. They responded by creating SABURA for the families in Brockton to reimagine education and recreation as a place where students and families thrive.

REFERENCES

Massachusetts Department of Education. "Culturally Responsive and Sustaining Schools and Classrooms." http://www.doe.mass.edu/odl/e-learning/culturally-resp -sust/content/index.html#/, n.d.

Matias, Cheryl E. "Check Yo'self Before You Wreck Yo'self and Our Kids: Counterstories from Culturally Responsive Teachers?...To Culturally Responsive Teachers!" *Interdisciplinary Journal of Teaching and Learning* 3, no. 2: 68–81, 2013.

Monteiro, L., & Monteiro, I. *Report on Cape Verdean (CV) Parents' Focus Group*, 2018.

SABURA. "SABURA Youth Programs: About Us." https://www.saburainc.org/ about.html, 2018.

Chapter 19

She Too, Dreams

Edna DaCosta

Born[1] in a village so remote, when it rained once in a great blue moon, the only road out of town became an endless horizon of floodwaters. She, like her siblings and all the children from that village somehow found joy in the arduous tasks of walking for miles to fetch water, and treasure hunted while collecting driftwood and tree branches so her mother would be able to cook what was, in most cases, the day's only meal. She was unaware that so early on in life she knew of an alternative fuel source, cow manure, which they used when driftwood was scarce. She and her sister collected it and dried it to be used as fuel for cooking. At the tender age of four or five, she took pride in being able to contribute to the daily chores of the house. She was able to wash dishes, sweep the concrete and stone-paved "poial," and even looked after her younger brother, who was two-and-a-half years younger. To this day, when she tells people she remembers the day he was born; she's looked at with skepticism. She is able to recount most of the details, and, at times, all, with the help of her older sister. She remembers having to become inventive, such as when the strap broke on the only pair of sandals she had. Together with her older siblings, they would carefully grab the loose strap, bring it up to a flame, let it melt a little, and quickly press it on the area where it was initially attached. That technique worked a few times until there were no more remedies, and she had to wait until her mother was able to save a little extra and went to the open market. The excitement of a new pair of sandals was so great that she did not mind joining her on the treacherous five-mile walk, barefoot. She also struggles with the memory of some experiences, which she later learned would be called "traumatic"—a trauma that paralyzes healthy emotions as it is concealed in the layered depth of family secrets for fear of embarrassment.

Fast forward to today and storing past and present memories and many experiences, some challenging, some sad, and some she joyfully recounts as blessings. She does not dwell on her hardships but looks at them as steppingstones, the arduous road of becoming that keep taking her to where she defines as her destination. In other words, her becoming has followed the poetic force of António Machado captured in his eloquent verses: "Caminante no hay camino, se hace el camino al andar" ("Traveler there is no road, one makes the road walking"). Thus, the fluidity of her being makes her free to dream, and her dreams of being free guide and shape her becoming. She dreams and is no longer afraid of sharing her dream, and for those who doubt her, she feels no necessity to prove them wrong, as she's too busy dreaming.

She is not the sole proprietor of her dream, as such is shared by the woman she values most. A woman who raised nine children on her own and left alone in a foreign country to raise five of her younger children, without money, without a job, without speaking the language, and without the technology of reading or writing but with the wisdom that transcends instrumental literacy at the highest level. What she lacked in conventional education she made up by her passion, compassion, and ethics. This woman of unmeasured courage was never blessed with the opportunity of an education and only learned how to write her name. Yet this same woman has had the ability to instill the importance of an education into her children as she shared her wisdom with them and modeled her defiance against the precariousness of life and thought them without lecturing the audacity of love.

I have been truly blessed, as along my journey I have met selfless individuals who have shared their knowledge with me, have mentored me, and have been a support system. I will forever be grateful to those individuals, but my dedication has a sole proprietor. Mom having you as my cheerleader and biggest supporter means more than my actual accomplishment. You have no idea how those phone calls on rainy days expressing your concern for my safety made my heart melt while my soul soared to its highest level. Your tiny eyes reflect so much pain, but yet infinite mounds of love. Your calloused hands spell resilience at its finest. Those three words "ai nha fidju," penetrate deep into my soul. You are and will always be my "Shero."

As a chapter of my life comes to an end, giving birth to the concretization of a dream, that of becoming a police officer, I reflect on all. I pray for the ability to perform to the best of my ability, to always apply the ethics instilled within me, to treat others as I would want to be treated, to strive for continuous learning while walking the path with humility, and to always come home safe to my loved ones.

NOTE

1. Edna DaCosta participated as a panelist at Poderoza I (2016). She reflects here on her Poderoza mother, her own journey, and the realization of her lifelong dream of becoming a police officer.

Part VIII

CONSEDJU ("ADVICE/WISDOM")

Chapter 20

Zau eh D'Pove

An Oral History of Isaura Tavares Gomes

Terza A. Silva Lima-Neves

THE IMPORTANCE OF AFRICAN ORAL HISTORY

In[1] an essay I wrote ten years ago, commemorating 550 years of Cabo Verde's discovery and 35 years of independence, I reflected on how most published accounts of Cabo Verdean history were reactionary and attached to colonial occupation and the subsequent struggles for survival.[2] I challenged this narrative because I had heard my family's stories and remembered my own happy childhood in São Vicente filled with fun nightly get-togethers at my grandmother's front steps, while an older prima/o or tia/o told scary stories as we cracked the shells and ate roasted peanuts. I also remember my grandmother's daily trips to the fish and vegetable markets, the various social activities she planned with her group of friends, how they would get up early to do daily walks to the beach, go for a swim, or catch up on the most recent town news or gossip. I yearned for more stories like these, of everyday Cabo Verdeans and how they lived their lives prior to and during colonial occupation, in spite of colonial occupation (Lima-Neves 2010). My concern was that these rich and important stories, which were not found in texts like the documented history of slavery and colonialism, would be forgotten and new generations of Cabo Verdeans, at home and abroad, would not know that their ancestors lived good for a living by design and with intention even in the face of oppressive structures or that among them existed brilliant women who kicked butt and took our nation's freedom during an armed struggled. Our family stories are part of the African oral history tradition that must be preserved.

African oral history is important because it tells the people's stories (Pilgrim 2008). It creates space for African people to reclaim our narratives in texts as well as assures that these stories get passed down through generations, preserving family history and cultural traditions, offering a counter-narrative to the existing scholarship on colonial history as the only way to tell Africa's stories. Now more than ever, African authors, filmmakers, and artists are documenting the continent's rich histories thus making a statement that personal accounts and experiences do matter and are important in telling stories and transmitting knowledge.[3] We see a new wave of critique of Western academia which has largely dominated knowledge production and set parameters around what is considered legitimate and true (Cohen et al. 2001; Patai et al. 1991; Romero 1987; Lima-Neves 2010).

In the case of Cabo Verde, its history has been immortalized through traditional songs by the queen of Finason, Nácia Gomi as well as poems, essays, and folk tales by Baltasar Lopes, Eugenio Tavares, and other members of the Claridade Movement, the Cabo Verdean Kriolu literary tradition from the early 1900s, and more recently, in the literary works of Vera Duarte and Germano Almeida (Lima-Neves 2012; Lopes 2019). Learning about the people in Cabo Verdean history is important in preserving national culture and pride. Still, the history of Cabo Verde written and told by the people of Cabo Verde remains limited. What does exist is largely in the Portuguese language and to a limited degree, in Kriolu, the language of the people. Kriola voices and experiences, however, have been largely absent in the history of Cabo Verde as historians, storytellers, and active participants.

CENTERING KRIOLAS IN CABO VERDE'S HISTORY

This chapter focuses specifically on the liberation movement from Portuguese colonial occupation in the 1960s and 1970s and centers on the voice of women during this period. I specifically focus on the life of pharmacist, politician, and women's rights activist, Isaura Tavares Gomes. Literature on African women has only increased in the last two decades. Although there is a surge of literature on African women, they remain marginalized and largely invisible in what Paul Tiyambe Zeleza (2005) calls "malestream African history" (11). We see this phenomenon, where the lives of African revolutionaries like Amilcar Cabral, Kwame Nkrumah, Nelson Mandela, Thomas Sankara, and Patrice Lumumba, for example, are documented in countless books and films but not the experiences of the women who also were actively involved in the same independence movements.

When explaining her choice to include men's work in her book on African American women in the civil rights movement in the United States, Belinda Robnett (1997) says, "no honest, and holistic account of the civil rights movement can and should exclude men" (6). Thus, in this same vein, we can argue that no honest and holistic account of any independence movement across

Africa should exclude women's voices. It's not that many women did not write, tell stories to their children, sing songs about their daily activities, or participate in the independence movement; many women did. The issue is that it hasn't been widely documented.

In the case of women in the Cabo Verdean independence movement, the only autobiographical published account that is available is Paula Fortes' *A Minha Passagem* (2013). In her book, she calls for "multiplication of the pages of our history, so that future generations can have a future that is simplified, by knowing the point of departure so that they can better know their destination" (Fortes 2013, 17). There are also popular articles and video interviews featuring other women who participated in the independence movement such as Zezinha Chantre, Lilica Boal, Elizabeth Reis, Dori Silveira, and Tutu Evora.[4] However, without proper documentation, we run the risk of a collective national erasure of a people's history inclusive of women's contributions to community and state, building, and development. Telling Isaura Tavares Gomes' story and her extensive contributions to her beloved homeland continues the tradition of centering the lives, voices, and experiences of Cabo Verdean women.

WHO IS ISAURA TAVARES GOMES?

Through two interviews, I document Gomes' personal and professional life (Lima-Neves 2012). The first section focuses on a chronological biographical sketch of her life and accomplishments. Consequently, in a conversational interview, the focus turns to her life's story in her own words. The goal of this essay is to document the life and contributions of Isaura Tavares Gomes as a woman of the people, one who joined the independence movement because she believed in freedom of expression for all Cabo Verdean citizens, one who pursued her dream of becoming a pharmacist because she was a girl who loved science, and one who often sacrificed motherhood and family life for the goal of creating a better society through the improvement of the nation's public health and nutrition infrastructures. Telling Isaura Tavares Gomes' story contributes to a growing body of oral history tradition that focuses on stories as imperative in documenting a complete history of African women, broadly speaking and Cabo Verdean society, in particular.

A committed Cabo Verdean citizen, daughter, mother, sister, and friend, "Zau" (Pronounced Zahh-ooooh) as she is known in her native island of São Vicente, is a bigger than life personality, who has dedicated herself to family, community, and country. It is this love and commitment to Cabo Verde and her people that has led her to a life well lived and of service.

A pharmacist, women's rights activist, and political figure, Isaura Tavares Gomes was born on the island of São Vicente, Cabo Verde, on February 22, 1944. Her mother, Maria da Luz Tavares Gomes sold goods at the local municipal market. Her father, João Lopes Gomes, whom she didn't meet, emigrated to Venezuela in 1947, never to return to Cabo Verde. Gomes was one of six children. She attended *Liceu Gil Eanes*, the country's first secondary school, graduating with distinction as the best student of her class in 1963. However, she did not receive a scholarship to continue her university studies in Portugal. A scholarship, instead, was awarded to a student with lower grades, a son of a Portuguese citizen, resident in São Vicente. This event affected her tremendously as she was a committed, young student. Without a scholarship and lack of education alternatives on the islands during the Portuguese colonial period, Gomes tutored high-school students in mathematics, chemistry, and physics to support herself and help her mother with household expenses. In October 1964, with the help of the island's only dentist, who would later become her longtime friend, Dr. Anibal Lopes da Silva, she was awarded a full scholarship to study pharmacy at the University of Coimbra in Portugal by the *Agencia Geral do Ultramar* ("General Overseas Agency"), which governed Portugal's overseas provinces. Gomes excelled as a university student, always at the top of her class. In addition to her academic scholarship, she was awarded additional scholarships as a top university student. This allowed her to travel during vacations to visit her mother in Cabo Verde. She also tutored classmates to earn extra money. Gomes completed her pharmacy studies, and subsequently, specialized in clinical analysis at the University of Porto. She worked in Portugal for a brief period, returning to Cabo Verde in 1970.

Gomes' political activism began as an adolescent in 1962, when she joined her fellow students at *Liceu Gil Eanes* in protesting the appointed Portuguese director of the school. Students were in favor of appointing a native Cabo Verdean, João Quirino Spencer, to this position. This protest resulted in the expulsion of many students, disciplinary action against some, and the involvement of the *Policia Internacional e de Defesa do Estado* (PIDE), the Portuguese secret police. During this time, Gomes' aunts were also involved in clandestine activities with the nationalist African Party for the Independence of Guiné-Bissau and Cape Verde (PAIGC), led by Amilcar Cabral (1924–1973). Their activities led to Gomes' family being harassed by PIDE. These events strengthened her desire to participate in the struggle against colonial rule in her homeland. Her university years in Portugal were informative as she learned more about colonial rule and political activism. The environment in Portugal was more conducive to student organizing and academic discussions on issues pertaining to colonial struggles around the world. Ironically, Portugal's universities were the training ground for many

African nationalists such as Amilcar Cabral, Aristides Pereira, and Pedro Pires of Cabo Verde, Agostinho Neto of Angola, and Joaquim Chissano of Mozambique, all who were to lead the armed struggle against Portugal's colonial rule in Africa.

Upon her return to Cabo Verde in 1970, Gomes led the clandestine PAIGC activities in São Vicente. In 1970, she would also marry Daniel Henrique Cardoso. He was the director of the *Chefe do Estado-Maior das Forças Armadas* ("Chief of Staff of the Armed Forces"). They had three children, Ernesto Daniel, Aleida Raquel, and Abel Djassi. They would later divorce in 1981.

After Cabo Verde's independence from Portugal on July 5, 1975, she worked with officials in Cabo Verde to transition from a single party to a multiparty system where the government could encourage development through tourism and allow citizens the right to vote for their leadership. Other members of her political party did not share her views. Disillusioned with PAIGC's lack of support for her ideas, Gomes left the party in 1981. As the first and only PAIGC female deputy, from 1975 to 1981, Gomes was responsible for the advancement of women's rights during her tenure with the PAIGC. In 1976, she co-founded the *Organização das Mulhers de Cabo Verde* (OMCV), the National Women's Organization of Cape Verde, and was a major player in passing the nation's abortion laws, making abortions legal. During the 1980s, she was instrumental in developing Cabo Verde's medical system and training its technical professionals. She was the director of pharmacy and trained the country's pharmacy and laboratory technicians. In 1989, she opened her own pharmacy, *Farmácia Jovem,* and clinical labora-tory, *Labo Jovem,* two years prior to Cabo Verde's transition to a democratic multiparty system leading to the privatization of state infrastructures. During the 1990s, she focused her attention on the advancement of women's rights. She rejected the existing patriarchal practices and spoke out against the suf-fering of women. Gomes believed all Cabo Verdean women should have access to the same opportunities as men, recognizing their own potential and accomplishing their own goals through education and training. She founded and served as the president of the *Associacão das Mulheres Empresarias de Cabo Verde* (AMECV), the Association of Women Entrepreneurs of Cape Verde, from 1997 to 2003. This organization offered education and training for women business owners. In 2001, Gomes also served as the president of the *Federação Caboverdiana das Associações de Promoção da Mulher* (FAM), the Cape Verde Federation of the Associations for the Promotion of Women.

In 2000, Gomes ran for, and lost, the mayoral race in São Vicente, as an independent. She finally won in 2004, becoming the country's first female mayor. In 2005, she formally joined the political party, *Movimento para*

Democracia (MpD), Movement for Democracy. In 2008, with the support of MpD, Isaura Gomes was re-elected as the mayor of São Vicente. In 2012, she resigned from the position due to health concerns. Now, during her retirement years, Gomes lives a quiet, simple life and exercises her duties as a Cabo Verdean citizen by giving her time and support to local organizations and social causes when need be.

FAMILY, CAREER, AND LIFE AFTER RETIREMENT

I sat down with Isaura Tavares Gomes at her home in São Vicente Island, Cabo Verde on February 3, 2019, for a conversational interview. We talked casually about her childhood, admiration for her mom, life as a student in grade school in São Vicente Island, and the obstacles she faced in pursuing university studies abroad, reasons why she joined the anticolonial movement as well as her sources of pride and joy. As a pioneering women's rights advocate, Gomes also commented on how far Cabo Verdean women have come since independence and offered her insight on the existing challenges.

Accompanied by my grandmother, I arrived at Tia (aunt) Zau's house on the morning of a sunny day in February, her birthday month. We sat in her beautifully large sun-lit living room, decorated with family pictures and exquisite art by African artists that she'd collected over the many years of travel. Tia Zau sat to my left on an ivory leather couch, and I sat on another couch with my grandmother, Maria. We began with chit-chat about the family, kids, work, and overall health. Once that was done, I nervously pressed "record" on my phone to begin the conversation.

Terza Lima-Neves (TLN): I'm interested to know what was your daily life like as a child?

Isaura Tavares Gomes (ITG): I had a happy childhood. I had an exceptional mother. I had a great second mom in your grandmother who is also an exceptional woman. I studied. I finished primary school. I was always a good student. Then in high school, I did well too. A child's life at that time was to play and study. So, we did homework and prepared to go to school. I consider that a happy childhood.

TLN: I heard that depending on the island on which you are raised, some families encouraged boys to go to school and not girls. Did your mom always encourage you to go to school?

ITG: In my time I don't think this was an issue, but everyone advanced based on their capacity.

Maria Rosario Silva (MRS): That was during my time. I remember that your (Isaura's) grandfather said that girls only went to school to find boyfriends (laughter)

ITG: That is interesting.

TLN: How did you decide what you wanted to study? Was it based on what was available at the time or what you chose?

ITG: It was both. I really liked chemistry. And that had a lot to do with pharmaceuticals. At that time, we pursued areas of studies that had available scholarships by Portugal. So, it was based on the availability of scholarships and the discipline I was interested in.

TLN: I find it interesting that you studied chemistry because of the current conversation about girls and women entering the fields related to science, technology, and math. And that your daughter, Aleida studied the same. My daughter Ema is interested in math.

ITG: That is very interesting and good.

TLN: Let's talk about your time at the University.

ITG: It was okay. I went to Portugal in a time where there was a lot of racism. I was there in 1963, way before the (Portuguese) revolution in 1974, that changed the ways of thinking and values in their people. But I suffered some racism. But the rest was normal university life.

TLN: But it didn't affect you in a way that made you want to come back to Cabo Verde?

IG: No. My desire to finish my studies and return was stronger than any reaction to racism. Also, Portugal as a society faced many difficulties. There were regions that I had visited where people had never seen a Black person before. So, it was normal that they'd have a different reaction.

TLN: Speaking of enduring racism, let's go back a little bit. I am very interested in daily life during colonial times. What were some of the things you could and could not do as Cabo Verdeans? For example, I heard that people couldn't walk barefoot on the city square.

ITG: Yes, that happened. There was also no freedom of the press. You couldn't say what you were thinking. In Santiago, for example, Batuku and Funana were not allowed. It was after independence that they could be expressed freely.

TLN: Now let's go forward a bit and discuss the challenges faced by women. I remember one time when you came to the United States to campaign and we were at a shopping center, I asked for your advice and opinion on when was the right time to have children. You told me, at the end of the day, the decision was up to me and my husband, that my mom, dad, and grandma weren't going to be there every single day to help with the children. So that helped with my decision.

ITG: It had to be a decision between you and your partner.

TLN: I always remembered that. And someone else that I spoke with was former Ambassador to the United States, Fatima Veiga who told me her professional decisions were based on the age of the children. She said she wanted to be in Cabo Verde during their formative years. That her international/diplomatic appointments came later. Was it a hard decision to study abroad, have children, and become a professional woman?

ITG: I finished my studies first and then I got married and had children. It was a normal decision after marriage to dream of having children.

TLN: In terms of being a working woman and getting into political life, was that hard?

ITG: I had a lot of support from my mother. She was my biggest supporter. To be able to have a professional, political, and personal life, you must have a supportive base. My mother supported me a lot in my children's education. This freed up a lot of my time to be in politics and a career.

TLN: To be outside of the country. I remember you were in Brazil one time . . .

ITG: It's always hard to leave your family, but you must create more options. I went to Brazil for additional training on nutrition and public health because I thought it would be important to the development of Cabo Verde.

TLN: And you traveled to Cuba as well, right?

ITG: Yes, for meetings during the movement. It was a Cuban women's congress. I also went to the (former) Soviet Union for trainings.

TLN: Did Cabo Verde receive a lot of support from the Cuban government and how important was it to our development?

ITG: It was very important. Many people received military and scientific training. Cuba has given us lots of support, and it continues today.

TLN: In terms of the women's congress, what were the topics discussed?

ITG: How to balance family life with political life because it was very important in the development of any country. We also talked about teen pregnancy, gender relations, family issues, education, women's involvement in the struggle for independence.

TLN: In terms of the comrades in the struggle—men and women, what could have been done differently? Were we fighting two colonialisms, the men and the Portuguese?

ITG: Yes, gender equality is a fairly modern concept so yes, it was present.

TLN: Did you ever feel less than or that men of the (political) party said that this is not a women's place?

ITG: No, never.

TLN: Based on what I have read on Cabral and others, women had an important role to play in the struggle.

ITG: Absolutely. He always defended women's rights.

TLN: We have made great gains in terms of women's rights don't you think?

ITG: We've made lots of advancement but still have many challenges.

TLN: What do you think are the biggest challenges that women face today in political life and society in general?

ITG: In political life, we have to strive for more women in political parties. Because when you start at the political party level, then you can ascend to other areas like parliament and national government. At the general level, I think Cabo Verdean women have fought tremendously for self-emancipation, but we must continue to fight to end violence against women. To spread the message not only to men but also to women. Women have to refuse to accept psychological and physical violence. This is a major challenge we must combat in our society.

TLN: Do you think the state has done enough to combat the challenge?

ITG: In terms of legislation, laws, yes. It's good but we know that laws are not enough. You must have conditions where these are applied. In this aspect, we are in an evolutionary process with the creation of the Institute for Gender Equality which is at the vanguard of the movement.

TLN: What is your biggest source of pride in your professional and your personal life?

ITG: In my professional life, opening my own companies Farmacia Jovem and Labo Jovem (pharmacy and laboratory). In my personal life, having a family and three children.

TLN: So what is the day-to-day life for Isaura Gomes during retirement?

ITG: I read a lot, romantic novels. I like to follow Cabo Verde and international politics. I like to watch the news. I like to listen to music.

TLN: In terms of authors, who do you like?

ITG: It's more about themes. I like to read Cabo Verdean history books. We have a new generation of historians who write our history very well.

TLN: Do you still love to dance?

ITG: I do like it but I don't dance anymore.

TLN: In terms of music? What and who do you like?

ITG: I like Elida Almeida, Cremilda Medina, Assol Garcia, Neusa . . . I love Cabo Verdean artists.

TLN: If you could go back in time, are there any regrets or anything you could've done differently?

ITG: Generally speaking, no. I don't have any issues that were not resolved.

TLN: What advice/lessons have you given your children about life in general?

ITG: Live life based on moral values, humility, honesty, and solidarity. The more you're willing to give, the more you receive. We have to be open to others so that we are able to receive help ourselves.

TLN: Do you feel valued by the Cabo Verdean society as someone who has done a lot for her country?

ITG: Yes, yes, I have received many medals and awards, and words from people recognizing what I have done.

TLN: What is your favorite place in the world, besides Cabo Verde?

MRS: She has been to many places.

ITG: Yes, I have. That's tough. I have visited many places, but I love Holland. I like Portugal too because it's familiar, since my university days.

TLN: Speaking of Portugal, the concept of neocolonialism. My students always ask me about the constant presence of foreigners like China and Portugal in Cabo Verde. What are your thoughts on the presence of Portugal and China in Cabo Verde?

ITG: This is sort of natural. Like France's privileged position with its former colonial subjects. There's the language connection too. England as well. But it doesn't always mean that it's colonialism. It's a natural relationship.

TLN: How about China in Africa?

ITG: China is following its international political agenda and diplomacy. When China plans, it does long-term planning. It is merely carrying out what it has been planning for a long time. But I am sure the United States is not very happy about it. China continues to gain space in Africa.

TLN: I have always admired your friendship (speaking and pointing to ITG and Mãe).

ITG: Yes? Like sisters.

TLN: I want my sisters and I to have this type of friendship. You can be in the same room without speaking to each other, but you feel each other. I have observed this since a young age.

ITG: Yes, we feel each other. She's like a second mom, an older sister.

MRS: We were five (siblings). The others left for a life abroad and the two of us stayed and became closer.

TLN: It affected me profoundly. My parents raised us to be close, but I also had your friendship as an example. Because of your friendship, I learned that family is not always about blood.

MRS: I don't mean to cut you off, but I was in conversation with (omitted name) and I don't remember why but we got on this topic, but she said, "Zau considers you family, you are her family."

ITG: I told her that? I don't remember that but if she said it then it's true. She is right.

MRS: We are not blood, but we were raised together. We are family.

ITG: That's right.

TLN: I think we're done, right? I think that's it . . .

ITG: Okay. Sonia, How's lunch coming along?

REVOLUTIONARY MOTHERING IN THE CONTEXT OF NATION BUILDING

Thanks to my grandmother's intervention, Tia Zau granted me the second interview; something she doesn't normally do nowadays. She prefers a quiet life surrounded by family after a long career in the public eye. As her sister and close confidant, I know that my grandmother would know how to approach Tia Zau to secure my interview. I was nervous about this visit because I knew it wasn't just the regular family visit to catch up on life over a delicious three-course traditional meal prepared by her longtime house manager, Sonia.

Tia Zau and my grandmother, Maria, known to family and close friends as "Mãe" or mother and locally as "Ia" (eeh-uh), grew up together in the 1950s. Born in São Nicolau Island, my grandmother was orphaned at an early age and has little memory of her birth parents.[5] She was sent to live in São Vicente with Tia Zau's family while other siblings were sent to Santiago Island. These two women developed a sisterly bond that continues today. It was important for me to include my grandmother in this conversation with Tia Zau for two reasons: (1) Without her, the interview wouldn't have taken place. It's the trust built between the two women over five decades of sisterhood that granted me entrance into Tia Zau's sacred space and to talk about moments in her life that may not have been easy to revisit and (2) I find it important to highlight supportive sisterhood between Cabo Verdean women as key in documenting African history, for our survival as well as essential in personal and professional development. Since I could remember, my grandmother has been Tia Zau's travel partner and confidant. I recall their weekend trips to a resort in nearby Santo Antão island as well as being closed up in their rooms holding serious decision-making conversations about topics I would try to unsuccessfully find out about as a child, through holding my ears close to the door. For me, their weekend trips and self-care Sundays represented an authentic sisterly bond. This carefully crafted sisterhood is not born from them being biological sisters but rather from the African tradition of Ujamaa, where people in communities take care of each other because they are part of the same community.

For African women, when doing work outside of the home, the personal has always been political. In light of the work Tia Zau was doing, framing family and community support in the larger context of women's rights, nation building, and development helps us to understand how difficult it was for women to be involved in political life without support, especially if they had children who needed to be cared for. This added a layer of responsibility that women had to consider as they made professional decisions. During our conversation, Tia Zau talked about the importance of her mother's support in her ability to complete studies in Portugal and later, continue professional training in Brazil, the Soviet Union, and Cuba. She discussed how hard it was to leave her children, but that her travel abroad was necessary in receiving training so that Cabo Verde would have more options in the areas of public health and nutrition. Thus, leaving her children behind was a sacrifice and responsibility she had to make for her country and its citizens. For Cabo Verdean women, nation building was necessarily a revolutionary community effort, in that some women would go abroad for training and others would stay home to care for their children, and both roles were equally important. The support Tia Zau received from her mom, my grandmother, and other women in her family, demonstrated that they understood the importance of her work in creating Cabo Verde's national infrastructure and improving the lives of Cabo Verdean citizens, particularly healthcare that impacted women's reproductive health. In a broad sense, these women understood and carried out, Ujamaa.[6] They understood that Zau belonged to them, but she was also a woman of the people of Cabo Verde. Documenting the complexities of these intricate relationships is essential for a nation's collective memory.

Isaura Gomes Tavares is one of many African women from Cabo Verde who made invaluable contributions to the development of their homeland as well as sacrificed their personal and professional lives for the greater good. Properly documenting their stories is imperative so that their accomplishments are cemented in their rightful place, the nation's collective memory.

NOTES

1. Portions of this chapter were originally published as Lima-Neves, Terza Silva (30 September 2012). "Gomes, Isaura." *Oxford African American Studies Center.*

2. Isaura Tavares Gomes is known as Zau (Zahhh-ooh) to the people of her home island, São Vicente. During her tenure as the first female mayor of Cabo Verde, she was known as *um amdjer de pove* or a woman of the people. She was always out and about in the streets of the city of Mindelo socializing with her fellow citizens, at local restaurants, and concerts. As an elected politician, everyone marveled at how easily accessible she was and how she genuinely connected with the people on a daily basis.

3. See and hear for example https://www.audible.com/blog/arts-culture/this-man-embodies-a-thousand-years-of-west-african-oral-history.

4. I wrote and published a popular article in English on my website, detailing the names and work of the women in the struggle for independence. It can be accessed here: https://www.terzalimaneves.com/the-tea-with-dr-t/heroinas-dnos-terra-cabo-verdean-women-34-years-after-independence. The existing accounts which include magazine and newspaper interview as well as video interviews are in Portuguese.

5. Most Black communities on the African continent and in the diaspora can relate to my story of families that have been born not out of biology but out of long-standing traditions that reflect the African proverb that *it takes a village to raise a child*. Families are often born out of necessity such as death of parents and migration. For my grandmother, her parents both passed away leaving behind three small children. This was common during the 1930s and 1940s, a period in the country's colonial history when half of the Cabo Verdean population perished from illness and hunger due to long periods of drought. Because of these harsh socio-economic conditions, children stayed with grandparents and other family members while their

parents emigrated in search of better opportunities. This continues to be a common occurrence among Cabo Verdean people, leading to new families being created.

6. I am thankful to my friend and colleague, Dr. Julia Jordan-Zachery for helping me develop this idea, the importance of collective mothering in the context of nation building.

REFERENCES

Fortes, Paula. *A Minha Passagem, Praia: Fundacao Amilcar Cabral*, 17, 2013.

Lima-Neves, Terza. "Commemorating Cabo Verde's 550 Years of Discovery and 35 Years of Independence: What is our True History?" (5 July 2010). https://www .terzalimaneves.com/the-tea-with-dr-t/commemorating-cabo-verdes-550-years-of -discovery-and-35-years-of-independence-what-is-our-true-history.

Lima-Neves, Terza Silva. "Almeida, Germano de." *Oxford African American Studies Center* (30 Sep. 2012). Accessed 30 June 2020. https://oxfordaasc.com/view/10 .1093/acref/9780195301731.001.0001/acref-9780195301731-e 48224.

Lima-Neves, Terza Silva. "Duarte, Vera." *Oxford African American Studies Center* (31 May 2015). Accessed 30 June 2020. https://oxfordaasc.com/view/10.1093/ acref/9780195301731.001.0001/acref-9780195301731-e-50507.

Lima-Neves, Terza Silva. "Gomes, Nácia." *Oxford African American Studies Center* (30 Sep. 2012). Accessed 30 June 2020. https://oxfordaasc.com/view/10.1093/ acref/9780195301731.001.0001/acref-9780195301731-e-48838.

Lima-Neves, Terza Silva. "Isaura Tavares Gomes." *Oxford African American Studies Center* (30 Sep. 2012). Accessed 30 June 2020. https://oxfordaasc.com/view/10 .1093/acref/9780195301731.001.0001/acref-9780195301731-e-48838.

Lopes, Baltasar. *Chiquinho*. Original Portuguese Text, 1947. Translated to English by Isabel Feo Rodrigues and Carlos Almeida. Tagus Press (UMass Dartmouth), 2019.

Pilgrim, Aminah. *"Free Men Name Themselves:" Cape Verdeans in Massachusetts Negotiate Race, 1900–1980*. Dissertation (History), Rutgers University, 2008.

Robnett, Belinda. *How Long? How Long? African American Women in the Struggle for Civil Rights*. Oxford: Oxford University Press, 1997.

Romero, Patricia. *Life Histories of African Women*. New York: Humanities Press, 1987.

Zeleza, Paul Tiyambe. "Gender Biases in African Historiography." In *African Gender Studies*, edited by Oyeronke Oyewumi. New York: Palgrave Macmillan, 2005.

Chapter 21

A Letter to Inez Santos Fernandes

Aminah Fernandes Pilgrim

Dear Mama,

I can hardly believe that it's been about thirty years since you left us. It still feels like yesterday, and the thought still brings tears to my eyes. I have a picture of us (1970's you, holding me as a wide-eyed baby, your granddaughter) on my dresser, my *"kombra."* I still hear you saying that word in your Brava-Fogo Kriolu that I loved to hear come off your tongue. It sounded like sweet honey, and I longed for it to drip from yours to mine so I could speak to you in the same sound. I long for every bit of your love, and I miss you so much! *Forti sodadi*!!! I'm beginning to cry as I write this, as I think of ALL you are!

Guess what? I can finally speak Kriolu (well, still learning every day) . . . I imagine our conversations sometimes—adult me talking with my muse. What a trip that would be! I shake my head. I take a deep breath; this is harder than I thought.

In this letter, I want to tell you about my journey and about *Poderoza*. Your picture was actually included on the 2020 media; we declared it the decade of the Kriola, and it felt like such a gift to be able to honor you in a very small way there. It was an aged picture of gorgeous, younger you; I wonder how old you were. I only have some fragments of your story. You eloped and married at age sixteen. You were a mother of fifteen children with Ben Fernandes, who was much older than you. You were born and raised in Onset, Massachusetts. You were the daughter of a well-known midwife and matriarch of the community. You became a matriarch in your own right. There wasn't a place I could go around the Cape where people didn't know your name. I loved that. It made me feel important growing up when I felt so unimportant in so many spaces. Anyway, I was then, and always have been, in awe of you and your life. I'll never forget the advice you gave me about education. You told me that, as a girl, at age twelve, you loved school (especially math), but you had to drop out to work in the cranberry bogs and the family store and support the home. You told young me to go as far as I could and to get all the education that I can. I remembered that when I was about to quit my Ph.D. program. I wanted to finish for you/ for us. As you already know, my angel, I did and so many doors have opened since then. But this letter is about the Poderoza Conference and my journey leading up to this moment, this collection.

You are my earliest introduction to the idea of feminism. Yet I don't think I had the vocabulary to name that thing until probably high school. In particular, I had a chance to do a literature project in which I could self-select the books, and I chose books by women of color. My focus was on *The Color Purple*. In reading reviews and analyses of the book, and also bios of the author Alice Walker, I found it. In fact, I fell in love. As you know, I was in a predominantly white school with a very white, colonized curriculum, and I suffered in that situation. But that project gave me a sense of finding home—both in the research and writing and in the exploration of women scholar-activists telling women's stories. I don't like "regrets," but if I have one, it's that I never recorded your story, in your own voice, before you passed away. I guess much of my work has been symbolic of trying to get back to that voice, ever since.

Yours has been the voice in my heart and mind for my entire life. Your values—our family and cultural values—are my compass. Your legacy set the bar high for me, and I work in your name. You taught me everything I know about being Cabo Verdean, being Kriola . . . When people tell me I act like I was born there, I know what they mean. They are telling me about your traditions. In fact, I think this is what Margaret Busby (2019) talked about in the great collection *Daughters of Africa* when she wrote about the ways Black women are nurtured by history and tradition in a spiritual way.

Indeed, we are. Indeed, I am nurtured by our collective history and by tradition. That book is just one of the books that paved the way for collections such as this one. Yet I digress.

First, let me share some personal reflections on some of the experiences that have informed my own feminism, as well as moments in my life history that led to the first Poderoza in 2016. You'll see that I made so many mistakes—ones I feared you'd be ashamed of had you lived to see them. Yet I always tried to live by the adage "to whom much is given, much is required." I tried and I try to serve, and to empower others, lift as I climb—what I learned from African American feminist pioneers like Anna Julia Cooper, Ida B. Wells, and Ella Baker (just three of my heroines).

There were many childhood wounds, Mama, some with scars so deep I can't seem to access them for healing. I coped by burying myself in work, and I poured myself into it all to wash my pain away. The idea of you kept me going at my lowest moments. It has all informed my teaching, research, community organizing, and youth work. Those wounds must mean nothing where you are, yet just to fill you in . . . so you know why I "go so hard." I experienced molestation, bullying, and racism in elementary and middle school and serious isolation. Each death in our family hit hard. I didn't feel the full brunt of losing you and losing family until college. There, in North Carolina, I confronted being "black," discovering I was "not black enough" in the U.S. south, and then young adulthood . . . sexual assault, more isolation, depression. But I met Maya Angelou in college, and I'll never forget that moment! I read her book one summer at your house, and then when I saw the made-for-TV film based upon the book, I had the first inkling of wanting to publish my writing. Anyway, I met many of my favorite authors and icons along the way—but no "star" ever impressed me as much as you did. Okay, meeting Rosa Parks came close . . . I'm making myself laugh! I just mention these as a way of saying I felt your hand on me always, experiencing exceptional grace and blessings in the midst of every trauma and challenge. I fell apart many times, and the thought of you, Ma, Dad, Ayana, Hasani (and the whole tribe) always knit me back together.

I got through college, graduate school, and moved back home to Massachusetts to only be told I'm not Cape Verdean, not Kriola, or I'm a "fake Cape Verdean." I didn't fully understand the comments then, but I get it now. I couldn't speak Kriolu fluently. I am Barbadian as well as Cabo Verdean born here, on and on, and on. I didn't seem to fit in anywhere in Brockton when I first arrived here (still living here now in the midst of the 2020 pandemic, the ongoing 400+ year pandemic of white supremacy and racism, and the global uprising). In 2007, I received the "Cape Verdean Woman of the Year" award from the Associação de Mulheres, led by Maria Eugenia DaSilva at the time, and the online news/community site Forcv.com. Mama, I was so filled with shame. I was in an emotionally abusive relationship at the time. I was navigating an experience of duality that so many women know all too well—one of simultaneous visibility and invisibility, voice and voicelessness, professional presence yet domestic oppression. How could I be an educator and community activist, working toward women's empowerment, and yet allow myself to be treated in this way? I felt like I truly was fake, and I worried that so many would lose respect for me.

My theories and practices were out of sync. I was, and in many ways still am, what Roxanne Gay (2014) calls "a bad feminist" (5). She writes:

> I embrace the label of bad feminist because I am human. I am messy. I'm not trying to be an example. I am not trying to be perfect. I am not trying to say I have all the answers. I am not trying to say I'm right. I am just trying—trying to

support what I believe in, trying to do some good in this world, trying to make some noise with my writing while also being myself. (Gay 2014, 5)

It's risky sharing this with you here, writing about the personal in this book, in this way is "messy" and in many ways too human for academia. Yet this is what has made Poderoza work, and this is the work it has done inside of me. This entire collection attempts to make some feminist noise and to do some good in the process. Besides, as the epigraphs I included at the top of the letter suggest, it's about time to take off the masks and contribute to moving the transnational Kriola Diaspora forward. I chose those quotes from that particular classic, feminist collection *This Bridge Called My Back*, because it's another model of the work this collection represents. There are historical letters in that collection that perform the same labor. I honor those sister-scholar-ancestors with this letter styled after theirs, in our book modeled upon their work.

My story—like yours, like each of ours—defies simple explanation. It has been a journey to get back to my roots and revolutionize the way I live. To do what "msafropolitan" Minna Salami compels us to do, that is, change our illusions. Poderoza has changed illusions about Kriolas and has built a movement around this #rebranding and #reclaiming what was lost.

If you were here, I would ask you what you lost? Or what was stolen from you in addition to school? What wages did you and our ancestors pay for our privileges? Thankfully we know from elders like Isaura, a Tia to Terza, whom I partnered with to co-create the Poderoza movement. Terza Alice Silva Lima-Neves is such a force! You would get a kick out of her, for sure! She and her work have made a true difference in my life and our journey together on the road to Poderoza and made a sisterhood out of a professional friendship.

We both know that Poderoza contributes to forging new intellectual and community ground. It's become a space that has given birth to a new kind of Kriola feminist consciousness. The first and second Poderoza Conference events were about lifting our voices, redefining our image in opposition to the well-rehearsed stereotypes, and healing the traumas that have plagued so many of us. 2020 Poderoza was about "Making History" and the "Decade of the Kriola." The intention was to create a thread that documents the work being done all over the Diaspora in this moment and that captures that momentum of the movement, that is clearly forging a kriola feminist consciousness—one that began with our ancestors in the Independence struggle who laid the groundwork and institutionalized women's rights into the framework of the new country. Ours is a feminism, similar to other, historical women of color feminisms, that represents both social and academic labor.[1] It is very clearly rooted in our beloved culture, and as such, it speaks truth to the power of the multiple patriarchies within which we live, work, and move. The (West) African, the Portuguese, the European, the Catholic, Christian, Jewish patriarchies, the colonial and postcolonial patriarchies, the U.S. white and black patriarchies, and all of those that appear wherever we exist in the world—including what bell hooks calls "the enemy within" which is the internalized sexism that we express ourselves toward one another. Thus our feminist work necessitates rigorous, intentional inter and/or trans-disciplinarity—history, political science, sociology, anthropology, oral history, ethnography, poetry, popular culture, African feminism, African American womanism, intersectional feminism, social media analysis, black studies, and so on. The Kriola feminist consciousness makes room for bold expressions of sensuality and style (true to African aesthetics), but insists upon respect for our equal power and positionality within the spaces where we live, work, love, and exist.

The Poderoza Conference and this collection of essays and scholarly articles is what feminist poet Chrystos (2015) has called "a theory in the flesh" (23). She states,

A theory in the flesh means one where the physical realities of our lives—our skin color, the land or concrete we grew up on, our sexual longings—all fuse to create a politic born out of necessity. Here, we attempt to bridge the contradictions in our experience:
We are the colored in a white feminist movement.
We are the feminists among the people of our culture . . . . (Chrystos 2015, 23)

The Kriola feminist consciousness is fractured, complex, multilayered, multicultural, and multilingual mirroring the individual and collective identities of Kriolas ourselves. Poderoza's intentional work is to unify and document, to be a bridge between and to us all. As Chrystos (2015) says above, and continues: "We do this bridging by naming ourselves and by telling our stories in our own words. The theme echoing throughout most of these stories is our refusal of the easy explanation to the conditions we live in" (23).

Mama, as I have been trying to tell you, this book has many sources of inspiration. For me, again, one of the most significant ones is the classic women of color feminist collection, *This Bridge Called My Back*. Words from the introduction by co-editor Cherríe Moraga (2015) could be easily related to the project of Poderoza in this book. She writes:

I think: what is my responsibility to my roots—both white and brown, Spanish-speaking and English? I am a woman with a foot in both worlds, and I refuse the split. I feel the necessity for dialogue. Sometimes I feel it urgently. But one voice is not enough, nor two, although this is where dialogue begins. It is essential that radical feminists confront their fear of and resistance to each other because without this, there will be no bread on the table. Simply, we will not survive. If we could make this connection in our heart of hearts, that if we are serious about a revolution—better—if we seriously believe there should be joy in our lives (real joy, not just "good times"), then we need one another. We women need each other. Because my/your solitary, self-asserting "go-for-the-throat-of-fear" power is not enough. The real power, as you and I well know, is collective. I can't afford to be afraid of you, nor you of me. If it takes head-on collisions, let's do it: this polite timidity is killing us. (Moraga 2015, 34)

Like Moraga (2015) said, "We need one another" (34). We need one another to work against and defeat the multiple patriarchies that oppress us. We need one another to affirm that we deserve more, that we *are* more. Indeed, the women of ICIEG (CV Institute for Gender Equality & Equity), led by Rosana Almeida, and the many active feminists in Cabo Verde (Clementina Furtado, Joana Rosa Amado, Idalina Freire Gonçalves, Laurença Tavares, Vicenta Fernandes, Carla Carvalho, Roselma Evora, & many others) have declared this very truth in the recent past, working and winning changes in parity laws in the archipelago in 2019. They also had hard-won victories to secure legal protections for children to prevent further generations suffering from incest or other forms of abuse. And since our Cabo Verdean Diaspora is a set of simultaneously overlapping, interlocking Diasporas including a very powerful and active digital diaspora, several movements have taken place along similar timelines in various spaces including participation in the current Black Lives Matter movement. Poderoza has intervened in this space, led by Terza, with her own dynamic online presence. The many examples of Kriola feminist consciousness, that have emerged online (many of which we believe have been inspired by the Poderoza Conference and its highly visible presence on social media), represent what Minna Salami describes of her own work: "feminism with critical reflections on contemporary culture from an Africa-centered perspective." She argues: "No one but African women ourselves can bear the responsibility to protect the histories of African women and to connect them to the situations of today" (Salami 2013, para. 4).

As Poderozas, we are the keepers of our own histories. We speak the history makers' names so that they no longer remain invisible. Who else would speak for us? Who else would bear witness to our pain? Who else can sing our song or laugh with us in a way that echoes what we know? We are the difference. The difference between Madonna leading the singing and performing of *Batuku* and Nha Nácia Gomi leading *Se Mosinhus y Batukadeiras,* is that traditional call and response that vibrates with over 500 years of history. We are the difference between "Rádio Kriola" (a 2018 album recorded by a *Portuguesa* who says she is influenced by sounds from Brazil, Nigeria, Cabo

Verde)—one of the results one finds when doing a search for "Kriola song writers". . . and Jenifer Solidade, Mayra Andrade, and Elida Almeida. We are the difference between the reality and the song lyrics and images of our bodies on music videos. Consider the following words, now so common and cliché, sang by various male artists in honor of Kriolas:

"Poderosa" Sung by Grace Evora (2010) by Studio Creola

Charmosa sin duvida
Poderosa sin duvida
Pode fazé tudu ... ku omi

"Kriola" Rap by Elji
Nha kuzinha doce
Bo e nha rainha

"Poderosa" Sung by Djodje
El e gostosa

I can only imagine what you would think of music like this; I hear you loved to dance. Yet I would tell you these songs reduce women to pretty little things only, to say the least. As Minna Salami explained in a blog post, we acknowledge and appreciate the recognition of physical beauty, yet we are tired of the constant objectification and reduction of our stories to that one aspect of our identities.

We are the difference between mainstream television news covering the cases of Jassy Correia and other young women of color, barely visible, and the *visitas* to their family homes, knowing the silences and cultural nuances that made them more vulnerable to interlocking oppressions and fatal gender-based violence. We are the many anonymous social workers, caseworkers, teachers, and community advocates in Boston and Brockton, Pawtucket, Newark, Bridgeport, and everywhere Cabo Verdeans reside . . . the Poderozas like Representative Liz Miranda and Labor Union director Dalida Rocha . . . who fight every day for a better existence for us all.

So we are paying our debts to our elders, and we are paying it forward to our daughters and sons. By the way, Mama, in 2010, I became a mother as you know (too handsome Akein). . . . This is the most important achievement/gift/honor I've been given, and it has brought me closer to you as each day; I seek to understand all that you sacrificed and all the love you poured out to raise fifteen! I'm seeking your presence and guidance with my one. And I have a spiritual daughter whose name is (a wink from the divine) Inês Amina!! She has truly been an angel and maybe another gift from you.

They are both in SABURA; I'll tell you about that another time . . . but it's a program we fill with love like yours and it's a treasure to join with Leny Monteiro & Ivette Monteiro and all of the others to do it!

I've written enough. I hope I/ we make you proud . . . You're part of our "feminist genealogy" which is one that includes the elders Terza has written about in her work, all those whom we have recognized at Poderoza, and each time we engage in this work (social and academic), we affirm what the feminist ancestor Anna Julia Cooper declared: "when and where I enter, the whole race enters with me" (Bailey 2004, 56).

I am not Kriola by birthplace. I was not born in the archipelago. I am Kriola because Cabo Verde, Kabuverdianidade, and the Diaspora, was born in and through me. I'm Kriola because YOU gave me the keys. I'm still sitting by your feet, hanging on your every word. I love you, my forever Poderoza.

NOTE

1. I am thinking here of collections such as *This Bridge Called My Back*, *Feminist Genealogies*, *Words of Fire*, and other collections, more recent, that articulate the work of women of color feminists, black and African feminists.

REFERENCES

Bailey, Cathryn. "Anna Julia Cooper: 'Dedicated in the Name of My Slave Mother to the Education of Colored Working People.'" *Hypatia* 19, no. 2, Women in the American Philosophical Tradition 1800–1930: 56–73, 2004.

Busby, Margaret. "Introduction." In *New Daughters of Africa: An International Anthology of Writings by Women of African Descent*, edited by Margaret Busby, xxvi. New York: Harper Collins, 2019.

Cherríe, Moraga. "La Güera." In *This Bridge Called My Back*, edited by Cherríe Moraga and Gloria Anzaldúa. Albany: SUNY Press, 2015.

Gay, Roxanne. *Bad Feminist: Essays*. United States: Harper Perennial, 2014.

Minna, Salami. "A Brief History of African Feminism." *www.msafropolitan.com*, July 2013. https://www.msafropolitan.com/2013/07/a-brief-history-of-african-eminism.html.

Index

Note: Page numbers in italics denote figures and tables.

About the Editors and Contributors

ABOUT THE EDITORS

Terza A. Silva Lima-Neves is a proud Kriola/Cabo Verdean woman, wife, mom, scholar, award-winning professor, African feminist, and community advocate. She was born and raised in Cabo Verde and immigrated to the United States with her parents and sisters as a teenager.

She is a graduate of Providence College and Clark Atlanta University and is currently associate professor of political science and chair of the Department of Social and Behavioral Sciences at Johnson C. Smith University. As a scholar, her research interests and published scholarship are interdisciplinary and straddle the fields of political science, sociology, African diaspora studies, and women and gender studies. Dr. Lima-Neves is one of a handful of scholars whose work focuses on the emerging field of Cabo Women's studies adding the voice, stories, and experiences of Cabo Verdean women to the larger body of literature on Lusophone African studies, African women's studies, African gender studies, and modern African diaspora politics. Terza is especially interested in Cabo Verdean women's understanding and expressions of self-identity, self-love, sexuality, womanhood, sisterhood, self-empowerment through social media, social movements, and beyond. As the co-founder of the Poderoza International Conference on Cabo Verdean Women and founding president of Cape Verdeans of The Carolinas Association, she is passionate about community work that empowers and inspires people. For more on Terza's work visit her website, terzalimaneves.com.

Aminah N. Fernandes Pilgrim is a Kriola who is also of Barbadian descent, a mother, educator, organizer, author, and artist. A graduate of Duke University and Rutgers University, she is currently affiliated with UMass

Boston and the Pedro Pires Institute for Cape Verdean Studies at Bridgewater State University. Her areas of research include late nineteenth and twentieth- century African-American history, African-American women's history, African Diaspora studies, Cabo Verdean studies, critical education research, and critical hip-hop studies.

She is a community organizer/activist, working on matters related to children, youth/gang violence, the school-to-prison pipeline, immigrant transitions, women's empowerment, and Cabo Verdean community concerns. She is an advocate of teaching using civic engagement and has empowered many students to make a difference in this field. She is the founder of the HIPHOP Initiative, MEMORIA Oral History Project, and the co-founder of SABURA Youth Program in Brockton, Massachusetts. For further information on her work and publications, see aminahpilgrim.com.

ABOUT THE CONTRIBUTORS

Elizabette Andrade M.Ed., M.S. is a first-generation Cape Verdean-American and native of Brockton, Massachusetts. Elizabette is a faculty of nutrition at Walnut Hill College and the founder and creative director of cooking alchemy, a family-based health and wellness business in Philadelphia, Pennsylvania, that offers classes, coaching, and specialty products to help others reclaim power over their well-being. Elizabette's life passion is focused on healing with plant-based foods and practices that promote holistic well care. With an emphasis on food and nutrition literacy, she leads interactive classes and workshops throughout the Philadelphia and New Jersey region. You can learn more about her work at cookingalchemy.com.

Stephanie Miranda Andrade is a proud Kriola born in Boston, Massachusetts. Her family comes from Fogo, Cabo Verde, where she has been fortunate to visit twice up to now. She holds a BA in African American Studies and a BS in journalism from the University of Massachusetts Amherst. She currently works in finance for a major online advertising company. Yet and still, she defines herself as "very much a creative who enjoys reimagining spaces, making things beautiful, practicing mindfulness, reading and writing."

Shauna Barbosa is the author of the poetry collection *Cape Verdean Blues* (University of Pittsburgh Press, 2018). Her poems have appeared or are forthcoming in *The New Yorker, Ploughshares, AGNI, Iowa Review, Virginia Quarterly Review, Boulevard, Poetry Society of America, PBS Newshour, Lit Hub, Lenny Letter*, and others. She was nominated for PEN America's 2019 Open Book Award and was a 2018 Disquiet International Luso-American fellow. Shauna received her MFA from Bennington College in Vermont and currently resides in Los Angeles, California, where she teaches creative writing in the Writers' Program at UCLA Extension.

Aleida Mendes Borges is a PhD candidate at King's College London. Her research interest focuses on the political participation and engagement of women, youth, and the diaspora in Lusophone Africa. Her current research project focuses on how youth navigate spaces of political marginalization in Cabo Verde and São Tomé e Principe through developing community projects and engaging the state. She comes from an interdisciplinary background and holds a BA in law with French, an LLM in international legal practice, and an MSc in research for international development. Her previous experience includes legal practice in human rights law, international development work as well as research and publications on women in politics, youth political participation in Lusophone Africa, governance in Africa, diaspora political participation, external citizenship, and minority rights in Brazilian law. Aleida is currently co-chair of the Youth Advisory Board of the Youth Bridge Foundation based in Ghana.

Iva Brito is an artist, poet, actress, educator, activist (also known as Iva B). As a native of Cabo Verde, Iva channels her nostalgic love of her birthplace, tapping into her culturally diverse identity, to call for justice, unity, and liberation through her artistic works. She is the author of the poetry book *Essence, Tones, Whispers and Shouts*, a collection of poetry in which she draws on nature, past experiences, and her vision for an illuminated and inclusive world. She has performed her pieces at universities, concerts, spoken word showcases, community outreach, and socio-political awareness events at various locations throughout the nation. Iva is a featured artist in the Women Anthem "Take Back the Power" music video, a partnership with the National Parks, celebrating the centennial anniversary of women's right to vote in 2020. Iva was awarded the prestigious Artist-in-Residence placement for the New Bedford Whaling National Parks, where she focused on New Bedford's unique ancestral connections to people of color and the Cape Verdean immigrant experience, working to create their first Cape Verdean Heritage Tours. Iva showcased both her painting and poetry at the Whaling Museum exhibit in honor of the late Judge George Leighton. Outside of being an artist, Iva is a licensed social worker and educator. Currently, she serves as the director of Bristol Community College Women's Center and adjunct faculty for the college. Iva holds a master of science degree from UMASS, Boston, and a certificate of advanced graduate studies in expressive arts from Salve Regina University, as part of their holistic counseling program. More information about Iva can be found on her website www.ivabrito.com or as Ivab5 on Facebook & Instagram.

Edna DaCosta was born and raised in Ribeirão Boi, Feguesia Santiago Maior. She left there at age 10, and migrated to the United States in 1989 when she settled in Cambridge, Massachusetts. In Cambridge, she joined her father and his family, until mom (Domingas Mendes) came four years later. She holds a BA in Latin American & Iberian Studies, with a concentration in translation, and a minor in anthropology from UMass Boston. She is currently pursuing an MS in criminal justice. A mother of two beautiful children (Zahra DaCosta-Gomes and Evan DaCosta-Gomes), she is also a hairstylist, writer, and creative. She is passionate about health and fitness, art, cooking, Cabo Verdean culture and most of all, family. She currently works as a police officer in the city of Somerville, Massachusetts.

Vera Duarte (Vera Valentina Benrós de Melo Duarte Lobo de Pina), former Chief Justice of the Supreme Court of Cabo Verde and writer, is one of the most prestigious Cabo Verdean public figures. She is a minister of education and higher education, president for the National Commission of Human Rights and Citizenship, judge counselor to the Supreme Court, attorney general and advisor to the President of the Republic. Her literary works cover various genres such as poetry, prose fiction, essays, travel writing, world literature, human rights, slavery and women's empowerment and have been translated to several languages. In 1993, she published her first poetry book, *Amanhã amadrugada*. This book was followed by several others, including *O arquipélago da paixão* (Cape Verde, poetry, 2001), *A candidata* (2004), *Preces e súplicas ou os cantos da desesperança* (2005), *Construindo a utopia* (2007), *Ejercicios poéticos* (2010), *A palavra e os dias* (2013), *A matriarca: uma estória de mestiçagens* (2017), *De risos & lágrimas* (2018), *A reinvenção do mar: antologia poética* (2018), *Cabo Verde, um roteiro sentimental: viajando pelas ilhas da Sodad, do Sol e da Morabeza* (2019). Her works are also part of prominent literary anthologies. In 2001, Duarte was distinguished with the Tchicaya U Tam'si Prize for African Poetry (Morocco). She has received several distinctions including Medalha de Mérito Cultural (Medal of Cultural Merit) by the Government of Cape Verde (2005) and Medalha do Vulcão (Vulcan Medal) awarded by the President of the Republic of Cape Verde for International Women's Day (2010).

Jess Évora is the founder of Ranja CV, a community organization that aims to unite and prepare the next generation of Cabo Verdean community leaders around the world. Jess is a Leadership Development professional with nine years of experience developing leaders at all levels, from high-school students to university scholars to full-time professionals. She specializes in the intersection of leadership development and diversity, equity, & inclusion. Jess teaches at the University of California Merced, where she is the associate director of the Margo F. Souza Student Leadership Center. She also develops leadership development curriculum for community organizations. In addition, Jess serves as director of content for Poderoza: International Conference on Cabo Verdean Women. Jess earned her bachelor's degree from Syracuse University, and her master of education from the University of Southern California. A native of Rhode Island, United States, Jess is passionate about uniting Cabo Verdeans to realize their individual dreams while giving back to the Cabo Verdean community.

Roselma Évora holds bachelor and master degrees in political science and doctorate in sociology from the Universidade de Brasília (UnB), Brasil. She is the author of two books and co-author of six books on topics related to political systems, electoral and party systems, democracy, political participation in Africa, particularly in Cabo Verde. She is an independent researcher and consultant on democracy, legal status, electoral and party systems, decision processes, good governance, state reform, transparency, citizenship and human rights, and questions of gender and women empowerment in Africa. Dr. Évora has published articles in journals in Cabo Verde and the United States as well as authored articles on local newspapers on questions of democracy. She has participated in multiple seminars as well as national and international conferences on democracy, political participation, women in politics, and other topics. Dr. Évora is a frequent political analyst on radio and television programs. She is a founding member of LusoForumForDemocracy and social activist. She is winner of the Center for Social Studies Young Researchers Program (CES) at the Universidade de Coimbra in 2008 and honored by the government of the República Federativa do Brasil on the 50th anniversary of the Program PEC as an exemplary successful alumna in November 2014. In January 2011, Dr. Évora received the distinguished diploma of professional merit by the Government of Cabo Verde

Clementina Baptista de Jesus Furtado is a PhD in political & social sciences, on the scope of the PIC from CUD (Uni-CV/ULB), under the topic, "Migrations from Western Africa in Cabo Verde: attitudes and representations". A teacher at the course Graduation in Geography & Spatial Planning, (LGOT) at the University of Cabo Verde and the Director of CIGEF (Center for the Research and Training on Gender and Family (Current position), since August 1, 2013. She has been a member of the Gender-Based Violence (GBV) Implementation and Evaluation Committee and the Focal Point for Gender issues at the Cabo Verdean Institute for Gender Equality and Equity (ICIEG) and member of National Committee of Immigration (CNI-DGI). She is also a member of the Parity Proposal Law Committee, approved in November 2019. She has organized and participated in several international and national congresses and seminars, always delivering communications. Current areas of research: migrations in the Cabo Verdean society, gender, and development.

Gina Sánchez Gibau is associate vice chancellor for faculty diversity and inclusion and associate professor of anthropology in the IU School of Liberal Arts at Indiana University Purdue University, Indianapolis. She earned a Ph.D. in anthropology from the University of Texas at Austin, specializing in the African Diaspora. Her research interests include racial and ethnic identity development, multicultural pedagogy, and professional development and advancement of underrepresented groups in higher education. She conducted fieldwork on identity formation among Cape Verdeans in Boston, Massachusetts. She has presented at numerous conferences in the United States and abroad and has published in several edited volumes and journals, including *Cimboa: Journal of Cape Verdean Letters, Arts, and Studies, Transforming Anthropology, Identities, the Journal of Women and Minorities in Science and Engineering, CBE Life Sciences Education, the Journal of Teaching and Learning with Technology, and Science Education.* She is a 2013 alumna of the Higher Education Resources Services (HERS) Bryn Mawr Leadership Institute. In her current role, Dr. Gibau is responsible for providing strategic vision to academic units in support of their efforts to attract, recruit, retain, and advance a more diverse faculty. She works collaboratively with deans and chairs to enhance the pathways toward diversifying the faculty and promoting inclusive excellence. She is the current co-director of the IUPUI Next Generation 2.0 program, a leadership and professional development initiative for women and underrepresented faculty and staff. She is also Co-PI on an ADVANCE adaptation grant, Project EPIC, and the IUPUI Team Lead for the APLU Aspire Alliance IChange Network initiative.

Rosilda Alves DePina James is a wife and mother of two amazing children, a licensed psychologist, an advocate and an educator. She was born in Fogo, Cabo Verde, and immigrated to Boston, Massachusetts, at age 10. She earned a bachelor of arts in psychology and sociology from Bridgewater State University. She then moved to San Francisco, California, where she earned a masters in marriage and family therapy from the University of San Francisco. She went on to earn a masters and doctorate in clinical psychology from The Wright Institute in Berkeley, California. Dr. James has dedicated over twenty-five years to the practice of providing an avenue for healing to survivors of trauma while also specializing in multiculturalism, acculturation, ethnic and racial identity, and immigrant issues. Dr. James has been with Kaiser Permanente since 2002 where she is currently a hospital-based psychiatric consultant. She also has a private practice where she treats couples, adults, and families. She was an adjunct professor for 5 years at The Wright Institute in Berkeley.

Anna Lima MA-SLP is a Speech and Language Pathologist who received her master's in communication disorders from the University of Massachusetts at Amherst. She is also known as The CV Genealogist, author of a blog by the same name, focusing on Cape Verdean genealogy and history. She is the founder and president of Cape Verde DNA, Inc. a nonprofit whose mission is to expand the understanding of Caboverdeanidade, to share our story with the world and to reaffirm and strengthen the Cape Verdean family and future generations.

Callie Watkins Liu an intersectional and critical race scholar-activist, dedicated to research and collaborations that prioritize social justice and center the socially vulnerable. Her expertise in social movements, social policy, urban planning, global development (especially Latin America and Africa), conflict resolution and social psychology equip her to navigate between theory and lived experiences, understand social problems, and identify interventions. Dr. Watkins Liu's work challenges power inequities and supports social justice-oriented systems, structures, and practices. As a social policy PhD and urban planner, Dr. Watkins Liu is acutely aware of how the environment and formal and informal social systems impact life chances and quality of life, especially for vulnerable populations. She uses critical analysis of society, social problems, and their implications to identify social justice-oriented interventions at cultural, organizational, policy, and practice levels. She uses theories such as critical race theory and intersectionality to advance her work in theoretical and practical ways. Areas of expertise include organizational theory for social movements, anti-racism, higher education, non-profit and community organizations.

Ivette Centeio Monteiro was born and raised in Dorchester, Massachusetts. She was born to Cabo Verdean parents from Fogo, Cabo Verde. She is a graduate of UMass Boston where she studied psychology and Africana Studies and earned M.Ed. in elementary education. She also holds a graduate certificate in family and community engagement in culturally and linguistically responsive education from Lesley University. Ivette currently lives in Brockton, Massachusetts, where she is a mother of three children, a wife, educator, and advocate for social justice.

Ayana Pilgrim-Brown is a Kriola raised in Onset, Massachusetts, who currently resides in Philadelphia, Pennsylvania. She holds an MBA in human resource management from Clark University as well as four professional coaching designations in the areas of career coaching, life purpose coaching, life coaching, and holistic health coaching. She is the founder and CEO of Purpose Rising Inc. and serves on the staff of Temple University's Fox School of Business. She is on a personal mission to educate, encourage, and empower job seekers to advance their careers with a sense of purpose and well-being. She was a corporate recruiting leader for twelve years conducting hiring efforts for some of the world's largest Fortune 100 companies, including Bank of America, Pfizer Pharmaceuticals, and Cigna Healthcare. Having an insider's perspective on how top-tier organizations recruit top talent has enhanced Ayana's ability to empower candidates with the skills needed to attract top employers. She fuses her personal, educational, and professional experiences to offer students and professionals clear, insightful, and relevant counsel on life purpose exploration, professional development, and maintaining work–life balance.

Idalina Pina is a creative writer, photographer, and gardener based in Boston, Massachusetts. Born and raised on the islands of Cape Verde, Idalina immigrated with her family to the United States at the age of 9. She acclimated well, eventually going to boarding school during her high-school years. She attends Davidson College pursuing a double major in anthropology and Africana Studies. Idalina enjoys traveling the world, taking pictures of her cat, Morgan, and long walks on the beach.

Aldegundes (Gunga) Tolentino Tavares working at the Consulate General of Cabo Verde for over twenty years, has been connecting the Cabo Verdean Community through grassroots cultural and social initiatives and helping build bridges among relevant players of our diverse community. Gunga Tavares is known as an experienced journalist with a long career that spans from the first Cape Verdean Newspaper *Voz di Povo* and the National Television in Cabo Verde, to Washington DC, where she worked for ten years as an international broadcaster and news editor at the international radio Voice of America and the international television WorldNet, two crucial programs that brought news and information to the Portuguese-speaking countries in Africa in the years after their independence. Coming to Boston in 1995, her communication skills helped establish solid relationships with the different generations of Cape Verdeans across the United States. Along with a group of scholars and educators, she was one of the founders of *Cimboa*, a Capeverdean journal of arts letters and studies (1996–2001), the first step to bring awareness about common issues and concerns within the academic and intellectual Cape Verdean and Capeverdean American Community. The momentum and the intellectual potential inspired by this magazine help her and another group of community activist found the Common Threads – Cape Verdean Community Conferences (2000–2005) to stimulate another level of dialogue among Cape Verdeans. Gunga Tavares continues to support and help create new programs to celebrate the Cape Verdean heritage and culture in New England and unique opportunities to showcase the history and culture of the Cape Verdean people.

Dawna Marie Thomas is a professor at Simmons University and jointly appointed in the Sociology and Women's and Gender Studies Departments. She is the chair of the Sociology Department and Director of the Law and Justice Minor. Her research interests include Cabo Verdeana, disability, gender, race, ethnicity, and class. She is one co-founder of the former Common Threads, grassroots community cultural initiative dedicated to the preservation and celebration of the cultural and historical traditions of the Cabo Verdean Diaspora in the United States and Transnational Cabo Verdean Community. Common Threads focuses on linking all communities in the United States, through conferences that celebrate and preserve Cabo Verdean culture. She is dedicated to the cultural and historical preservation of the Cabo Verdean Diaspora. She brings her community-based research to the academy and blends theory and practice.

Candida Rose is a vocal artist who was born and raised in New Bedford, Massachusetts, and captivates her audiences with the golden aura of her radiant presence and stirs them with a uniquely compelling voice that combines the overtones and undertones of jazz, rhythm, and blues, and gospel with just the right touch of international spice. Candida Rose's 10-song debut CD entitled "KabuMerikana: The Sum of Me", combines her Cape Verdean musical roots with her American influences to bring a fresh new take on world/jazz music which she calls "KabuJazz". A recent review in "Global Rhythm Magazine" will attest to the beauty and depth of both the CD's production and Candida Rose's vocal abilities. Candida Rose is a recent graduate of the University of Massachusetts, Dartmouth, where she graduated "Summa Cum Laude" with a bachelor of arts degree, majoring in Music (African-American/World music) and a minor in African and African/American Studies. Candida has been and continues to be a dedicated teacher and mentor to many of New Bedford's aspiring young vocalists. Aside from her work with youth, Candida currently travels the SouthCoast region of Massachusetts and Rhode Island as a Life Enrichment Entertainer singing for nursing home, assisted living and adult day-care facilities, as well as for various senior groups and associations. Whether at a gospel revival, jazz night, Cape Verdean festival, R&B Revue, anniversary, wedding, birthday celebration, or whatever event you can think of, Candida Rose continues to amaze audiences with her diverse vocal performances. But more importantly, she reaches out with her heart and soul and touches everyone in her presence. Wherever you happen to catch her performance, be prepared to catch your breath!!

www.ingramcontent.com/pod-product-compliance
Lightning Source LLC
Chambersburg PA
CBHW050635280326
41932CB00015B/2648